CW00408692

MASTERING MATHEMATICS

NUMBER

Series Editor: Roger Porkess

HODDER
EDUCATION
AN HACHETTE UK COMPANY

Series contributors:

Bola Adiboye, Caroline Clissold, Ruth Crookes, Heather Davis, Paul Dickinson, Alan Easterbrook, Sarah-Anne Fernandes, Dave Gale, Sophie Goldie, Steve Gough, Kevin Higham, Sue Hough, Andrew Jeffrey, Michael Kent, Donna Kerrigan, Nigel Langdon, Linda Liggett, Robin Liggett, Andrew Manning, Nikki Martin, Chris Messenger, Richard Perring, Grahame Smart, Alison Terry, Sam Webber, Colin White

Some activities from Formula One Maths, used with permission of author. Some SMILE activities © RBKC, used with permission

The publisher would like to thank the following for permission to reproduce copyright material:

Photo credits:

p. 2 © Kirill Zdorov – Fotolia.com; **p. 10** © Ernest Prim – Fotolia.com; **p. 16** © Photodisc/Getty Images/ Business & Industry 1; **p. 23** © whiteaster – Fotolia.com; **p. 40** © lassedesignen – Fotolia.com; **p. 45** © Gina Sanders - Fotolia.com; **p. 51** © Brebca - Fotolia.com; **p. 57** © Kadmy – Fotolia.com; **p. 64** © Ingram Publishing Limited / Business Platinum Vol 1 CD 1; **p. 71** © Pete Saloutos - Fotolia.com; **p. 78** © NASA; **p. 84** © amphotolt – Fotolia.com; **p. 90** © Ulrich Müller – Fotolia.com; **p. 97** © HugoCCampos – Fotolia.com; **p. 104** l Elizabeth Warren, **c** and **r** © Steve Connolly; **p. 110** © hipgnosis - Fotolia.com; **p. 114** © .shock – Fotolia – Fotolia.com; **p. 120** © Scott Griessel – Fotolia.com; **p. 125** © Alexandr Mitiuc – Fotolia.com; **p. 129** t © Food photo – Fotolia.com, b © Coprid – Fotolia.com; **p. 136** © pumpuija – Fotolia.com; **p. 139** © bonzodog - Fotolia.com **p. 144** Heather Davies; **p. 148** © Elaine Lambert; **p. 153** © gemphotography – Fotolia.com; **p. 162** © Rich Lindie – Fotolia.com; **p. 168** © Yali Shi – Fotolia.com; **p. 175** © Anne Wanjie; **p. 183** © Imagestate Media (John Foxx) / Vol 18 Golddisc I; **p. 190** © tinteapetrica – Fotolia.com; **p. 197** © Brian Jackson – Fotolia.com; **p. 205** © yanlev -Fotolia.com; **p. 212** © Pavel Losevsky – Fotolia.com; **p. 221** © cherries – Fotolia.com; **p. 226** © Marek Kosmal – Fotolia.com; **p. 232** t © matka_Wariatka – Fotolia.com, b © Sue Hough **p. 236** © Anne Wanjie; **p. 238** © Florin Capilnean – Fotolia.com; **p. 245** Dave Gale; **p. 253** © Alexander Khripunov – Fotolia.com; **p. 260** Dave Gale; **p. 262** © helenedevun – Fotolia.com; **p. 268** © Minerva Studio -Fotolia.com; **p. 273** © paulmz – Fotolia.com; **p. 279** © Adam Cunningham and John Ringland – Wikipedia Creative Commons (http://creativecommons.org/licenses/by-sa/3.0/deed.en); **p. 284** © Simon Smith/iStockphoto.com; **p. 289** © Rawpixel -Fotolia.com

Every effort has been made to trace all copyright holders, but if any have been inadvertently overlooked, the Publishers will be pleased to make the necessary arrangements at the first opportunity.

Although every effort has been made to ensure that website addresses are correct at time of going to press, Hodder Education cannot be held responsible for the content of any website mentioned. It is sometimes possible to find a relocated web page by typing in the address of the home page for a website in the URL window of your browser.

Orders: please contact Bookpoint Ltd, 130 Milton Park, Abingdon, Oxon OX14 4SB. Telephone: (44) 01235 827720. Fax: (44) 01235 400454. Lines are open 9.00–17.00, Monday to Saturday, with a 24-hour message answering service. Visit our website at www.hoddereducation.co.uk

© Hodder & Stoughton 2014

First published in 2014 by

Hodder Education

An Hachette UK Company,

Carmelite House

50 Victoria Embankment

London EC4Y 0DZ

Impression number	5	4		
Year	2018	2017	2016	2015

Cover photo © Dreaming Andy – Fotolia

Typeset in 10/11.5pt ITC Avant Garde Gothic by Integra Software Services Pvt. Ltd., Pondicherry, India

Printed in Italy by Printer Trento S.r.l.

A catalogue record for this title is available from the British Library

ISBN 978 1471 805912

How to get the most from this book

This book covers the Number that you need for your key stage 3 Maths course.

The material is split into **seven strands**:

- Calculating
- Using our number system
- Accuracy
- Fractions
- Percentages
- Ratio and proportion
- Number properties

Each strand is presented as a series of units that get more difficult as you progress (from Band c through to Band h). In total there are 44 units in this book.

Getting started

At the beginning of each strand, you will find a 'Progression strand flowchart'. It shows what skills you will develop in each unit in the strand. You can see:

- what you need to know before starting each unit
- what you will need to learn next to progress

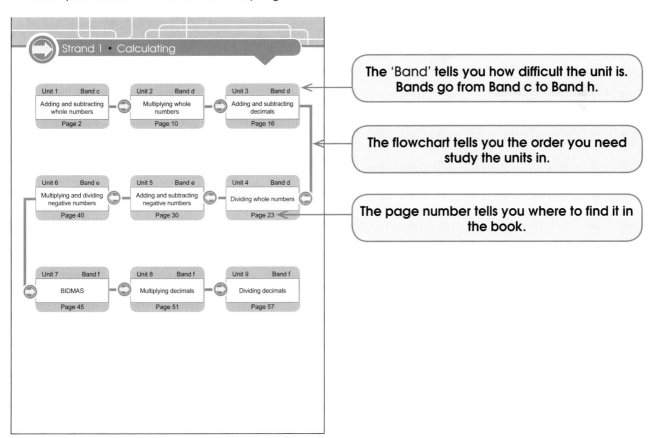

When you start to use this book, you will need to identify where to join each strand. Then you will not spend time revisiting skills you have already mastered.

If you can answer all the questions in the 'Reviewing skills' section of a unit then you will not have to study that unit.

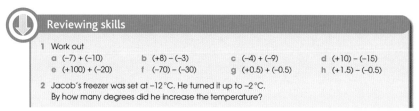

Reviewing skills

1 Work out
  a (−7) + (−10)   b (+8) − (−3)   c (−4) + (−9)   d (+10) − (−15)
  e (+100) + (−20)   f (−70) − (−30)   g (+0.5) + (−0.5)   h (+1.5) − (−0.5)

2 Jacob's freezer was set at −12 °C. He turned it up to −2 °C.
  By how many degrees did he increase the temperature?

When you know which unit to start with in each strand you will be ready to start work on your first unit.

Starting a unit

Every unit begins with a **'Building skills'** section:

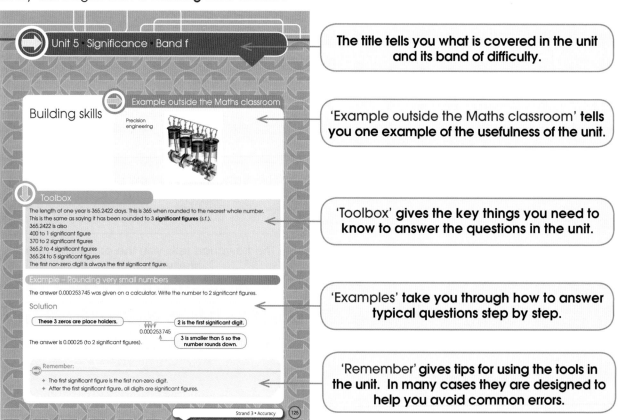

The title tells you what is covered in the unit and its band of difficulty.

'Example outside the Maths classroom' **tells you one example of the usefulness of the unit.**

'Toolbox' **gives the key things you need to know to answer the questions in the unit.**

'Examples' **take you through how to answer typical questions step by step.**

'Remember' **gives tips for using the tools in the unit. In many cases they are designed to help you avoid common errors.**

Now you have all the information you need, you can use the questions to develop your understanding.

Skills practice A

1 Look at these diagrams.

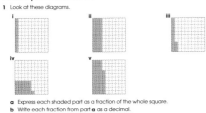

a Express each shaded part as a fraction of the whole square.
b Write each fraction from part **a** as a decimal.

> **'Skills practice A' questions** are all about mastering essential techniques that you need to succeed.

Skills practice B

1 Here is a message in a code. You need to work out the code. What does the message say?

2 Susan and Gary are contestants in a number quiz.
a Susan's target number is 358. The numbers she has are 100, 10, 8, 6, 4 and 3.
   She can use the operations +, −, ÷ and × and brackets as many times as she wishes.
   How can she make the target number?
b Gary's target number is 278. The numbers he has are 75, 50, 8, 4, 3 and 2.
   How can he make the target number?

> **'Skills practice B' questions** give you practice in using your skills for a purpose. Many of them are set in context. The later questions are usually more demanding.

Wider skills practice

1 If you add up the numbers in any row, column or diagonal in this magic square, you should always get the same total. Unfortunately one of the numbers is incorrect. Can you find it?

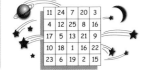

2 In one very strange cricket match, the scores of all 11 batsmen are consecutive numbers.
a What is the smallest total they could have scored?
b What are the scores of the batsmen if the total is
   i 121 runs   ii 374 runs   iii 616 runs?
c Could the total be
   i 84 runs   ii 95 runs?

> **'Wider skills practice' questions** require you to use maths from outside the current unit. In some cases they use knowledge from other subjects or the world outside.
>
> You can use this section to keep practising other skills as well as the skills in this unit.

Applying skills

1 Avonford School orders new tables for the dining hall. There is a choice of two designs.

£30   £32

The dining hall is to seat 336 pupils.
a How many tables does the school need if they are
   i hexagonal   ii octagonal?
b Which design of table is cheaper for the school to order?
   How much money does the school save?

2 Tom and Lucy have each worked out 236 × 48.

Tom   Lucy

Without working out the calculation explain why both Tom and Lucy are wrong.

> **'Applying skills' questions** give examples of how you will use the Maths in the unit to solve problems:
> - in the real world
> - in other subjects
> - in personal finance
> - within Maths itself.
>
> These are more demanding questions, so only one or two are provided in each unit. Together they form a bank of questions.

When you feel confident, use the **'Reviewing skills'** section to check that you have mastered the techniques covered in the unit.

You will see many questions labelled with (Reasoning) or (Problem solving)

These are the general mathematical skills that you need to develop. You will use these skills in all areas of Maths.

They will help you think through problems and to apply your skills in unfamiliar situations. Use these questions to make sure that you develop these important skills.

About 'Bands'

Every unit has been allocated to a Band. These bands show you the level of difficulty of the Maths that you are working on.

Each Band contains Maths that's of about the same level of difficulty.

This provides a way of checking your progress and assessing your weaker areas, where you need to practise more.

Moving on to another unit

Once you have completed a unit, you should move on to the next unit in one of the strands. You can choose which strand to work on next but make sure you complete all the units in a particular Band before moving on to the next Band.

A note for teachers

Bands have been assigned to units roughly in line with the previous National Curriculum levels. Here they are, just to help in giving you a reference point.

Band	Approximate Equivalent in terms of Old National Curriculum Levels
b	Level 2
c	Level 3
d	Level 4
e	Level 5
f	Level 6
g	Level 7
h	Level 8

Answers and Write-on sheets

Write-on sheets to aid completion of answers are denoted by . These and Answers to all the questions in this book are available via **Mastering Mathematics Teaching and Learning Resources** or by visiting

www.hodderplus.co.uk/masteringmaths

Contents

Contents

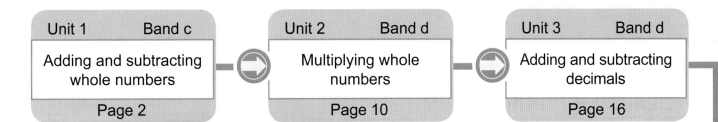

Unit 1	Band c
Adding and subtracting whole numbers	
Page 2	

Unit 2	Band d
Multiplying whole numbers	
Page 10	

Unit 3	Band d
Adding and subtracting decimals	
Page 16	

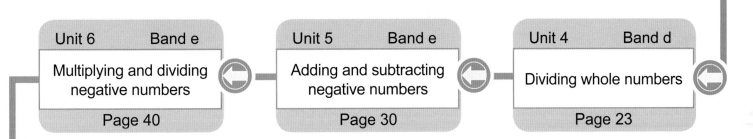

Unit 6	Band e
Multiplying and dividing negative numbers	
Page 40	

Unit 5	Band e
Adding and subtracting negative numbers	
Page 30	

Unit 4	Band d
Dividing whole numbers	
Page 23	

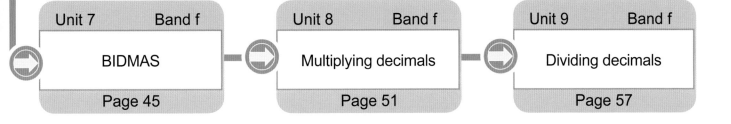

Unit 7	Band f
BIDMAS	
Page 45	

Unit 8	Band f
Multiplying decimals	
Page 51	

Unit 9	Band f
Dividing decimals	
Page 57	

Unit 1 • Adding and subtracting whole numbers • Band c

Building skills

Example outside the Maths classroom

Taking stock

Toolbox

There are several different methods you can use for addition and subtraction.
Here are three of the main methods:

- using columns
- using a number line – count on or back from the number
- partitioning – break up one or both numbers into hundreds, tens and units.

Think about subtracting 63 from 122 using each of the three methods.

Columns

```
      11 1
  X    2   2
 −     6   3
      _____
       5   9
```

A number line
Count on from 63 to 100 and then to 122.

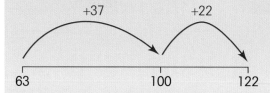

```
      +37           +22

  63          100   122
```

The difference between 63 and 122 is 37 + 22 = 59.
So 122 − 63 = 59.

Partitioning

$$122 - 63 = 122 - 60 - 3$$
$$= 62 - 3$$
$$= 59$$

> **To subtract 63, you can take away 60 and then 3.**

Example – Calculating profits

Avonford School holds a school talent show to raise money. It raises

- £156 from pupils entering the competition
- £218 from ticket sales
- £63 from refreshments.

a How much does the school raise altogether?

b The school uses the money to buy a table tennis table costing £349. How much money does it have left over?

Solution

a You need to work out £156 + £218 + £63. Here are three methods.

Columns

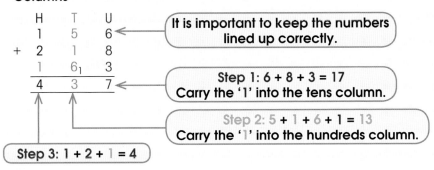

It is important to keep the numbers lined up correctly.

Step 1: 6 + 8 + 3 = 17
Carry the '1' into the tens column.

Step 2: 5 + 1 + 6 + 1 = 13
Carry the '1' into the hundreds column.

Step 3: 1 + 2 + 1 = 4

Number line

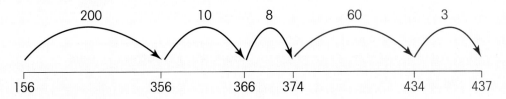

Partitioning

	Hundreds	Tens	Units
156	100	50	6
218	200	10	8
63		60	3
Add	300	120	17

Add the numbers in each column and then add along the bottom row.
The school raised a total of £437.

b You need to work out £437 minus £349. Here are three methods.

Columns

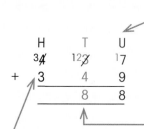

Step 1: You can't do 7 – 9 so borrow 1 ten from the tens column. 17 – 9 = 8

Step 2: **Borrowing** 1 ten **leaves** 2 tens **here. You can't do** 2 tens – 4 tens **so borrow 1 hundred from the hundreds column.** 12 – 4 = 8

Step 3: 3 – 3 = 0 So you have finished.

Number line

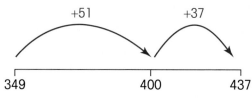

You counted on 51 + 37 = 88. So they have £437 – £349 = £88 left.

Partitioning

	Hundreds	Tens	Units
437	400	30	7
349	300	40	9
Subtract			

You can't do 7 – 9 so borrow 10 from the tens column.

Borrowing 10 leaves 20 here.

	Hundreds	Tens	Units
437	400	20 30	17
349	300	40	9
Subtract			8

You can't do 20 – 40 so borrow 100 from the hundreds column.

	Hundreds	Tens	Units
437	300 400	120	17
349	300	40	9
Subtract	0	80	8

80 + 8 = 88

Answer £88

Remember:

✦ Look out for these words for addition: total, sum, plus.
✦ Look out for these words for subtraction: take away, difference, minus.

Skills practice A

1 Pick out five pairs of numbers that each add up to 10.
   3 2 6 5 9 1 7 5 4 8

2 Pick out five pairs of numbers that each add up to 30.
   12 17 9 25 11 18 13 21 19 5

3 Pick out five pairs of numbers that each add up to 50.
   39 22 27 37 46 28 11 13 23 4

4 Work out these additions.
   a 63 + 22   **b** 145 + 251   **c** 205 + 473
   d 149 + 38   **e** 576 + 47   **f** 603 + 98

5 Work out these subtractions.
   a 68 – 21   **b** 140 – 50   **c** 186 – 78
   d 245 – 168   **e** 503 – 279   **f** 1000 – 364

6 The table shows the distances that Meena and Sophie travel during their
   holiday in a car.

	Monday	Tuesday	Wednesday	Thursday	Friday
Morning	96 km	132 km	128 km	103 km	127 km
Afternoon	80 km	86 km	77 km	98 km	85 km

   a Work out how far they travel each day.
   b Find out how far they travel altogether.

7 Copy and complete these number walls.
   The number in each brick is found by adding the numbers in
   the two bricks below it.

   a | 24 | 65 | **b** | 73 | 54 | **c** | 521 | 456 |

   d | 23 | 37 | 58 | **e** | 384 | 297 | 512 | **f**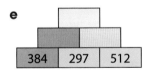

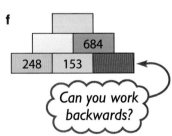

Can you work backwards?

8 Find the sum of each of these pairs of numbers.
   a 321 and 123   **b** 451 and 73   **c** 285 and 472

9 Find the difference between each of these pairs of numbers.
   a 632 and 586   **b** 327 and 115   **c** 418 and 329

10 Suzanne wins a holiday in a competition. The prize is worth £2499. If she wishes
   she may upgrade to the deluxe holiday which costs £3249. How much extra must she pay?

Reasoning

Skills practice B

1 India have a score of 218 runs. England are batting. They have 176 runs.
How many more runs do they need
   a to draw level   **b** to win?

2 Humza has four pieces of wood, each 1 m long.
He cuts off the following lengths, one from each piece.   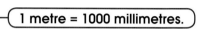 1 metre = 1000 millimetres.
What lengths remain?
   a 970 mm   **b** 420 mm   **c** 235 mm   **d** 815 mm

3 Copy and complete these calculations.

   a 75
      65
      37 +

   b 340
      270
      460 +

   c 1413
      324
      165 +

   d 634
      796
      952 +

   e 10 445
          776 +

   f 703
      196 −

   g 2023
      1070 −

   h 42 707
      17 398 −

   i 2640
      1890 −

   j 2304
      1837 −

4 Copy the cross-number grid.
Fill in the answers with one digit in each square.

Across	Down
1 638 − 200	**2** 734 − 699
5 303 − 287	**3** 1000 − 784
6 418 − 328	**4** 850 − 46
8 953 − 432	**7** 615 − 583

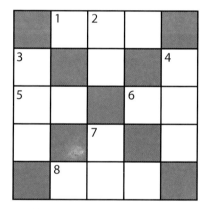

5 Copy and complete these number walls.
The number in each brick is the sum of the numbers in the two bricks below it.

a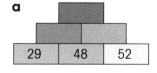

b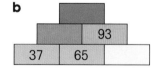

c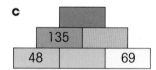

d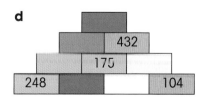

e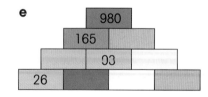

6 Play this subtraction game with a friend.

Starting with 123, players take turns to subtract numbers using only one digit in the preceding answer.

The first player can choose 33, 2, 111, for example.

You are not allowed to subtract 0.

The winner is the first player to reach zero.

Play a few games. Try starting with different numbers.

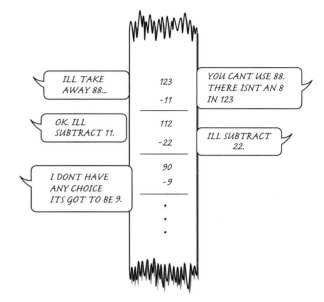

7 What is the price difference between a car costing £12 995 and a car costing £7925?

8 John is collecting money for new shirts for his football team. They cost £454.
How much more does he need when he has collected:

   a £242   **b** £272   **c** £293   **d** £324   **e** £353?

9 Four mountain bikes in a shop cost £599, £649, £700 and £859. How much do they cost altogether?

10 The table shows the distances, in miles, between some towns in Britain.
Work out the distances travelled on each of these journeys.

Bristol	Gloucester	Leeds	Manchester	Norwich	Nottingham	York	London
36							
213	178						
172	137	44					
233	211	172	185				
145	110	74	71	119			
220	191	24	71	181	87		
120	102	198	202	116	131	211	

   a Bristol to Gloucester then Gloucester to Nottingham

   b Leeds to Manchester then Manchester to Nottingham

   c Nottingham to Norwich then Norwich to London

   d Bristol to Gloucester then Gloucester to Nottingham then Nottingham to York

   e York to Leeds then Leeds to Nottingham then Nottingham to London

   f London to Norwich then Norwich to Nottingham then Nottingham to Manchester

Wider skills practice

1 If you add up the numbers in any row, column or diagonal in this magic square, you should always get the same total. Unfortunately one of the numbers is incorrect. Can you find it?

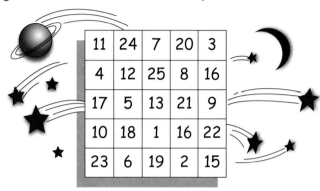

11	24	7	20	3
4	12	25	8	16
17	5	13	21	9
10	18	1	16	22
23	6	19	2	15

2 In one very strange cricket match, the scores of all 11 batsmen are consecutive numbers.

  a What is the smallest total they could have scored?

  b What are the scores of the batsmen if the total is

    i 121 runs   **ii** 374 runs   **iii** 616 runs?

  c Could the total be

    i 84 runs   **ii** 95 runs?

3 Copy the diagram. Arrange the numbers 1, 2, 3, 4, 5 and 6 in the circles so that each line of three numbers has the same total.

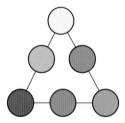

4 Copy the diagrams. Arrange the numbers 1, 2, 3, 4, 5, 6 and 7 in the circles so that each line of three numbers has the same total.

  a

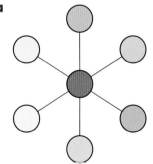

  b

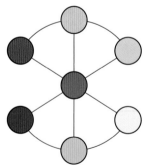

Applying skills

1 Draw nine circles in a 3 × 3 grid arrangement.

Roll a die. Write the result in any one of your circles. Do this eight more times. When all the circles are filled, treat each of the three rows as a three-digit number. Add the numbers.

Play this game with a friend, on separate grids. The winner is the one who gets nearest to 1000. What strategy should you use to win?

2 Mary opened a bank account on Tuesday with £100. On Wednesday she withdrew £56, on Thursday she deposited £232, on Friday she withdrew £67 and on Saturday she deposited £378. How much was in her account on Sunday?

3 Michelle takes £350 spending money on a weekend away.

a She spends £22 on a meal. How much has she left?

b Then she spends £127 on an outing. How much is left now?

c She buys a dress for £98. How much is left now?

d She also buys some perfume for £59. How much is left?

e A scarf costs £45. Can she afford it?

Reviewing skills

1 Without a calculator, work out these.

   a 12 + 13   **b** 74 + 83   **c** 24 + 68 + 121   **d** 263 + 354 + 455

2 Without a calculator, work out these.

   a 12 – 7   **b** 76 – 28   **c** 256 – 142   **d** 321 – 289

3 The chart shows the distances between some UK airports.

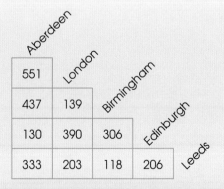

a How far would you travel if you flew from Aberdeen to Edinburgh, then from Edinburgh to Leeds?

b How far is it to travel from Aberdeen to Leeds directly?

c What is the difference between the answers to part **a** and part **b**?

Example outside the Maths classroom

Building skills

Painting

Toolbox

Here are three methods you can use to multiply two numbers together.

- the column method
- partition one or both numbers

$8 \times 34 = 8 \times 30 + 8 \times 4 = 240 + 32 = 272$

- a grid

Consider multiplying 123 by 26.

The **column method**

```
      1   2   3
  ×       2   6
  2   4   6   0  ←  ( 123 × 20 )
      7₁  3₁  8  ←  ( 123 × 6 )
  3   1   9   8
  1
```

Partitioning

$123 \times 26 = 100 \times 26 + 20 \times 26 + 3 \times 26$

$= 100 \times 20 + 100 \times 6 + 20 \times 20 + 20 \times 6 + 3 \times 20 + 3 \times 6$

$= 2000 + 600 + 400 + 120 + 60 + 18$

$= 3198$

The **grid method**

×	100	20	3
20	2000	400	60
6	600	120	18
	2600	520	78

$2600 + 520 + 78 = 3198$

Look carefully. You will see that partitioning and the grid method are really just the same.

The answer is 3198, whichever method you use.

Example – Calculating the total cost

A school orders 28 new laptops at £465 each. How much do they cost in total?

Solution

The total cost is 28 × £465.

First, use estimation to check roughly what the answer should be:

$28 × £465 ≈ 30 × £500 = £15\,000$

Either use the column method.

```
        4   6   5
    ×       2   8
  ─────────────────
    9₁  3₁  0   0      465 × 20
    3   7₅  2₄  0      465 × 8
  ─────────────────
1   3   0   2   0
    1
```

Or use the grid method.

	400	60	5
20	8000	1200	100
8	3200	480	40
	11200	1680	140

11200 + 1680 + 140 = 13020

The total cost of the laptops is £13 020.

Remember:

+ You should always make an estimate to check your answer.
+ You can use a division to check a multiplication.
+ Look out for these words for multiplication: times, product, multiply.

Skills practice A

1 Copy and complete these calculations.

a $2 × 7 = \boxed{}$
b $\boxed{} × 6 = 48$
c $4 × \boxed{} = 36$
d $8 × 9 = \boxed{}$

e $\boxed{} × 6 = 72$
f $7 × \boxed{} = 56$
g $6 × \boxed{} = 18$
h $\boxed{} × 6 = 0$

2 Work out these calculations.

a i $3 × 4$ **ii** $3 × 40$ **iii** $3 × 400$

b i $5 × 7$ **ii** $5 × 70$ **iii** $5 × 700$

c i $6 × 8$ **ii** $60 × 8$ **iii** $600 × 8$

d i $7 × 9$ **ii** $70 × 9$ **iii** $700 × 9$

3 Work out these.

    a 3 × 10   **b** 5 × 100   **c** 8 × 1000

    d 17 × 100   **e** 20 × 10   **f** 90 × 1000

4 Work out these.

    a 5 × 30   **b** 30 × 40   **c** 50 × 20

    d 80 × 50   **e** 400 × 3   **f** 70 × 40

5 Work out these.

    a 17 × 4   **b** 17 × 400   **c** 239 × 8

    d 239 × 8000   **e** 69 × 7   **f** 69 × 70

6 Many things are sold in packs.

    a How many cereal boxes are there in

        i 3 packs   **ii** 8 packs?

    b How many greetings cards are there in

        i 7 packs   **ii** 9 packs?

Greetings cards: packs of 5

    c How many dog treats are there in

        i 5 packs   **ii** 14 packs?

7 A coach trip costs £65 per person.

How much does a trip for a family of three people cost?

8 Six friends go out together in Paris.

Find the total cost of

    a their meal

    b their tickets to the theatre

    c their ice-cream.

9 Freya works out that 414 ÷ 18 = 23.

    a Use Freya's answer to find the answer to 18 × 23.

    b Explain how you know.

Reasoning

Skills practice B

1 Look how Lucy works out 19 × 24.
Work out these using Lucy's method.

  a 29 × 15

  b 11 × 23

  c 9 × 47

  d 21 × 33

  e 43 × 19

  f 37 × 17

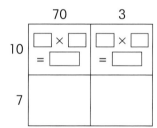

> I know 10 lots of 24 is 240
> So 20 lots of 24 is 480
> So 19 lots of 24 is 480 − 24
> So 19 × 24 = 456

Lucy

2 Copy and complete these multiplications.

  a 54 × 18 =

	50	4
10	50 × 10 = 500	4 × 10 = ☐
8	☐ × ☐ = ☐	☐ × ☐ = ☐

  b 73 × 17 =

	70	3
10	☐ × ☐ = ☐	☐ × ☐ = ☐
7		

Remember: To find the product you multiply.

3 Find the product of each pair of numbers.

  a 43 and 35   **b** 621 and 78   **c** 507 and 93

  d 477 and 23   **e** 517 and 88   **f** 4091 and 238

4 A holiday company offers the following prices per person for return flights.

  a Amsterdam for £79.

  b Montego Bay for £290.

  c Bermuda for £369.

  d Rio de Janeiro for 312 euros.

How much would each holiday cost for eight people?

5 A group of six friends are considering the holidays listed below.

  a How much would each cost the group of friends?

    i A weekend break in New York for £269 per person.

    ii 12 days in the Rockies for £1145 per person.

    iii A 7-day Mediterranean cruise for £699 per person.

  b How much would it cost, in the currency given, to stay for 17 days at each of these rates?

    i £65 per day   **ii** 187 euros per day   **iii** 97 dollars per day   **iv** 238 euros per day.

6 A cinema has 37 rows of seats. Each row seats 25 people.
How many people can watch a film at the same time?

7 A wood has 25 rows of trees. Each row has 17 trees.
How many trees are there in the wood?

Reasoning

8 In these calculations each ☐ stands for a missing digit.

Can you find them? (One cannot be done.)

a 35 × 57 = 1 ☐☐ 5   **b** ☐ 3 × 59 = 767   **c** 1 ☐☐ × 23 = 3013

d 36 × 4 ☐ = 169 ☐   **e** 56 × 7 ☐ = 4 ☐ 32   **f** ☐ 9 × ☐ 7 = 1 ☐☐ 3

g 48 × ☐ 7 = 2 ☐☐ 6   **h** 1 ☐ × ☐ 9 = 4 ☐ 6   **i** 36 × 4 ☐ = 69 ☐

j ☐ 3 × ☐ 7 = 41 ☐☐   **k** ☐ 7 × ☐ 3 = 1591

Wider skills practice

Problem solving

1 An ounce is approximately 28 grams.

A muffin weighs 4 ounces.

a How many grams does one muffin weigh?

b How many grams would six muffins weigh?

2 In each of these calculations, the letters (A, B, etc.) stand for different single digits (but not zero). Work out what they can be. There are two possible sets of answers for parts **a** and **b** but only one for part **c**.

a
```
    A
×   A
─────
  B A
```

b
```
    C
×   C
─────
  D 6
```

c
```
  2 L M
×     M
───────
L M N L
```

Problem solving

3 In these multiplications, each letter represents a missing digit. Find the missing digits.

a
```
    A 7 B
×       3
─────────
  C 4 D 5
```

Hint: Find B first, then D, then A and C.

b
```
    E 6 4
×       F
─────────
  6 1 G 2
```

c
```
  H I J K
×       7
─────────
  3 6 7 2 9
```

Reasoning

4 Find a route from START to FINISH that totals 100 exactly.

Which route from START to FINISH has the lowest total?

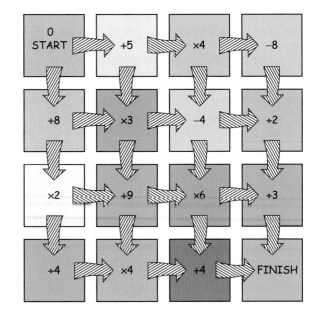

14

Applying skills

1 Avonford School orders new tables for the dining hall. There is a choice of two designs.

£30

£32

The dining hall is to seat 336 pupils.

  a How many tables does the school need if they are
     i hexagonal   **ii** octagonal?

  b Which design of table is cheaper for the school to order?
     How much money does the school save?

2 Tom and Lucy have each worked out 236 × 48.

 The answer is 1328

 No, the answer is 11 329

  Tom   Lucy

  Without working out the calculation explain why both Tom and Lucy are wrong.

3 You can make different products using the digits 1, 2, 3, 4 and 5 exactly once, for example 123 × 45 or 34 × 125.
  What is the largest product you can make using those digits?
  Explain your answer.

Reviewing skills

1 Find the product of each pair of numbers.
  a 3 and 90   b 30 and 90   c 30 and 900

2 Work out these.
  a 56 × 3   b 56 × 30   c 56 × 33

3 Find the product of 217 and 12.

4 A train has 16 coaches. Each coach seats 64 people.
  How many people can sit on the train?

5 A gardener plants 13 rows of 25 tulip bulbs and 15 rows of 17 daffodil bulbs.
  How many bulbs does he plant altogether?

Building skills

Example outside the Maths classroom

Carpontry

Toolbox

Use the same methods to add and subtract decimals as you use for whole numbers.

- **Column method**

  Use the column method to add 11.23 and 4.58

  Make sure you line up the numbers with the decimal point:

  ```
      1  1  .  2  3
  +      4  .  5  8
  ─────────────────
      1  5  .  8  1
                 1
  ```

- **Number line**

  5.7 + 3.2 = 5.7 + 3 + 0.2

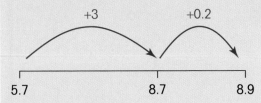

So 5.7 + 3.2 = 8.9

- **Partitioning**   break up one or both numbers into units, tenths, hundredths and so on.

  Use partitioning to subtract 0.57 from 10.3

  $$10.3 - 0.57 = 10.3 - 0.3 - 0.2 - 0.07 = 10 - 0.2 - 0.07$$
  $$= 9.8 - 0.07$$
  $$= 9.73$$

Example – Working out change

Joseph decides he needs all of these items before he goes back to school.

BACK TO SCHOOL

Geometry set	£3.70
Fountain pen	£6.50
Calculator	£5.25

Special Offer

a How much does it cost altogether?

b Joseph pays with two £10 notes. How much change should he receive?

Solution

a
```
    3 . 70
    6 . 50
+   5 . 20
───────────
   15 . 45
```

Make sure you line up the numbers with the decimal point.

b Write £20 as £20.00

```
£ ¹2 ¹0 . ¹0⁹ ¹0
− £ 1 5 . 4  5
─────────────────
£      4 . 5  5
```

Remember:

✦ When you use the column method, make sure you line up numbers with the decimal point.

Skills practice A

1 Work out

   a 0.11 + 6 units   **b** 0.11 + 3 tenths

   c 0.11 + 7 hundredths   **d** 0.11 + 9 tenths

2 Work out

   a 3.4 + 0.3   **b** 5.7 + 6.2   **c** 4.1 + 5.8   **d** 7.2 + 8.8

   e 9.4 + 7.3   **f** 12.2 + 13.9   **g** 6.6 + 3.7   **h** 5.6 + 4.1

3 Work out

   a 5.4 − 0.2   **b** 5.8 − 2.2   **c** 4.1 − 2.0   **d** 8.7 − 5.3

   e 9.4 − 8.6   **f** 11.7 − 10.9   **g** 26.4 − 13.6   **h** 5.3 − 3.9

4 Subtract each of these numbers from 10.

   a 6.1   **b** 4.8   **c** 7.3   **d** 5.9   **e** 8.7

Reasoning

5 Work out

   a 3.6 + 2.9   **b** 7.5 + 5.7   **c** 23.3 + 3.5

   d 22.45 + 0.53   **e** 31.56 + 78.45   **f** 34.065 + 2.303

   g 1.2345 + 2.3456   **h** 0.567 + 0.789   **i** 3.332 + 0.393

6 Work out

   a 3.6 − 2.9   **b** 7.5 − 5.7   **c** 23.3 − 3.5

   d 22.45 − 0.53   **e** 78.45 − 31.56   **f** 34.065 − 2.303

   g 2.3456 − 1. 4567   **h** 0.789 − 0.567   **i** 3.332 − 0.393

7 For each of the calculations below, write six more number sentences you can work out using them. In each case an example has been done for you.

   a 3.8 + 6.2 = 10   **b** 0.65 + 0.35 = 1   **c** 0.09 + 0.01 = 0.1

Examples:

    3.81 + 6.22 = 10.03   1.65 + 0.35 = 2   0.49 + 0.01 = 0.5

Skills practice B

1 David has £23.98 in his money box. He uses it to buy the following items. Find the amount he has left after each purchase.

   a flowers for Granny's birthday, £6.95

   b ticket and programme for Goliaths v Spartans, £8.50

   c Easter eggs and card, £3.98

2 Find the total cost of each set of items.

   a T-shirt £17.99   **b** Trainers £54.99

      Shorts £19.99   Sports bag £35.99

      Sunglasses £27.99   Sweatshirt £39.99

3 Work out

   a £7.39 + £21.25 + £12.30   **b** 24.65 m + 17.34 m + 5.08 m   **c** 29.01 + 7.37 + 16.92

   d £10.71 − £3.46   **e** 12.35 m − 4.82 m   **f** 16.03 − 9.77

4 Work out

   a 2.3 + 3.72   **b** 2.04 + 4 + 2.2   **c** 62.3 + 6.23 + 0.62

   d 0.19 + 0.01 + 0.8   **e** 0.90495 + 0.00205 + 0.093   **f** 10.92 − 6.3

   g 2 − 0.05   **h** 0.602 − 0.25

5 Add these numbers.

   a 24.02 + 13.4   **b** 36.234 + 25.68   **c** 27.567 + 32.62

6 Subtract these numbers.

   a 24.54 − 17.33   **b** 36 − 14.7   **c** 42.5 − 17.834

7 Work out these calculations.

Match your answers to the letters to crack the code.

5.14	5.80	7.77	9.78	9.89	10.78	16.96	17.56	26.21	31.41
E	D	A	L	S	C	I	N	O	M

a	b	c	d		e	f		g	h	i	j	k	l	m	n

a   12.34
   + 4.62

b   8.04
   + 2.74

c   5.13
   + 2.64

d   14.50
   + 3.06

e   2.56
   + 3.24

f   22.78
   + 3.43

g   17.86
   − 12.06

h   10.69
   − 5.55

i   19.99
   − 9.21

j   19.28
   − 2.32

k   43.24
   − 11.83

l   9.35
   − 1.58

m   14.10
   − 4.32

n   10.21
   − 0.32

8 Play this game with a friend. You will need a six-sided die.

Each player starts with a score of 0. First player to 10 or more wins.

On your turn:

- Roll as many times as you like
- Use the table to find out what your throw means

Number thrown	This means you ...
1	lose everything you have scored this turn and end your turn!
2	add 0.2
3	add 0.3
4	add 0.4
5	add 0.5
6	subtract 0.6 if your total is 0.6 or more

- If you throw a 1 your turn ends and you go back to your score before the turn.
- Throw again or end your turn by banking your score

9 Sarah wants to buy all these items to decorate her bedroom.

Find the total cost.

- Paint £15.99
- Pillowcases £10.99
- Curtains £29.99
- Duvet cover £23.99
- Sheet £24.99
- Table lamp £14.99

10 Amanda and Lionel are in the pharmacy.

a Amanda buys some emery boards, cotton wool, nail scissors and nail polish.

   i How much does this cost altogether?

   ii How much change will she get from a £10 note?

b Lionel buys some hair gel, deodorant and soap.

   i How much does this cost altogether?

   ii How much change will he get from a £10 note?

emery boards   99p
cotton wool   £1.45
nail scissors   £2.49
nail polish   £4.50
hair gel   £2.19
deodorant   £2.29
soap bar   £2.35

11 For her new flat, Tara needs to buy all these kitchen utensils.

   a What is the total cost of her shopping list?

   b Tara has £100 to spend. How much does she have left?

4 mugs	at £ 1.49 each
4 glasses	at £ 1.49 per pack of 4
1 teapot	at £ 3.99
A set of crockery	at £ 10.99
A wok set	at £ 17.99
A kettle	at £ 14.99
A toaster	at £ 12.49

Wider skills practice

1 Work out the perimeter of each of these triangles.

a

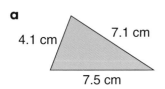

4.1 cm   7.1 cm   7.5 cm

b

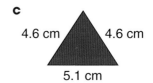

4.2 cm   8.5 cm   6.6 cm

c

4.6 cm   4.6 cm   5.1 cm

2 The number in each rectangle is the total of the numbers in the circles it is joined to.

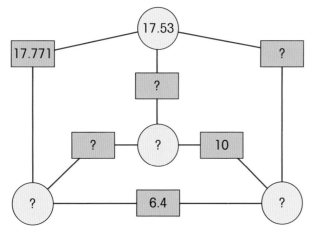

Copy the diagram and fill in all the missing numbers.

Reasoning

Applying skills

1 Ali buys all of these computer games with money he has been saving.

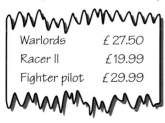

Warlords	£27.50
Racer II	£19.99
Fighter pilot	£29.99

a How much do the games cost him altogether?

b Later that same year he sells them to a friend for these amounts. How much does he lose?

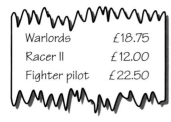

Warlords	£18.75
Racer II	£12.00
Fighter pilot	£22.50

c With the money from the sale he wants to buy a new soundboard for his computer.
The new card costs £75.99. How much more money does he need to buy the card?

2 Rachel is given £100 for doing well in her exams. She decides to spend it on new clothes.

This is a list of clothes she would like to buy. She realises she cannot buy all of them!

What combination of clothes can she choose to spend as much of her £100 as possible?

She does not want to buy more than one of any item.

Shoes	£27.75
Skirt	£14.99
Blouse	£12.99
Trainers	£32.49
Crop top	£9.99
Jacket	£33.45
Sweatshirt	£14.99
T-shirt	£6.99

Reasoning

Reviewing skills

1 Work out these calculations.

   a 4.6 + 5.1   **b** 3.7 + 3.5   **c** 8.1 + 2.59   **d** 4.76 + 8.9

2 Work out these calculations.

   a 2.7 − 1.1   **b** 8.7 − 3.8   **c** 9.75 − 2.19   **d** 4.31 − 2.9

3 Carlo's father goes shopping with £200. He goes to the fishing shop and buys all of these items.

Carbon fishing rod   £ 84.99

Thigh waders   £ 59.99

Fixed spool red   £ 34.99

a How much does this cost altogether?

b How much money has he still to spend?

c He decides to buy a bite alarm for £36.99.

How much money will he need to pay, in addition to the vouchers he has left?

Building skills

Example outside the Maths classroom

Bulk catering

Toolbox

Here are two formal methods you can use for working out a division problem

- short division
- long division.

Use short and long division to divide 276 by 6

Short division

$$\begin{array}{r} 46 \\ 6{\overline{)27^36}} \end{array}$$

6 into 2 doesn't go
6 into 27 goes 4 times with 3 left over
6 into 36 goes 6 times

Long division

$$\begin{array}{r} 46 \\ 6{\overline{)276}} \\ -24 \\ \hline 36 \\ -36 \\ \hline 0 \end{array}$$

← (**4 × 6 = 24, leaving 3**)

← (**6 × 6 = 36**)

Some people use an informal method know as multiplying up.

Use multiplying up to work out 276 divided by 6

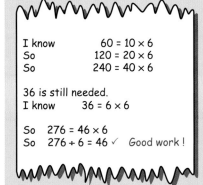

I know   60 = 10 × 6
So   120 = 20 × 6
So   240 = 40 × 6

36 is still needed.
I know   36 = 6 × 6

So   276 = 46 × 6
So   276 ÷ 6 = 46 ✓   *Good work !*

Example – Using long division

Work out 4439 ÷ 17

Solution

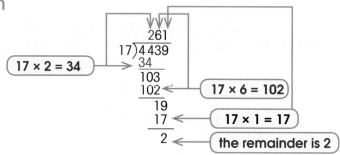

$17 \times 2 = 34$

$17 \times 6 = 102$

$17 \times 1 = 17$

the remainder is 2

4439 ÷ 17 = 261 remainder 2

Check: 261 x 17 = 4437

Add the remainder 2 to get 4439 ✔

Example – Short division

Work out 635 ÷ 5

Solution

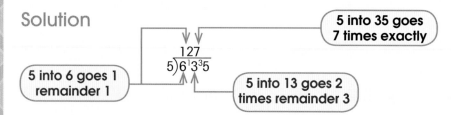

5 into 35 goes
7 times exactly

5 into 6 goes 1
remainder 1

5 into 13 goes 2
times remainder 3

So 635 ÷ 5 = 127

Check: 127 x 5 = 635 ✔

Example – Multiplying up

Poppy is making some bracelets.

Each bracelet needs 24 beads. Poppy has 320 beads.

How many bracelets can she make?

Solution

You need to work out $320 \div 24$.

You know that $10 \times 24 = 240$. Count up using a number line.

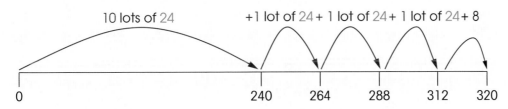

So Poppy can make 13 bracelets and will have 8 beads left over.

Notice that you have to round down because Poppy doesn't have enough beads for 14 bracelets.

Check your answer is about right: $320 \div 24$ is about $300 \div 20 = 15$

Remember:

✦ Check your answer by multiplying. If there is a remainder add it on.
✦ You can also use estimation to check your answer.

Skills practice A

1 Find the missing number in each of these calculations.

  a $24 \div 8 = \square$ **b** $64 \div \square = 8$ **c** $36 \div 9 = \square$

  d $\square \div 9 = 1$ **e** $48 \div \square = 6$ **f** $\square \div 7 = 8$

  g $\square \div 9 = 9$ **h** $45 \div \square = 9$ **i** $72 \div \square = 9$

2 Look at these numbers: 592, 713, 834, 1055, 1068.

  a Which of them are even numbers?

  b Divide all your answers to part **a** by 2.

  c Can you divide any of them by 2 again?

3 Speed test! See how quickly you can answer these.

  a $736 + 203 = \square$ **b** $14 + 23 + 17 = \square$ **c** $99 + 98 = \square$ **d** $230 - 96 = \square$

  e $300 - 97 = \square$ **f** $180 - 153 = \square$ **g** $\square \times 7 = 56$ **h** $421 \times 5 = \square$

  i $72 \div \square = 8$ **j** $324 \div 4 = \square$ **k** $6 \times 12 = \square$ **l** $7 \times 7 = \square$

4 Speed test! See how quickly you can answer these.

a 25 + 60 + 18	**b** 41 + 173 + 68	**c** 514 + 307 + 266	**d** 399 + 28 + 514
e 19 – 8	**f** 65 – 32	**g** 236 – 197	**h** 1050 – 688
i 403 × 6	**j** 589 × 7	**k** 327 × 63	**l** 516 × 88
m 210 ÷ 6	**n** 2891 ÷ 7	**o** 832 ÷ 8	**p** 832 ÷ 16
q 27 × 8	**r** 27 × 16	**s** 1764 ÷ 9	**t** 1764 ÷ 36

5 Calculate these divisions.

a 138 ÷ 3	**b** 245 ÷ 5	**c** 156 ÷ 2	**d** 234 ÷ 3
e 530 ÷ 5	**f** 186 ÷ 6	**g** 528 ÷ 4	**h** 756 ÷ 6
i 176 ÷ 8	**j** 864 ÷ 3	**k** 378 ÷ 9	**l** 7695 ÷ 5
m 504 ÷ 14	**n** 552 ÷ 24	**o** 884 ÷ 17	**p** 1957 ÷ 19

Skills practice B

1 Three friends share £156 between them.
How much should they get each?

2 Four friends share some takeaway pizza. The takeaway costs £28.
How much should each friend pay?

3 Humza and seven of his friends have gone out for a meal. The meal costs £184.
How much should each person pay?

4 Isobel has £12.40 worth of credit on her mobile phone.   ← (Hint: Change pounds to pence.)
A phone call costs her 15p per minute.
How many whole minutes of phone calls can she make?

5 658 football fans are going to see an away match. Each coach can seat 54 fans.
How many coaches do they need to hire?

6 Millie is planning a trip to the Space Museum for her Youth Group.
She has £430 to spend.
How many people can go?

SPACE MUSEUM
Tickets £15 per person

7 326 students sign up for a school trip.   ← (Remember: all the students want to go!)
How many minibuses are needed?

Maximum
load
16 people

8 A group of friends go to Avonford
Adventure Park.
How many are in the group?

Avonford Adventure Park
£24 per person

Total: £336

Reasoning

Reasoning

9 In these number pyramids, the number in each brick is found by multiplying together the numbers in the two bricks underneath it. Find the missing numbers.

a

112

4   7

b

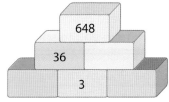

648

36

3

10 How much is the cost per day of each of the following holidays?

a an 11-day ski holiday in the Alps for £1375

b a 16-day holiday in Canada for £2048

c a 14-day Greek island cruise for £1386

d a 28-day Andes trek for £1484

Wider skills practice

Reasoning

1 Use the fact that 2664 ÷ 72 = 37 to find the answers to these calculations.

a 2664 ÷ 37   **b** 2664 ÷ 74   **c** 2664 ÷ 36   **d** 2664 ÷ 9

e 37 × 72   **f** 37 × 36   **g** 370 × 36   **h** 37 000 × 18

Reasoning

2 Use the fact that 2080 ÷ 32 = 65 to find the answers to these calculations.

a 2080 ÷ 65   **b** 2080 ÷ 16   **c** 32 × 65

d 64 × 65   **e** 20 800 ÷ 64   **f** 2 080 000 ÷ 64

Reasoning

3 Mercy and Karl are working out 330 ÷ 12.

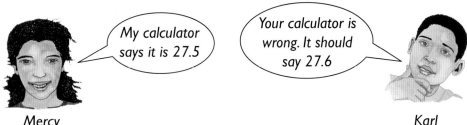

My calculator says it is 27.5

Your calculator is wrong. It should say 27.6

Mercy   *Karl*

a What is 330 ÷ 12? What is the remainder?

b Mercy uses her calculator to check her answer. Who is right? Why?

Problem solving

4 In these divisions, each letter represents a missing digit. Find the missing digits.

a L M 5
3)9 7 N

b   5 3 8
P)4 Q 4 R

c   6 5 3
7)S T U V

Applying skills

1 Give your answers to these problems as accurately as you can. Assume every year has 365 days.

  a How long would it take you to spend £1 000 000 if you spent £25 every day?

  b If a £10 note weighs about 1 gram, how much would £1 000 000 in £10 notes weigh?

  c The Moon is about 250 000 miles away. How long would it take you to walk there?

  d How many seconds old are you? If you have a 'birthsecond' party every 100 million seconds, when will your next party be?

2 A teacher draws a number line exactly 1 metre long on the board.
At one end of her number line she writes 0 and at the other end she writes 1 billion.

```
 ┌──────────────────────────────────┐
 0                            1 billion
```

  a How far from 0 should the teacher write 1 million on the number line?

  b How long would the teacher need to make her number line so that she can add 1 trillion to it?

3 Jo and Andy are playing 'Remainder bingo'. They take a card from a pack and answer the question. When the remainder is on their grid they can cross it off. The winner is the first person to get a line of three crossed out.

  a Here are the first card and their grids.

| 427 ÷ 17 |

Jo's grid:

1	0	9
4	3	8
5	6	2

Andy's grid:

7	0	10
6	1	4
3	2	8

Jo's grid   *Andy's grid*

  i What is the remainder? Who can cross off a number?

  ii Here are the next four cards. Who wins?

| 260 ÷ 15 | | 430 ÷ 13 | | 172 ÷ 18 | | 228 ÷ 12 |

  b Play your own game of 'Remainder bingo' with a partner.
Draw a 3 × 3 grid. Each choose nine numbers from 0 to 15 and write them in your grid.
Answer the following questions in turn.

  a 290 ÷ 18   **b** 161 ÷ 12   **c** 380 ÷ 17   **d** 317 ÷ 22
  e 352 ÷ 18   **f** 517 ÷ 23   **g** 423 ÷ 17   **h** 418 ÷ 14
  i 192 ÷ 12   **j** 211 ÷ 14   **k** 75 ÷ 8   **l** 160 ÷ 13
  m 223 ÷ 15   **n** 216 ÷ 11   **o** 316 ÷ 14   **p** 182 ÷ 21

Reviewing skills

1 Work out
   a 455 ÷ 7　　　　b 150 ÷ 6　　　　c 518 ÷ 14　　　　d 1445 ÷ 17

2 Work out
   a 985 ÷ 15　　　　b 460 ÷ 19　　　　c 315 ÷ 8

3 The cost of hiring a car for 12 days is £504. What is the cost per day?

4 Mrs Jones has £6000 to spend on laptops. Each laptop cost £325.
   How many laptops can she buy?
   How much money does Mrs Jones have left over?

Building skills

Example outside the Maths classroom

Accounts and finance

	A	B	C	D	E	F	G
1							
2		Monco Ltd					
3							
4		PROFIT AND LOSS ACCOUNT					
5			Year 1	Year 2	Year 3		
6							
7		Sales	£ 46,543	£ 52,128	£ 62,554		
8		Cost of Sales	£ 5,426	£ 5,643	£ 5,869		
9		Gross Profit	£ 41,117	£ 46,485	£ 56,685		
10							
11		Overheads					
12		Staff	£ 31,245	£ 37,494	38,994		
13		Premises	£ 7,785	£ 8,564	8,907		
14		Transport	£ 1,290	£ 1,342	1,395		
15		General expenses	£ 709	£ 737	767		
16		Total overheads	£ 41,029	£ 48,137	50,062		
17							
18		Net Profit/(Loss)	£ 88	-£ 1,652	£ 6,623		
19							

Toolbox

- When you add a positive number, you move to the right on the number line.
- When you add a negative number, you move to the left on the number line.

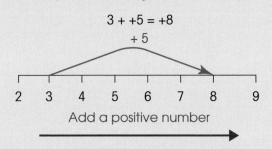

$$3 + {+5} = +8$$

Add a positive number

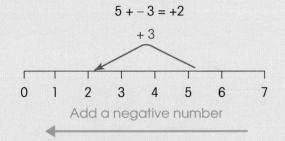

$$5 + {-3} = +2$$

Add a negative number

- When you subtract a positive number, you move to the left on the number line.
- When you subtract a negative number, you move to the right on the number line.

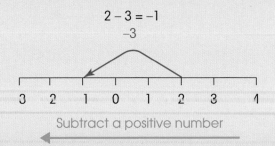

$$2 - 3 = -1$$

Subtract a positive number

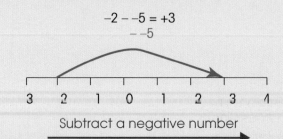

$$-2 - {-5} = +3$$

Subtract a negative number

Example – Adding a negative number

On Saturday the temperature was 3 °C.
On Sunday the temperature was –1 °C.
What was the average temperature over the weekend?

Solution

Calculate $\dfrac{3 + -1}{2}$

$3 + -1 = 3 - 1 = 2$

so $\dfrac{3 + -1}{2} = \dfrac{2}{2} = 1$

The average temperature was 1 °C.

Add a negative number

Example – Subtracting a negative number

Amy owes her sister £6. Her mum pays off £4 of Amy's debt.

a What calculation would represent the amount of money Amy now has?

b Calculate how much money Amy now has. Show your working out.

Solution

a Amy owes £6, so she has £(–6). Amy's mum has taken away £4 of debt. So Amy now has less debt than before.
   This can be written as –6 – (–4).

b

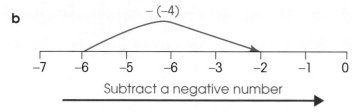

Subtract a negative number

Amy now owes £2.

> Remember:
>
> ✦ When a number is positive you do not need to write its sign.
> ✦ Adding a negative is the same as subtracting a positive; you move to the left on the number line.
> ✦ Subtracting a negative is the same as adding a positive; you move to the right on the number line.

Skills practice A

1 What number is

  a i 4 more than 5   **ii** 4 less than 5

  b i 3 more than 3   **ii** 3 less than 3

  c i 8 more than 7   **ii** 8 less than 7

  d i 10 more than 3   **ii** 10 less than 3?

2 Write these questions using positive and negative numbers. Take West as negative numbers and East as positive numbers. Work out where the finishing point is each time.

  a West 4 and then East 3   **b** East 1 and then West 6

  c East 3, East 4 and then West 5   **d** East 3 and then East 2

  e West 2 and then West 1   **f** West 1 and then West 7

3 Copy and complete these number patterns.

  a $3 - 2 = 1$ **b** $6 - 4 = 2$ **c** $4 - 4 = \square$

      $3 - 1 = 2$ $6 - 5 = \square$ $4 - 3 = \square$

      $3 - 0 = \square$ $6 - 6 = \square$ $4 - 2 = \square$

      $3 - (-1) = 4$ $6 - 7 = \square$ $4 - 1 = \square$

      $3 - (-2) = \square$ $6 - 8 = -2$ $4 - 0 = \square$

      $3 - (-3) = \square$ $6 - 9 = \square$ $4 - (-1) = \square$

      $3 - (-4) = 7$ $6 - 10 = -4$ $4 - (-2) = \square$

4 Work out

  a i $(+3) + (+2)$ **ii** $(+3) + (-2)$

  b i $(+5) + (+5)$ **ii** $(+5) + (-5)$

  c i $(+6) + (+8)$ **ii** $(+6) + (-8)$

  d i $(+2) + (+10)$ **ii** $(+2) + (-10)$

5 Work out

  a $(-5) + 7$ **b** $(-3) - 2$ **c** $8 - 11$

  d $6 + 4$ **e** $6 - 9$ **f** $(-3) + 5$

  g $(-2) + 3 + 1$ **h** $4 - 6 - 3$ **i** $(-5) - 2 + 3 + 1$

6 Copy and complete the table.

Temperature in morning (°C)	Change in temperature (°C)	Temperature in afternoon (°C)
+4	up 2	
+3	down 4	
−1	up 5	
−2	down 3	
−10	up 8	
−3	down 1	
0	down 4	
+1		+5
−2		−3

7 Simplify these.

a –(+2) **b** –(–3) **c** –(–6) **d** –(+1)

e –(–1) **f** –(–4) **g** –(+7) **h** –(+11)

8 Show these calculations on a number line.

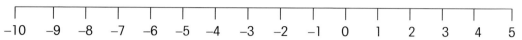

a (+3) + (–2) **b** (–5) + (–1) **c** (–3) + (+1) **d** (–1) + (–2)

e (+4) + (–6) **f** (–3) + (–6) **g** (+9) + (–4) **h** (–7) + (+3)

i (+20) + (+4) + (–18) **j** (–11) + (–5) **k** (–8) + (–14) **l** (+5) + (–3) + (–7)

9 Work out

a (–5) – (+2) **b** (–1) – (+3) **c** (+6) – (+2) **d** (+7) – (+6)

e (+7) – (+8) **f** (+5) – (–1) **g** (+3) – (–2) **h** (–6) – (–3)

i (–2) – (–2) **j** (–4) – (–1)

Use your calculator to check your answers.

10 Find the missing numbers.

a 8 – ☐ = 3 **b** 5 + ☐ = –9 **c** (–7) + ☐ = (–4)

d 8 + ☐ = 3 **e** 6 – ☐ = 8 **f** (–4) + ☐ = 1

g ☐ + 7 = 2 **h** ☐ – 7 = –10 **i** ☐ + 2 = –8

j (–1) – ☐ = (–6) **k** (–15) + ☐ = –9 **l** ☐ + 4 = –5

Skills practice B

1 Work out these calculations.

a (–1) + 7 **b** (–3) + 6 **c** 3 – 4 **d** 5 – 8

e (–5) + 7 **f** 5 + –7 **g** (–1) + –2 **h** (–4) – (–3)

i (–1) – (–1) **j** (–1) + (–1) **k** (–3) + 4 **l** 4 + (–2)

m (–3) + 1 **n** 1 – (–3) **o** 5 + –4 **p** (–6) + 9

q 2 + (–3) **r** (–2) – 2 **s** 2 – (–3) **t** 2 – (–4)

u (–5) + 8 **v** (–3) + 2 **w** (–2) + (–1) **x** 1 – (–1)

y (–1) – 1 **z** 6 + (–5)

Match your answers to the letters to complete the message below.

There are three types of mathematician in the world: those…

A	C	D	E	F	H	I	L	N	O	P	S	T	U	W
2	–3	4	5	–6	3	–5	7	–2	–1	–7	–4	1	0	6

2 Copy and complete this number wall.

The number in each brick is found by adding the numbers in the two bricks below it.

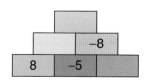

3 Calculate the difference between each pair of temperatures.

a Highest   Lowest   **b** Highest   Lowest

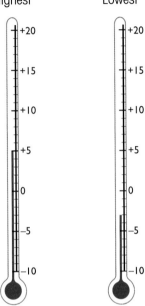
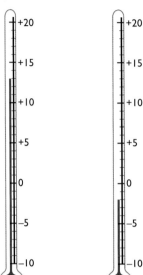

c Highest –1 °C, lowest –4 °C   **d** Highest +20 °C, lowest –5 °C
e Highest +2 °C, lowest –6 °C   **f** Highest –3 °C, lowest –10 °C

4 Each of these problems can be worked out using an addition sum.
For each problem, write down the addition and then solve the problem.
Example: The temperature is –5 °C. What will it be after a rise of 8 °C?
(–5) + (+8) = 3. The temperature will be 3 °C.

a I have €25 in my savings bank. I pay a bill for €34. How much money do I have?
b A lift starts in the basement (floor –1) and goes up four floors. What floor is it on?
c A seagull dives 20 m from a height of 15 m above the water.
How far below the surface does it dive?
d The temperature inside my shed is 10 °C more than outside. The outside temperature is –4 °C.
What is the inside temperature?

5 Mrs Green has £150 in her bank account. She receives a cheque for £50 from an insurance company. She has a phone bill of £95 to pay.
Mrs Green records her finances on this account sheet.

Credits (+)	Debits (–)	Balance (£)
		150
50		200
	95	?

a Copy the account sheet and fill in the missing balance.
b Extend your copy of the account sheet. Write these items in the correct column.
- Payment for dress £85
- Payment to hairdresser £40
- Competition win £100
- Payment for car repairs £150
- Payment for food £25
- Sale of old car £400

Work out the balance each time.

6 These are the temperatures in four cities recorded on 18 January.

London: 5 °C   Moscow: −9 °C   Rome: 7 °C   New York: −3 °C

   a What was the difference between the temperature in London and the temperature in Moscow?

   b How many degrees warmer was it in Rome than in New York?

   c How many degrees colder was it in Moscow than in New York?

   d On 19 January the temperature in New York fell by 5 °C.

      What was the temperature in New York on 19 January?

7 Copy and complete these addition grids.

a

+	7	3	−4	10
−1				
4				
−8				
−12				

b

+	5	−6		−4
−3				
9		6		
	−13			
				−2

8 The coldest temperature ever recorded was −89 °C, in Antarctica in 1988.

The hottest temperature ever recorded was 58 °C, in Libya in 1922.

What is the difference between these two temperatures?

Wider skills practice

1 In a magic square, you get the same answer when you add up the numbers in any row, column or diagonal. Copy and complete this magic square.

−4			−5
		2	
	1	2	−4
4	−6		7

Reasoning

2 Look at this puzzle. The total for each line of three is 2.

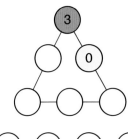

Copy these puzzles and choose numbers to complete them.
a The total for each row of three is 2.

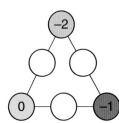

b The total for each row of three is −1.

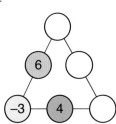

c The total for each row of three is −3.

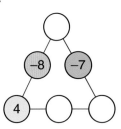

3 Use your calculator to work out these.
   a 14.4 − 29.7   **b** (−8) − 11.2   **c** 117 − (−351)   **d** (−67.8) − 32.2
   e 42.8 − (−22.9)   **f** 30 + (14.8 − 15.2)   **g** (−14.1) − (−26.7)   **h** (−6) − 62.7

Applying skills

1 On Monday morning a snail is 7 inches up a wall.
Every day the snail climbs 3 inches up the wall.
Every night it slips 1 inch down the wall.
The wall is 14 inches high.
What day does the snail reach the top?

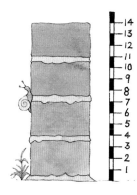

2 Here is the start of a cave system.

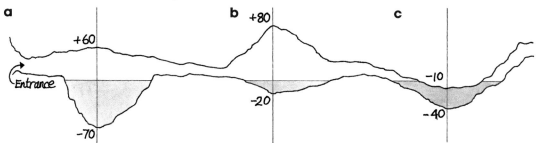

The other caves, in order, are at

	Top	Bottom
d	+15	−35
e	+25	−15
f	+70	−50

i Draw a possible version of the complete system on graph paper.

ii Work out the size, from top to bottom, of each cave.

Write a subtraction for each. The first one is done for you.

a (+60) − (−70) = 130

3 The manager of a bank opens his safe by turning a numbered dial.
The number 0 is at the top.
The turns needed to open the safe are written as
(+2) + (−4) + (+6) + (−2) + (−3)
Which number is at the top after the first turn of the dial?
......after the second turn?
Which number is at the top when the manager opens the safe?
The code for a different safe is written
+2, −1, +5, +1, −3, −5
These are the numbers that must appear at the top after each turn.
Write this code in words.
Write down a sequence of numbers for your own code.
Ask a friend to crack your code by describing the turns needed.

4 Chris is fed up. This letter has just arrived from the bank. He has been pretty bad at checking his online balance and it looks like he has been spending way too much.

> Dear Mr Cross
>
> I regret to inform you that your account is overdrawn and hence subject to a charge of £15 for an unauthorized overdraft. We have also been unable to honour the monthly payment for your mobile phone contact, which attracts an £8 administration charge.
>
> Please contact us at your earliest convenience to make arrangements to repay the money owed.
>
> Kind regards,
> Anthony Paine

He quickly goes through online security and takes a screen shot of his most recent transactions so he can work out what is going on.

Today's date: 21st April 2014   12 transactions found for the last 30 days

Date	Description	Money In	Money out	Balance
21.4.2014	Returned transaction fee		−8.00	−117.65
11.4.2014	Returned transaction – Phones4Him	35.00		−109.65
11.4.2014	Direct Debit – Phone4Him		−35.00	−109.65
21.4.2014	Unauthorised overdraft fee		−15.00	−74.65
20.8.2014	Lovinit clothing		−98.00	−59.65
19.4.2014	PizzaPlanet		−30.34	38.35
19.4.2014	Direct Debit – SafeCar Insurance		−35.87	68.69
18.4.2014	MusicMan Online – guitar		−256.00	104.56
10.4.2014	Premium Petrol		−56.00	360.56
9.4.2014	ChoccyWoccyKins nut selection		−12.50	416.56
3.4.2014	Sainsco Groceries		−76.56	429.06
30.3.2014	Lees Autos – BACS	825.56		505.62

a Chris decides to see if he can send anything he has bought back to get a refund into his account. Take a look at the statement. What items has he paid for? List them in order of cost. Tick those that you think he could get the money back for.

b Chris is not sure how he stands on returning things. His Aunt Lisa works at the Citizens Advice Bureau and tells him that if he bought anything online, he has the chance to send it back for a refund within 7 working days. Which items do you think might qualify?

c What would you advise Chris to do about returning any items? What would his new balance be if he followed your advice? Would he be able to get 'out of the red' and restore his balance to a positive rather then a negative number?

d Chris has been very foolish by spending money he has not got and not keeping an eye on his bank balance. What other problems might he have caused for himself by going 'into the red'? What do you think he should do differently in future?

Reviewing skills

1 Work out
   a (−7) + (−10)   b (+8) − (−3)   c (−4) + (−9)   d (+10) − (−15)
   e (+100) + (−20)   f (−70) − (−30)   g (+0.5) + (−0.5) h (+1.5) − (−0.5)

2 Jacob's freezer was set at −12 °C. He turned it up to −2 °C.
   By how many degrees did he increase the temperature?

3 One afternoon last winter the temperature in York was 4 °C at 2 pm.
   Between 2 pm and 2 am the temperature fell by 12 °C.
   What was the temperature at 2 am?

Unit 6 • Multiplying and dividing negative numbers • Band e

 Example outside the Maths classroom

Building skills

Modelling in science

Toolbox

- When you multiply or divide two numbers with the same sign, the answer is positive.

    $7 \times 3 = 21$ $(-7) \times (-3) = 21$

    $12 \div 4 = 3$ $(-12) \div (-4) = 3$

- When you multiply or divide two numbers with different signs, the answer is negative.

    $(-3) \times 2 = -6$ $3 \times (-2) = -6$

    $15 \div (-3) = -5$ $(-15) \div 3 = -5$

Example – Multiplying and dividing negative numbers

Work out

a $4 \times (-2)$ **b** $-4 \times (-3)$ **c** $-10 \div (+2)$ **d** $-9 \div (-3)$

Solution

Ignore the signs at first, and work out the calculation. Then decide on the sign of the answer.

a $4 \times 2 = 8$, so $4 \times (-2) = -8$ ⟵   **Different signs, so the answer is negative.**

b $4 \times 3 = 12$, so $-4 \times (-3) = 12$ ⟵   **Same signs, so the answer is positive.**

c $10 \div 2 = 5$, so $-10 \div 2 = -5$ ⟵   **Different signs, so the answer is negative.**

d $9 \div 3 = 3$, so $-9 \div (-3) = 3$ ⟵   **Same signs, so the answer is positive.**

Example – Calculating negative numbers and powers

Evaluate these.

a $(-3)^2$ **b** $(-2)^3$

Solution

a $(-3)^2 = (-3) \times (-3) = 9$ ⟵   **Same signs so the answer is positive. When a negative number is squared, the answer is positive.**

b $(-2)^3 = (-2) \times (-2) \times (-2)$

     $= 4 \times (-2)$ ⟵   **$(-2) \times (-2) = +4$ The signs are the same so the answer is positive.**

     $= -8$ ⟵   **$4 \times (-2) = -8$ The signs are different so the answer is negative. The cube of any negative number is negative.**

Remember:

✦ The order in which you multiply and divide does not affect the sign of the answer.

✦ Check the signs:

$(+) \times (+) = +$ $(-) \times (-) = +$ $(+) \times (-) = -$ $(-) \times (+) = -$

$(+) \div (+) = +$ $(-) \div (-) = +$ $(+) \div (-) = -$ $(-) \div (+) = -$

positive × positive = positive
positive ÷ positive = positive

positive × negative = negative
positive ÷ negative = negative

negative × negative = positive
negative ÷ negative = positive

negative × positive = negative
negative ÷ positive = negative

Skills practice A

1 Copy and complete these patterns.

a
$6 \times 3 = \boxed{}$
$6 \times \boxed{} = 12$
$6 \times 1 = \boxed{}$
$6 \times 0 = \boxed{}$
$6 \times (-1) = \boxed{}$
$6 \times \boxed{} = -12$
$6 \times (-3) = \boxed{}$

b
$2 \times 3 = 6$
$2 \times 2 = \boxed{}$
$2 \times 1 = \boxed{}$
$2 \times 0 = \boxed{}$
$2 \times (-1) = -2$
$2 \times (-2) = \boxed{}$
$2 \times (-3) = \boxed{}$

c
$(-3) \times 3 = \boxed{}$
$(-3) \times 2 = \boxed{}$
$(-3) \times 1 = -3$
$(-3) \times 0 = 0$
$(-3) \times (-1) = 3$
$(-3) \times (-2) = \boxed{}$
$(-3) \times (-3) = \boxed{}$

2 Make a copy of this multiplication grid.

a Fill in the missing numbers in the green areas.

b Describe the pattern of numbers in
  i the (−2) row
  ii the (−1) row.

c Continue these patterns into the red area.
  Look for more patterns.
  Then fill in all the numbers in the red area.

×	+3	+2	+1	0	−1	−2	−3
+3							
+2							
+1							
0							
−1							
−2							
−3							

3 Work out
a $(+2) \times (-5)$ **b** $(+3) \times (-7)$ **c** $(-6) \times 5$ **d** $(-9) \times 4$
e $(-5) \times (-1)$ **f** $(-8) \times (-9)$ **g** $0 \times (-7)$ **h** 6×0
i $(-4) \times 3$ **j** $5 \times (-6)$ **k** $(-7) \times (-7)$ **l** $(-1)^2$

4 Work out
a $(-8) \times (-6)$ **b** $(+2) \times (+6)$ **c** $(+5) \times 7$ **d** $0 \times (-3)$
e $(-3) \times 4$ **f** $7 \times (-9)$ **g** $(-2) \times (-2)$ **h** $(-9) \times (-10)$
i $25 \times (-4)$ **j** $(-4)^2$

5 $(-4) \times (-6) = (+24)$
Use this to work out
a $(+24) \div (-6)$
b $(+24) \div (-4)$

6 $(-5) \times (+6) = (-30)$
Use this to work out
a $(-30) \div (+6)$
b $(-30) \div (-5)$

7 Work out $(-2) + (-2) + (-2) + (-2)$. Why does this give the same answer as $(-2) \times 4$?

8 Work out
a $(-8) \div 2$
b $(-10) \div 5$
c $(-6) \div (+3)$
d $8 \div (-4)$
e $16 \div (-8)$
f $(-24) \div (-3)$
g $(-30) \div (-6)$
h $(-42) \div (-6)$
i $42 \div (-3)$
j $48 \div 3$
k $(-26) \div (-13)$
l $(+20) \div (+5)$
m $36 \div 3$

9 Work out
a $(-36) \div 12$
b $(-28) \div (-7)$
c $(+10) \div (+10)$
d $(-26) \div 2$
e $(-12) \div (-12)$
f $52 \div (-4)$
g $63 \div (-9)$
h $(-72) \div (-9)$
i $100 \div (-4)$
j $(-100) \div 20$
k $(-60) \div (-5)$
l $(-1) \div (-1)$
m $14 \div (-2)$

Skills practice B

1 Evaluate these.
a $(-3) \times (-2) \times (-1)$
b $(-2) \times (+5) \times (+4)$
c $(-2) \times (-2) \times (-2)$
d $(-3)^3$
e $(+10) \times (-3) \times (-7)$
f $\dfrac{(-2) \times (-3)}{6}$
g $\dfrac{(-3) \times (-2)}{(-6) \times (-1)}$
h $\dfrac{(-2) \times (-2) \times (-2)}{(-2)^2}$

2 $(-4)^2 = (-4) \times (-4) = +16$
a Work out
i 6^2
ii $(-6)^2$
iii 10^2
iv $(-10)^2$
b What can you say about the square of a negative number?
c Write down the square roots of these numbers. Each of them has two answers.
36   49   81   144   256

3 Copy and complete this multiplication grid.

×			6		12
5					
4	−16				
−2					
−3		9			
−10				−70	

4 George multiplies two numbers together. He gets the answer –18.

$$18 \times (-1) = -18$$

George

a What other whole numbers can he use? Find three more pairs.

b George multiplies two more whole numbers together. He gets 24.
   What numbers can he use? Find all the different pairs.

5 Work out

   a i $(-2)^4$ **ii** $(-4)^2$

   b i $(-2)^6$ **ii** $(-6)^2$

   c i $(-1)^4$ **ii** $(-4)^1$

   What do you notice?

Wider skills practice

1 Copy and complete this multiplying magic square.
   The numbers in each row, column or diagonal have the same product.

2	–9	–12
–36		
	18	

2 Copy and complete this table of values for $y = 4x$. Plot the points and join them up.

x	–3	–2	–1	0	1	2	3
$y = 4x$							

3 The formula $\dfrac{A + B}{2}$ gives the number that is exactly half way between A and B.

   Copy and complete the following table.

A	B	$A + B$	$\dfrac{A + B}{2}$
–1	–2		
–4	–10		
–7	3		
–12	5		
–3.5	–4.5		
–6.3	–6.4		

Reasoning

Reasoning

Reasoning

4 The formula $v = u + at$ is often used in physics. Use the formula to find v when

  a $u = 2$, $a = 5$ and $t = 6$
  b $u = 4$, $a = -10$ and $t = 3$
  c $u = -30$, $a = -0.5$ and $t = 6$
  d $u = 3.5$, $a = -1.5$ and $t = 4$

Applying skills

1 These are the midday temperatures during one week on Ben Nevis.
Work out the mean temperature for the week.

> Sunday −10 °C
>
> Monday −7 °C
>
> Tuesday −5 °C
>
> Wednesday 0 °C
>
> Thursday 2 °C
>
> Friday 2 °C
>
> Saturday −3 °C

2 Each question in an examination has four possible answers. Only one answer is correct.
A candidate receives 5 marks for a correct answer and (−2) marks for a wrong answer.
This formula gives a candidate's total mark.

$M = 5C - 2W$

  a Explain the formula.

  b Copy and complete the table to show the mark obtained by each candidate.

	C	W	$5C$	$-2W$	$5C - 2W$
Jane	10	10			
Edward	12	8			
Jessica	9	11			
Davinda	5	15			

  c George knows he chose the correct answer for eight of the questions and that one of his answers is wrong. He guessed the other 11 answers.

   i What is the highest mark that he can get?

   ii What is the lowest mark?

Reviewing skills

1 Calculate
  a $(+3) \times (-2)$
  b $(-3) \times (-2)$
  c $0 \times (-2)$
  d $(-5) \times (-4)$
  e $(-9)^2$

2 Calculate
  a $(+24) \div (-8)$
  b $(-24) \div (+8)$
  c $(-36) \div (-3)$
  d $\dfrac{(-20)}{(-5)}$
  e $\dfrac{-10}{2 \times (-5)}$

Example outside the Maths classroom

Building skills

Electricity bills

Toolbox

The order that operations should be carried out in is

- **B**rackets
- **I**ndices (powers, such as cubes or square roots)
- **D**ivision
- **M**ultiplication
- **A**ddition
- **S**ubtraction.

You can use the word **BIDMAS** to help you remember the right order.

Example – Using brackets

Work out these.

a $(8 + 5) \times 4$ **b** $50 - 2 \times (9 + 6)$

Solution

Remember BIDMAS.

a $(8 + 5) \times 4$ **Brackets**

     $= 13 \times 4$

     $= 52$ **Multiplication**

b $50 - 2 \times (9 + 6)$

     $= 50 - 2 \times 15$ **Brackets**

     $= 50 - 30$ **Multiplication**

     $= 20$ **Subtraction**

Example – Using powers

a Work out $(20 + 7) \div 3^2 + 4$ **b** $(10 - 3) \times 2^3 - 4$

Solution

a $(20 + 7) \div 3^2 + 4$

$= 27 \div 3^2 + 4$ ⟶ **Brackets**

$= 27 \div 9 + 4$ ⟶ **Indices**

$= 3 + 4$ ⟶ **Division**

$= 7$ ⟵ **Addition**

b $(10 - 3) \times 2^3 - 4.$

$= 7 \times 2^3 - 4$ ⟵ **Brackets**

$= 7 \times 8 - 4$ ⟵ **Indices**

$= 56 - 4$ ⟵ **Multiplication**

$= 52$ ⟵ **Subtraction**

Example – Using a fraction bar

Work out $\dfrac{6 \times 8}{14 - 2}$

Solution

The fraction bar counts as a bracket.
So this is the same as $(6 \times 8) \div (14 - 2)$

$= 48 \div 12$ ⟶ **Brackets**

$= 4$ ⟵ **Division**

Remember:

✦ When there is a mixture of + and −, you work from left to right.

✦ It is always helpful to use brackets to show the order of operations you mean.

✦ A fraction bar counts as a bracket.

Skills practice A

1 Work out these.

a $(2 + 3) \times 5$ **b** $(3 - 2) \times 100$ **c** $(2 + 1) \times 10$

d $(9 + 1) \times 10$ **e** $(12 - 2) \times 4$ **f** $(6 + 6) \times 3$

g $5 \times (8 - 4)$ **h** $(10 + 2) \div 3$ **i** $(7 + 3) \div 2$

j $9 \times (11 - 10)$ **k** $(5 + 2) \div 7$ **l** $(16 - 2) \div 7$

m $(4 - 1) \div 3$ **n** $(10 + 10) \times 5$ **o** $(6 \div 3) \times 5$

2 Work out these.

a $(5 + 4) \times (9 - 7)$ **b** $(9 - 1) \times (8 - 1)$ **c** $(100 - 10) \div (2 + 1)$

d $(3 + 2) \times (2 + 3)$ **e** $(5 - 4) \times (9 - 8)$ **f** $(6 + 6) \times (5 + 5)$

g $(3 - 2) \times (4 + 1)$ **h** $(6 - 2) \times (8 - 3)$ **i** $(9 - 4) \times (8 - 6)$

j $(7 - 1) - (8 - 6)$ **k** $(36 \div 3) \div (18 \div 9)$ **l** $(17 + 3) \div (8 - 3)$

m $(12 - 6) - (6 - 4)$ **n** $(12 \div 6) \div (6 \div 3)$ **o** $(9 \div 3) \times (5 - 2)$

3 Write in brackets to make each of these number sentences correct.
You may need more than one set of brackets.

a $5 + 2 \times 8 = 56$ **b** $9 + 42 - 6 \div 3 = 21$

c $14 - 8 \div 2 + 1 = 2$ **d** $7 + 3 \times 4 - 31^2 = 81$

e $7 - 5^2 - 1^3 = 27$ **f** $6 - 2 \times 8 - 3 = 20$

g $3 \times 5 + 4 - 8 + 12 \div 6 - 1 = 23$

4 Work out

a $(2 + 3) \times 6$ **b** $2 \times 6 + 3 \times 6$ **c** $(2 + 3) \times (5 + 1)$

d $2 \times (5 + 1) + 3 \times (5 + 1)$ **e** $(2 + 3) \times 5 + (2 + 3) \times 1$ **f** $2 \times 5 + 2 \times 1 + 3 \times 5 + 3 \times 1$

5 Work out

a $3 \times 10 + 4$ **b** $3 \times 100 + 4$ **c** $3 \times (10 + 100) + 4$

d $4 \times 10^2 + 5 \times 10 + 1$ **e** $4 \times 10^2 + 5 \times 10$ **f** $4 \times 10^2 + 1$

g $3 \times 10^3 + 4 \times 10^2 + 6 \times 10 + 9$ **h** $3 \times 10^3 + 6 \times 10 + 9$ **i** $3 \times 10^3 + 4 \times 10^2 + 9$

j $3 \times 10^3 + 9$ **k** $3 \times 10^3 + 4 \times 10^2 + 6 \times 10$ **l** $3 \times 10^3 + 4 \times 10^2$

Skills practice B

1 Here is a message in a code. You need to work out the code. What does the message say?

$3 + 5 \times 4$	$(5 + 5) \div 2$	$(2 + 1) \times (2 + 2)$
$2^2 \times 3$	$3 \times 2 - 6$	$2^4 \div 4$
$3 \times (4 + 1)$	$(4 + 3) \times (14 \div 7)$	$3^2 - 2^2$

2 Susan and Gary are contestants in a number quiz.

a Susan's target number is 358. The numbers she has are 100, 10, 8, 6, 4 and 3.
She can use the operations +, −, ÷ and × and brackets as many times as she wishes.
How can she make the target number?

b Gary's target number is 278. The numbers he has are 75, 50, 8, 4, 3 and 2.
How can he make the target number?

Reasoning

3 Work out

a $\dfrac{160 - 120}{5 \times 8}$

b $\dfrac{(16 - 12) \times 10}{40}$

c $\dfrac{(4 - 3) \times 40}{4 \times 10}$

4 Find the correct operation (+, −, ÷ or ×) to replace * and ○ in these statements.

a 17 * 17 ○ 17 = 306

b 38 * 47 ○ 58 = 49

c (47 * 53) ○ 10 = 1000

d 27 * (5 ○ 5) = 675

e 34 * (37 ○ 18) = 700

f (437 * 2) ○ 126 = 1000

g 91 * 7 ○ 13 = 49

h (47 * 34) ○ 27 = 3

i 768 * (43 ○ 37) = 128

j 1116 * (23 ○ 47) = 35

Wider skills practice

1 Find the value of

a $3(x + y)$ when
  - **i** $x = 2$ and $y = 8$
  - **ii** $x = 4$ and $y = 1$
  - **iii** $x = 2$ and $y = 0$
  - **iv** $x = 5$ and $y = -1$

b $5(x - y)$ when
  - **i** $x = 10$ and $y = 8$
  - **ii** $x = 10$ and $y = 9$
  - **iii** $x = 10$ and $y = 0$
  - **iv** $x = 5$ and $y = 5$

c $(x + y)(x - y)$ when
  - **i** $x = 5$ and $y = 2$
  - **ii** $x = 4$ and $y = 3$
  - **iii** $x = 6$ and $y = 0$
  - **iv** $x = 4$ and $y = 1$

d $(a + b + c) \div 3$ when
  - **i** $a = 5$, $b = 6$ and $c = 7$
  - **ii** $a = 1$, $b = 1$ and $c = 1$
  - **iii** $a = 2$, $b = 1$ and $c = 0$
  - **iv** $a = 9$, $b = 6$ and $c = -6$

2 Find the value of

a $x^2 + y$ when
  - **i** $x = 2$ and $y = 3$
  - **ii** $x = 4$ and $y = 3$
  - **iii** $x = 1$ and $y = 1$
  - **iv** $x = 5$ and $y = 2$

b $x + y^2$ when
  - **i** $x = 2$ and $y = 3$
  - **ii** $x = 4$ and $y = 3$
  - **iii** $x = 1$ and $y = 1$
  - **iv** $x = 5$ and $y = 2$

c $(x + y)^2$ when
  - **i** $x = 2$ and $y = 3$
  - **ii** $x = 4$ and $y = 3$
  - **iii** $x = 1$ and $y = 1$
  - **iv** $x = 5$ and $y = 2$

d $2(x + y)$ when
  - **i** $x = 2$ and $y = 3$
  - **ii** $x = 4$ and $y = 3$
  - **iii** $x = 1$ and $y = 1$
  - **iv** $x = 5$ and $y = 2$

Problem solving

3 Use a calculator and your judgement to find the correct operation (+, −, × or ÷) that belongs in each circle.

a (37 ◯ 21) ◯ 223 = 1000

b (756 ◯ 18) ◯ 29 = 1218

c 27 ◯ (36 ◯ 18) = 675

d 31 ◯ (87 ◯ 19) = 2108

e 476 ◯ (2040 ◯ 24) = 391

f (3461 ◯ 276) ◯ 101 = 37

g (967 ◯ 34) ◯ (1023 ◯ 654) = 369369

h $(2^9 ◯ 8^2) ◯ 9 = 64$

i (619 ◯ 316) ◯ 425 ◯ 196 = 924

j 6975 ◯ (36 ◯ 39) = 93

Applying skills

Problem solving

1 These numbers are being held prisoner. Their only means of escape is shown on the right.

a Can they all escape?

b Change the escape rules. Can all the numbers escape?

c Can you make up a rule so that

   i no numbers escape

   ii only some numbers escape

   iii only prime numbers escape?

Problem solving

2 Here are four cards with numbers on them.

  | 1 | −2 | −3 | 4 |

Using each card once and any of the operators below, other numbers can be made.

+ − × ÷ ( )

Work out these expressions.

a | 1 | × | −3 | + | 4 | − | −2 |

b | 1 | + | −2 | × | −3 | − | 4 |

c (| 1 | − | −2 |) ÷ (| −3 | + | 4 |)

Make every number from 1 to 15 using the cards above.

For each number:

- Use all four cards.
- Do not use any number card more than once.
- Do not use any operator more than once.

3 Mo is running a small building company, buying goods at lots of local shops. He rushed out to a small local builders merchants and bought himself a new hammer for £10 and 5 bags of nails at £2 per bag. He paid £30 and continued with his work.

Later that week, Joe – his partner, was checking the accounts, 'Why did you pay £30 for this Mo' – you have been overcharged!' No, that's right says Mo – and got out his calculator, look…. Sure enough – the total is £30.

a What buttons did Mo press on the calculator?

b Who is right and what is the correct bill?

c What will Mo have to be careful to do in the future so this does not happen again?

d Would Mo get the items cheaper if he buys the hammer last? Is that a rule he can work with in future?

e What can Mo and Joe do with their accounts to make sure they get their calculations right in the future?

Reviewing skills

1 Copy and complete this cross-number grid.

Across	Down
1 $14 + 120 \times 2$	**1** $2 \times 10^4 + 3 \times 10^3 + 2 \times 10^2 + 1$
4 $3 \times (11 \times 1000 + 1)$	**2** $(50 + 50) \div 2$
6 3×2^2	**3** $200^2 + 3 \times 200 + 1$
7 $(2 + 2)^3$	**4** $(1000 − 58) \div 3$
8 $(21 \times 10 − 9)^2$	**5** $(3 \times 10 + 1) \times (12 − 1)$
10 $1000 \div 5 − 9$	**9** $(4 + 3 \times 2) \times 5 − 1$

Building skills

Example outside the Maths classroom

Laying a lawn

Toolbox

When you multiply decimals you have two things to think about:
- getting the correct digits
- getting the decimal point in the right place.

Here are three methods you can use.
- rewriting the decimals so you are working with whole numbers.
  For example

  $0.03 = 3 \div 100$

  $8 \times 0.03 = 8 \times 3 \div 100 = 24 \div 100 = 0.24$

- the grid method
- long multiplication.

Example – Rewriting the decimals

Work out these calculations.

a 6×0.3

b 12×0.005

Solution

> 0.3 is rewritten as 3 ÷ 10

a $6 \times 0.3 = 6 \times 3 \div 10$

$= 18 \div 10$

$= 1.8$

> 0.005 is rewritten as 5 ÷ 1000

b $12 \times 0.005 = 12 \times 5 \div 1000$

$= 60 \div 1000$

$= 6 \div 100$

$= 0.06$

Example – The grid method

Calculate 4.36 × 23

Solution

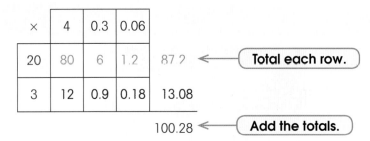

×	4	0.3	0.06	
20	80	6	1.2	87.2 ← **Total each row.**
3	12	0.9	0.18	13.08

100.28 ← **Add the totals.**

Example – Using long multiplication

Work out 12.36 × 1.5

Solution

We can treat 12.36 × 1.5 as 1236 × 15 as long as you adjust the number of decimal places at the end.

There are 2 + 1 decimal places here… → **…so put 3 decimal places in your answer.**

Work out 1236 × 15

```
        1  2  3  6
     ×        1  5
```
1 × 1236 →
```
     1  2  3  6  0    ←  This zero is a placeholder.
        6  1  8  0
     1  8  5  4  0
```

Now locate the decimal point.

12.36 × 1.5 is between 12 × 1 = 12 and 12 × 2 = 24.

So the answer should have two digits before the decimal point.

It is 18.540 or 18.54

Another way to locate the decimal point is to count the number of digits to the right of the decimal point. This should be the same in the question and the answer.

12.36 × 1.5 has 3 digits to the right, so the answer is 18.540
　12　　3　　　　　　　　　　　　　　　　　　　　　　　3 2 1

Remember:

✦ The number of digits after the decimal point in the answer is the same as the number of digits after the decimal points in the question.

Skills practice A

1 Work out the answers in these patterns.

a 180 × 300 = 54 000
    18 × 300 =
    1.8 × 300 =
   0.18 × 300 =
 0.018 × 300 =

b 180 × 3   =
   180 × 0.3   =
   180 × 0.03 =
   180 × 0.003 =

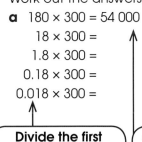

> **Divide the first number by 10...**
> **and so divide the answer by 10.**

> **Divide the second number by 10 and work out the answers.**

2 a Multiply each of these numbers by 0.5
    i 4   **ii** 8   **iii** 10   **iv** 7   **v** 3   **vi** 9

  b Copy and complete this sentence:
    Multiplying by 0.5 is the same as dividing by ☐.

3 Work out

  a 14 × 0.5   **b** 50 × 0.4   **c** 5 × 0.8   **d** 100 × 0.7
  e 15 × 0.4   **f** 4 × 0.9   **g** 64 × 0.2   **h** 16 × 0.2

4 Work out

  a 0.3 × 0.2   **b** 0.5 × 0.2   **c** 0.1 × 0.3   **d** 0.6 × 0.8
  e 0.01 × 0.4   **f** 0.06 × 0.3   **g** 0.07 × 0.07   **h** 0.005 × 0.005

5 Sally and Monique are shopping.

  a Sally buys three hairslides.
    How much is this altogether?

  b Monique buys two perfume sprays.
    How much is this altogether?

Perfume £23.68

Hairslides £5.95

6 Work out

  a i 10 × 6   **ii** 1 × 6   **iii** 0.1 × 6   **iv** 0.01 × 6   **v** 0.001 × 6
  b i 30 × 4   **ii** 3 × 4   **iii** 0.3 × 4   **iv** 0.03 × 4   **v** 0.003 × 4
  c i 20 × 7   **ii** 2 × 7   **iii** 0.2 × 7   **iv** 0.02 × 7   **v** 0.002 × 7

  What do you notice about the numbers of decimal places in the questions and the answers?

7 Work out the cost of each of these.

  a 6 rolls of wallpaper at £4.35 per roll
  b 4 toothbrushes at £1.59 each
  c 5 packets of toffees at 79p each
  d 9 rolls of parcel tape at £1.62 each

8 Work out these.

  a 0.3^2 **b** 0.5^2 **c** $0.4^2 × 10$
  d 0.4 × 0.5 × 0.6   **e** 0.23 × 1.4   **f** 11.2 × 0.7

Skills practice B

1 A rectangular carpet measures 4.3 m × 5.7 m. Calculate the area of the carpet in m².

2 The digits in these multiplications are correct, but there are no decimal points in the answers. Copy the calculations and put the decimal points in the correct place.
For example, 7.6 × 5.31 = 40356 can be corrected to 7.6 × 5.31 = 40.356.

  a 6.1 × 0.9 = 549   **b** 15.6 × 0.04 = 624   **c** 0.79 × 0.03 = 237   **d** 1.4 × 2.68 = 3752

  e 0.816 × 13.7 = 111792   **f** 0.98 × 3.71 = 36358   **g** 5.8 × 5 = 29   **h** 7.92 × 6 = 4752

3 This page shows Alan's answers to a maths test. Copy it out and mark it.
Correct any answers that Alan has got wrong. What is Alan's mark out of 10?

Maths Test
Name: Alan Wilson
(1) 3.2 × 0.4 = 12.8
(2) 0.04 × 4.2 = 0.168
(3) 0.8 × 0.6 = 4.8
(4) 5.6 × 0.5 = 2.6
(5) 1.4 × 1.4 = 1.96
(6) 0.05 × 6.8 = 0.34
(7) 4.2 × 0.8 = 3.36
(8) 8.2 × 5 = 4.1
(9) 0.3 × 6.3 = 1.89
(10) 7.5 × 0.2 = 1.5

4 Calculate

  a 2.4 × 0.2   **b** 128 × 0.3   **c** 5.6 × 2.4   **d** 9.24 × 0.25

5 Work out

  a 8.3 × 0.6   **b** 0.69 × 7   **c** 15.3 × 0.8   **d** 2.29 × 0.05

  e 2.8 × 0.17   **f** 0.34 × 5.6   **g** 18.7 × 0.61   **h** 0.12 × 0.12

6 Use the fact that 28 × 59 = 1652 to write down the correct answer to each of these.

  a 2.8 × 59   **b** 2.8 × 5.9   **c** 0.28 × 59

  d 0.28 × 0.59   **e** 0.028 × 5.9   **f** 0.028 × 0.59

  g 28 × 0.059   **h** 2.8 × 0.59   **i** 0.59 × 28

7 Without doing any multiplying, for each of the multiplications in column A identify the multiplication in column B that would give the same answer.

	Column A	Column B
a	5.7 × 98	0.057 × 9.8
b	5.7 × 0.98	57 × 0.98
c	0.57 × 98	0.57 × 9.8
d	0.57 × 0.98	57 × 9.8

Reasoning

8 A rectangle is 5.24 m long and 6.35 m wide.
  a What are these measurements in cm?
  b Calculate the area of the rectangle in cm².
  c How many cm² are there in 1 m²? Use this to work out 5.24 × 6.35.

9 A rectangle is 5.5 cm long by 2.4 cm wide.
  a What are these measurements in mm?
  b Calculate the area of the rectangle in mm².
  c How many mm² are there in 1 cm²?
  d Use this fact to convert the area in mm² to cm².

Wider skills practice

1 On one day the exchange rates are £1 = 1.57 US dollars and £1 = 2.35 Swiss francs.
   Convert these amounts into **a** US dollars **b** Swiss francs
   i £50   **ii** £80   **iii** £130

2 Copy and complete:
   $0.7^2 = 0.7 × 0.7 = 0.49$. So $\sqrt{0.49} = \square$
   Find the square root of each of these numbers.
   a 0.64   **b** 0.36   **c** 1.21   **d** 0.81
   e 0.04   **f** 1.44   **g** 0.0144   **h** 0.0025

3 A rectangle is 3.7 cm long and 2.3 cm wide.
   a What are these measurements in mm?
   b Calculate the area of the rectangle in mm².
   c How many mm² are there in 1 cm²?
      Use this to work out 3.7 × 2.3.

2.3 cm

3.7 cm

Applying skills

1 Find the total cost of each of these shopping bills. (Each price shown is for one article.)

a

Discount Shopper

1 × Cereal   @ £ 1.75
2 × Soap   @ £ 0.62
2 × Plant   @ £ 1.99
5 × Cat food   @ £ 0.32
1 × Biscuits   @ £ 0.99
3 × Pen   @ £ 0.17
2 × Milk   @ £ 0.60

**Thank you for
shopping with us**

b

Pets U Like

8 × Cat food   @ £ 0.33
1 × Cat litter @ £ 4.99
2 × Dog chew   @ £ 0.25
2 × Dog bowl   @ £ 2.75
1 × dog food   @ £ 0.37
3 × Nibbles   @ £ 1.16
2 × Collars   @ £ 1.99

**You need it,
we have it!**

Reasoning

Reasoning

2 A double sheet of newspaper measures 72.5 cm × 60 cm.

a Rewrite these lengths in metres.

b Calculate the area of this double sheet in m².

c The newspaper contains six double sheets.

What is the area of paper needed to make one copy of this newspaper?

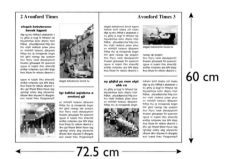

60 cm

72.5 cm

Reviewing skills

1 Copy these calculations. Put the decimal point in the correct place in each answer.

a 6.4 × 2.7 = 1728

b 9.83 × 0.014 = 13 762

c 5.26 × 41.7 = 219 342

d 0.025 × 0.68 = 1700

e 21.13 × 48.7 = 1 029 031

f 0.004 × 0.28 = 112

g 0.9 × 2.6 = 234

h 0.01 × 35.6 = 356

i 0.2 × 16 = 32

j 0.47 × 0.03 = 141

2 Work out these calculations.

a 0.4 × 0.1

b 0.32 × 0.4

c 2.2 × 0.03

d 2.4 × 0.8

e 0.04 × 0.04

f 1.6 × 0.05

g 8.3 × 0.6

h 0.69 × 7

i 15.3 × 0.8

j 2.29 × 0.05

3 Five of the rectangular tiles pictured are used to make the pattern below.

What is the area, in cm², of this pattern?

31.5 cm

10.5 cm

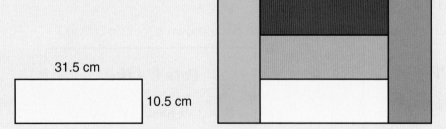

Building skills

Example outside the Maths classroom

Building quantities

Toolbox

Here are two methods you can use for working out a division problem:

- using equivalent fractions
  Start by writing the division as a fraction.
  Then multiply the top and bottom by a power of 10 so that both become whole numbers.
  You now have an easier equivalent fraction to work with.
  Here is how to find $0.6 \div 0.05$:

$$\times 100$$

$$\frac{0.6}{0.05} = \frac{60}{5} = 12 \quad \longleftarrow \quad \boxed{\frac{0.6}{0.05} \text{ and } \frac{60}{5} \text{ are equivalent fractions.}}$$

$$\times 100$$

- short division

Here is how to find $4.4 \div 6$ using short division:

$$6 \overline{)4.4^20} \longrightarrow 6 \overline{)4.4^20^2} \longrightarrow 6 \overline{)4.4^20^20}$$
$$\quad 0.7 \qquad\qquad 0.73 \qquad\qquad 0.733$$

You can also use long division.

Example – Using equivalent fractions

Work out these calculations.

a $3 \div 0.2$

b $1.2 \div 0.03$

Solution

a Write this as a fraction $\dfrac{3}{0.2}$

Now multiply both the numbers (top and bottom) by 10. That makes them into whole numbers.

$\times 10$

$$\frac{3}{0.2} = \frac{30}{2} = 15$$

$\times 10$

You can see this result on the number line from 0 to 3. It is divided into 15 pieces each 0.2 long

0   1   2   3

b $1.2 \div 0.03 = \dfrac{1.2}{0.03}$

$\times 100$

$$\frac{1.2}{0.03} = \frac{120}{3} = 40$$

$\times 100$

Example – Using short division

Work out $3 \div 8$

Solution

$$8\overline{)3.\,0^60^400}$$
$$\quad\;0.375$$

You can write extra zeros at the end of the number, after the decimal point.

This extra zero wasn't needed.

Answer 0.375

Remember:

✦ Always give answers involving money to 2 decimal places.
✦ Use estimation to check your answers are roughly right.
✦ When you divide a number, you can write extra zeros after the decimal point to help you.

Skills practice A

1 Monique and Karen love shopping.
They buy several things together and share the cost by dividing by 2.
How much do they each pay when the total cost is
  a £1.30   **b** £2.50   **c** £7.00?

2 Divide each of these numbers by 2.
  a 1.3   **b** 2.5   **c** 7
  d 6.75   **e** 0.45   **f** 43.6

3 Divide each of these numbers by 5.
  a 1.3   **b** 2.5   **c** 7
  d 6.75   **e** 0.45   **f** 43.6

4 Divide each of these numbers by 4.
  a 3.4   **b** 2.7   **c** 5.6
  d 0.07   **e** 1.9   **f** 9

5 Divide each of these numbers by 8.
  a 5.2   **b** 7.3   **c** 0.5
  d 0.17   **e** 15.8   **f** 11

6 Divide each of these numbers by 6.
  a 1.2   **b** 2.34   **c** 1
  d 5   **e** 3.5   **f** 43.6

7 Write each of these numbers as a decimal.
  a 6 ÷ 10   **b** 0.6 ÷ 10   **c** 0.06 ÷ 10
  d 6 ÷ 100   **e** 6 ÷ 1000   **f** 0.06 ÷ 100
Describe in words the effect of dividing a decimal by 10, 100 and 1000.

8 a How many 2p pieces are there in
    i £2   **ii** £5
    iii £7   **iv** £9?
  b Divide each of these numbers by 0.02
    i 2.00   **ii** 5.00
    iii 7.00   **iv** 9.00

9 a How many half hours are there in
    i 3 hours   **ii** 7 hours
    iii 15 hours   **iv** 18 hours?

  b Divide each of these numbers by 0.5
    i 3   **ii** 7
    iii 15   **iv** 18

10 The diagram illustrates $4.0 \div 0.8$. The line has been split into 5 parts. So $4.0 \div 0.8 = 5$.

  Use this method to carry out the following divisions
  i $4 \div 0.5$ **ii** $3.5 \div 0.7$
  iii $3.6 \div 0.6$ **iv** $3.3 \div 1.1$
  In each case
  a draw a copy of the line (or part of it)
  b split it up as in the example above
  c give the answer to the division.

11 Work out
  a $8.4 \div 0.4$ **b** $7.5 \div 0.5$ **c** $6.9 \div 0.3$
  d $7.2 \div 0.3$ **e** $3.76 \div 0.8$ **f** $4.626 \div 0.9$

12 Alice wonders what happens when you divide by a number less than 1.
  She tried these calculations. Do them yourself and see what she discovered.
  a $4.2 \div 0.1$ **b** $4.2 \div 0.02$
  c $4.2 \div 0.01$ **d** $4.2 \div 0.003$
  e $4.2 \div 0.002$ **f** $4.2 \div 0.0004$
  g $4.2 \div 0.0003$

13 Calculate these.
  a $2.36 \div 4$ **b** $17.34 \div 3$ **c** $8.246 \div 0.2$
  d $5.75 \div 0.5$ **e** $0.344 \div 0.4$ **f** $16 \div 0.04$
  g $56.25 \div 0.05$ **h** $0.894 \div 0.002$

Skills practice B

1 Copy and complete this table:

Number	3.6	6	12.9	17.1	105
÷ 3		2			
÷ 0.3	12				
÷ 0.03					3500

2 Instead of dividing a number by 0.13, Jamie divides by 13. His answer is 6.5.
  What should his answer be?

Reasoning

3 Work out

a 0.224 ÷ 0.07   b 1.542 ÷ 0.06   c 24.75 ÷ 0.05

d 2.912 ÷ 0.08   e 0.861 ÷ 0.07   f 32.76 ÷ 0.09

4 Work out, showing all your working clearly.

a 24.5 ÷ 0.07   b 268 ÷ 0.8   c 15.05 ÷ 0.7   d 39.42 ÷ 0.03

e 2.1 ÷ 0.6   f 80.08 ÷ 0.2   g 78.5 ÷ 0.5   h 84 ÷ 0.4

i 79.2 ÷ 0.09   j 53.6 ÷ 0.8

5 How many textbooks 1.2 cm thick will fit onto a shelf 132 cm long?

6 A pack of 24 coloured pencils costs £2.88.

a How much does each pencil cost?

b Another pack of 18 pencils costs £1.98. Which set has the cheaper pencils in it?

7 Change each of these to a decimal by dividing.

a $\frac{3}{4}$ b $\frac{1}{4}$

$$\frac{3}{8} = 8\overline{)3.000} = 8\overline{)3.\,^30\,^60\,^40} = 0.\,3\,7\,5$$

8 a 1.5 ÷ 0.5   b 2.5 ÷ 0.5   c 1.6 ÷ 0.4   d 0.9 ÷ 0.9

e 3.2 ÷ 0.4   f 2.4 ÷ 1.2   g 3.6 ÷ 0.6   h 2.8 ÷ 0.4

i 2.7 ÷ 0.3   j 1.3 ÷ 0.1   k 3.8 ÷ 0.2   l 3.6 ÷ 0.3

m 2.4 ÷ 0.1

Match your answers to the letters to solve this riddle.

I	`	M	A	D	O	T	I	N	P	L	A	C	E	!
19		2	3	5	13	24		8	12	9	7	6	1	4	

Wider skills practice

1 Calculate these, correct to 1 decimal place.

a 286.4 ÷ 0.7   b 42.5 ÷ 0.9   c 81.81 ÷ 0.8

d 98.9 ÷ 0.6   e 101 ÷ 0.3   f 73.9 ÷ 0.07

2 a i Divide 4 by 11, giving the first 6 decimal places.

ii Do the same for 7 divided by 11.

iii Add your answers to **i** and **ii** together

iv Comment on part **iii**

b Repeat part **a** for **i** 2 ÷ 11   **ii** 9 ÷ 11

c Find another pair of divisions by 11 that give the same pattern.

3 In each of these divisions, a letter represents a decimal number.

Work out the value of the letter to make the division correct.

a $\frac{0.6}{p} = 20$ b $\frac{3.5}{q} = 7$ c $\frac{4}{r} = 200$

d $\frac{0.4}{s} = 4$ e $\frac{0.32}{t} = 0.8$ f $\frac{6.3}{u} = 70$

Reasoning

Applying skills

Problem solving

1 Is it possible to fit 26 magazines each 0.7 cm thick into a magazine rack 18 cm wide?
Show how you would work this out.

Problem solving

2 Perfume is sold in bottles containing 30 ml.
   a What is this volume in litres?
   b How many bottles of perfume can be
   filled from a tank containing 1500 litres?

Problem solving

3 There is 400 g of hot chocolate in this jar.
   a What is this in kilograms?
   b A factory produces 10 000 kg of hot
   chocolate in one day.
   How many of these jars can be filled?

Problem solving

4 **a** Work out 1 ÷ 13, 2 ÷ 13, and so on, up to 12 ÷ 13.
   b Comment on the patterns in your answers.
   c Complete these number circles and explain
   how they work.

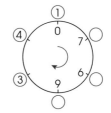 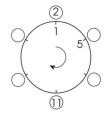

Reviewing skills

1 Work out
   a 22.72 ÷ 0.4
   b 51.6 ÷ 0.06
   c 0.65 ÷ 0.001
   d 11.2 ÷ 0.2
   e 2 ÷ 0.005
   f 7.2 ÷ 0.4

2 Work out
   a 1.95 ÷ 0.006
   b 2.24 ÷ 0.004
   c 0.4496 ÷ 0.008
   d 42 ÷ 0.005
   e 4.1157 ÷ 0.009
   f 3.3152 ÷ 0.007

3 Select the correct answer to each of the calculations.
   a 256 × 0.02
   b 256 ÷ 0.02

   | 5.12 | 12 800 |

4 How many magazines 0.6 cm thick will fit into a magazine rack 9.6 cm wide?

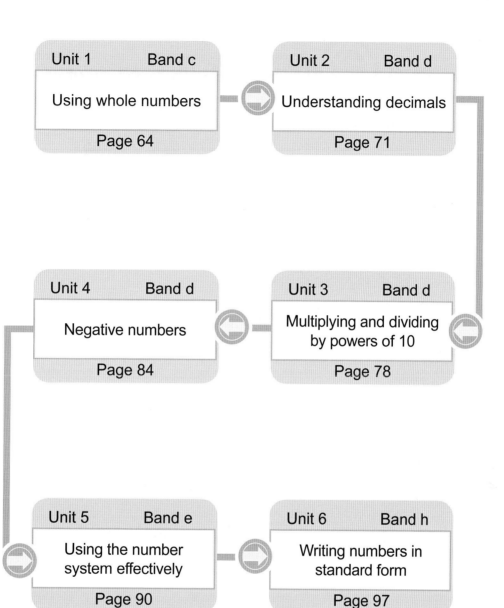

Unit 1	Band c
Using whole numbers	
Page 64	

Unit 2	Band d
Understanding decimals	
Page 71	

Unit 4	Band d
Negative numbers	
Page 84	

Unit 3	Band d
Multiplying and dividing by powers of 10	
Page 78	

Unit 5	Band e
Using the number system effectively	
Page 90	

Unit 6	Band h
Writing numbers in standard form	
Page 97	

Example outside the Maths classroom

Building skills

Money

 Toolbox

The further to the left a digit is, the greater its value. Each step left is worth 10 times as much. The 7 in 70 is worth 10 times as much as the 7 in 7 because it is one step further left.

It is sometimes helpful to label digits to keep track of their value using a place-value table.

Th	H	T	U
	4	6	7

Here the 4 means 400, the 6 means 60 and the 7 represents seven ones (or units). The total number is four hundred and sixty-seven.

Multiplying by 10 moves all of the digits left one step while dividing by 10 moves them all right. Looking at 467 multiplied by 10, each digit in 467 moves left and the gap is filled by a zero.

Th	H	T	U
4	6	7	0

Symbols can help to show which of two values is larger. When using inequality signs, the larger value goes on the larger side. So 70 > 7 is true, as is 4 × 10 < 50.

The equals sign means that the two values are the same, so 30 = 3 × 10.

Example – Using inequalities

Place the numbers 10, 11, 103, 103, 13 and 130 into the boxes to make three true statements.

$$\square > \square$$
$$\square < \square$$
$$\square = \square$$

Solution

There are several different correct answers. One is

11 > 10 ⟵ **In the inequality signs the larger end of the arrow is with the larger value and the smaller end is with the smaller value.**

13 < 130

103 = 103 ⟵ **The = sign means that the two values are the same.**

Example – Multiplying and dividing by 10 and 100

Work out the answers to these calculations.

a 3200 × 100

b 3200 × 1000

c 3200 ÷ 10

d 3200 ÷ 100

Solution

	M	HTh	TTh	Th	H	T	U
				3	2	0	0
a 3200 × 100		3	2	0	0	0	0
b 3200 × 1000	3	2	0	0	0	0	0
c 3200 ÷ 10					3	2	0
d 3200 ÷ 100						3	2

Million → M

Hundred thousand → HTh

Ten thousand → TTh

These two zeros are place holders. They fill the gaps.

× 100 moves the digits 2 places to the left.

× 1000 moves the digits 3 places to the left.

÷ 10 moves the digits one place to the right.

÷ 100 moves the digits 2 places to the right.

Remember:

✦ Multiplying by 10 moves all digits left one step.

✦ Dividing by 10 moves all digits right one step.

✦ The = sign means that the two things have the same value.

Skills practice A

1 The number 325 can be thought of as 3 hundreds 2 tens and 5 ones, or 300 + 20 + 5.

So 325 = 300 + 20 + 5.

Write these numbers in the same way.

a 498   **b** 694   **c** 703

d 314   **e** 87   **f** 1234

g seven thousand, three hundred and fifty-eight

h two thousand and thirty-four

2 Copy and complete this multiplication table.

×	1	2	3	4	5	6	7	8	9
1	1	2	3	4	5	6	7	8	9
10	10	20	30	40	50				90
100	100	200		400		600			900
1000	1000		3000		5000			8000	
10000	10000	20000					70000		
100000	100000	200000		400000					

a What calculation do you use to move from the numbers in one row to the numbers in the row below?

b What calculation do you use to move from the numbers in one row to the numbers two rows below?

c What calculation do you use to move from the numbers in one row to the numbers in the row above?

3 Multiply each number in Chart A by 10. Write your answer in a copy of Chart B.

Chart A

HTh	TTh	Th	H	T	U
			6	4	2
		9	8	4	3
		4	5	6	2
	8	6	3	6	4

Chart B

HTh	TTh	Th	H	T	U

4 Multiply each number in Chart A by 100. Write your answer in a copy of Chart B.

Chart A

HTh	TTh	Th	H	T	U
			5	3	2
			4	2	8
		5	6	4	0
		3	5	9	2

Chart B

HTh	TTh	Th	H	T	U

5 Divide each number in Chart A by 10. Write your answer in a copy of Chart B.

Chart A

HTh	TTh	Th	H	T	U
			1	8	0
		6	3	5	0
	9	6	4	2	0
8	6	8	7	0	0

Chart B

HTh	TTh	Th	H	T	U

6 Divide each number in Chart A by 100. Write your answer in a copy of Chart B.

Chart A

HTh	TTh	Th	H	T	U
			3	0	0
		3	4	0	0
	3	8	0	0	0
5	5	8	1	0	0

Chart B

HTh	TTh	Th	H	T	U

7 Copy and complete these charts.

a

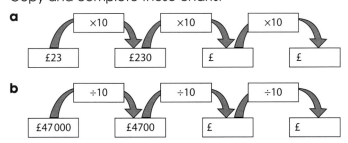

	×10		×10		×10	
£23		£230		£		£

b

	÷10		÷10		÷10	
£47 000		£4700		£		£

8 Sarah wants to change 42 into 4200.

Using the operation × 10, Sarah can change 42 into 4200 in two steps as follows:

42 × 10 = 420

420 × 10 = 4 200

How can Sarah change 42 into 4 200 using the operations × 10 and ÷ 10

a in four steps

b in eight steps?

c Explain why Sarah can't solve the problem using three steps.

9 In each part, fill in the box with one of <, > or =.

a 7 × 10 ☐ 7000 ÷ 10

b 200 × 100 ☐ 2 million

c 2050 ÷ 10 ☐ 25 × 10

d 8000 ☐ 80 × 100

e Five thousand ☐ 500000 ÷ 1000

Skills practice B

1 Look at the digit cards.

5 1 7 0 3 8

What is the smallest 3-digit number you can make with these cards?

Jo

*It is **one hundred and three.** What is the largest?*

Karl

	Smallest	Largest
4-digit number		
5-digit number		
6-digit number		

Use them to make the smallest and largest four-, five- and six-digit numbers you can. Write your numbers in a copy of the table.

2 Write each set of numbers in order from smallest to largest.

a 2345, 3245, 5324, 2543, 3425, 4235

b 2098, 9802, 9820, 9280, 2089, 2890, 2980, 8092, 9082

Reasoning

3 Write these numbers using digits

   a Five hundred and twenty six

   b Eight hundred and twelve

   c Five thousand three hundred and eight

   d Fifteen thousand and eighty one

   e Twenty thousand four hundred

4 Write these numbers in words

   a 735

   b 1009

   c 1407

   d 24008

   e 5000206

5 Look at these notes and coins.

   a How many 1p coins would you need, to have the same amount as each of these notes?

   b How many 10p coins would you need, to have the same amount as each of these notes?

6 Choose numbers to complete these inequalities.

   a ☐ × 10 > ☐ × 10   **b** ☐ × 10 > ☐ ÷ 10

   c ☐ ÷ 10 < ☐ ÷ 10   **d** ☐ ÷ 10 > ☐ × 10

   e ☐ ÷ 100 > ☐ × 10   **f** ☐ ÷ 100 < ☐ × 10

   g ☐ ÷ 100 = ☐ × 10

7 James thinks of a single-digit number. He puts his number through this set of steps.

   n ⟶ ×10 ⟶ ×10 ⟶ ÷10 ⟶ ×10 ⟶ ÷10 ⟶ Output

   Which of these could be the output?

   a 70   **b** 700   **c** 7000   **d** 7

   e 90   **f** 900   **g** 120   **h** 0

8 Use the operations × 100 and ÷ 10 to create a set of steps that will turn 67 into 67 000. How many solutions can you find?

Reasoning

Reasoning

Reasoning

Wider skills practice

Reasoning

1 Here are some cards with digits 0 to 9 written on them:

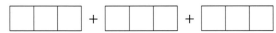

Place the cards into the boxes to make three 3-digit numbers (you'll have one left over).

☐☐☐ + ☐☐☐ + ☐☐☐

Add your three numbers together.

Find the three 3-digit numbers that make the answer

   a as large as possible   **b** as small as possible

Reasoning

2 Use your cards from question **1** and arrange them into each of these sets of boxes so that the result is:

  a as large as possible

  b as small as possible.

    i   ☐☐☐☐ × ☐☐

    ii ☐☐☐☐ ÷ ☐☐

Applying skills

Problem solving

1 a Play this game with a friend.

   Start by making one set of digit cards

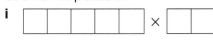

   and a game card like this for each player.

   Game 1

   ☐☐☐☐

- Place the cards face down on the table.

- One player chooses a card and turns it over.
  Each player writes that digit in one of the boxes on their game card.

- The next player chooses a card and turns it over.
  Each player writes that digit in one of the boxes.

- Carry on until each player has made a four-digit number.

- The winner is the person with the largest four-digit number.

  b Repeat the game several times.
  What strategies did you use for winning? Write your three top tips for another player.

Reviewing skills

1 In each part fill in the box with one of <, > or =
a 900 × 1000 ☐ one million
b 5000 ÷ 100 ☐ 5 × 10
c 25 × 1000 ☐ 205000 ÷ 10

2 a Write these numbers in digits
i Eight hundred and five
ii Six thousand and forty
iii One million four thousand and nine

b Write these numbers in words
i 1729
ii 4001
iii 620510

3 Copy and complete this trail of calculations.

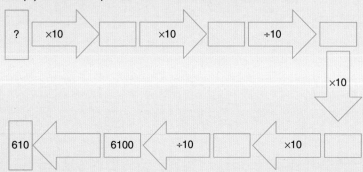

4 Copy the diagram. Write these numbers in the boxes so that all four inequalities are true.
940, 409, 490, 904

Building skills

Example outside the Maths classroom

Recording times in athletics

 Toolbox

The further to the left a digit is, the greater its value. Each step left is worth 10 times as much. The 7 in 1.7 is worth 10 times as much as the 7 in 0.17 because it is one step further left. The decimal point never moves. Any gaps can be filled in with a 0.

Although you don't have to, it is sometimes helpful to label the digits to keep track of their value using a place-value table.

T	U	.	$\frac{1}{10}$	$\frac{1}{100}$
	4	.	6	7

Here the 4 means four ones (units), the 6 means six tenths and the 7 represents seven hundredths.

The complete number is 4.67 and is made from 4 + 0.6 + 0.07

The place-value table also helps when ordering numbers.

Think about the numbers 4.67 and 4.8.

T	U	.	$\frac{1}{10}$	$\frac{1}{100}$
	4	.	6	7
	4	.	8	

Both of the numbers have four units and so are between 4 and 5. But 4.67 has six tenths while 4.8 has eight tenths, and so 4.8 is the larger of the two numbers.

Place-value tables are also helpful when converting decimals to fractions.

$4.8 = 4 + 0.8, 4 + \frac{8}{10}$ or $4\frac{8}{10}$.

$4.67 = 4 + 0.6 + 0.07, 4 + \frac{6}{10} + \frac{7}{100}$ or $4\frac{67}{100}$.

Being able to think of the same number in different ways – as a decimal, a fraction, or a collection of fractions – gives you much more flexibility when trying to solve problems.

Example – Ordering decimals

Place these decimals in order, from smallest to largest.

0.3   0.31   0.7   0.13   0.71   0.07

Solution

U	.	$\frac{1}{10}$	$\frac{1}{100}$
0	.	3	
0	.	3	1
0	.	7	
0	.	1	3
0	.	7	1
0	.	0	7

> A place-value table can help to show which digits represent the greatest value.

Looking at the place-value table, there is only one number that has no tenths, 0.07, so this is the smallest number.

The next smallest value in the tenths column is 1 so 0.13 is next.

There are two numbers that have 3 tenths, 0.3 and 0.31.
0.3 has no hundredths and 0.31 has 1 hundredth, so 0.31 is very slightly larger than 0.3.

Using the same reasoning 0.71 > 0.7.

So the order is

0.07   0.13   0.3   0.31   0.7   0.71

Example – Converting decimals to fractions

Convert these decimals to fractions.

0.3   0.31   0.7   0.13   0.71   0.07

Solution

You can use exactly the same place-value table as in the previous example to convert the decimals to fractions.

1	.	$\frac{1}{10}$	$\frac{1}{100}$	Explanation	Answer
0	.	3		0.3 has no units and 3 tenths, so it can be written as $\frac{3}{10}$	$\frac{3}{10}$
0	.	3	1	0.31 has no units, 3 tenths and 1 hundredth, so it can be written as $\frac{3}{10} + \frac{1}{100}$ or $\frac{31}{100}$	$\frac{31}{100}$
0	.	7		$0.7 = \frac{7}{10}$	$\frac{7}{10}$
0	.	1	3	$0.13 = \frac{1}{10} + \frac{3}{100} - \frac{13}{100}$	$\frac{13}{100}$
0	.	7	1	$0.71 = \frac{7}{10} + \frac{1}{100} = \frac{71}{100}$	$\frac{71}{100}$
0	.	0	7	$0.07 = \frac{7}{100}$	$\frac{7}{100}$

Remember:

✦ 0.1 is the same as $\frac{1}{10}$, 0.01 is the same as $\frac{1}{100}$.

✦ The decimal point is fixed.

✦ Most numbers can be written as a decimal or a fraction.

Skills practice A

1 Look at these diagrams.

i 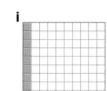   **ii**    **iii**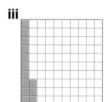

iv 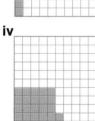   **v**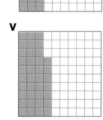

  a Express each shaded part as a fraction of the whole square.

  b Write each fraction from part **a** as a decimal.

2 Write each number in the table as a decimal.

H	T	U	$\frac{1}{10}$	$\frac{1}{100}$	$\frac{1}{1000}$
		4	6		
	1	5		3	
					9
3		1	2		7
				5	9

3 What is the value of the blue digit in each number?

Examples: In 6143.71 the 4 is worth 4 tens or 40. In 8.394 the 9 is worth $\frac{9}{100}$.

  a 16.32   **b** 4.78   **c** 19.74   **d** 11.308

  e 3.61   **f** 62.094   **g** 8.63   **h** 5.0019

4 Look at this number line. What decimal numbers do the arrows point to?

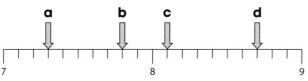

Reasoning

5 Copy this number line.

7.0   7.1   7.2

Put these numbers in the correct places:
7.05   7.02   7.14   7.16   7.19

6 a Write down a number between 6 and 7.

  b Write down a different number between 6 and 7 that doesn't have a 5 in it.

  c Write down a different number between 6 and 7 that doesn't have a 5 in it and is five digits long.

  d Write down a different number between 6 and 7 that doesn't have a 5 in it, is five digits long and has at least one 0.

  e Write down a different number between 6 and 7 that doesn't have a 5 in it, is five digits long, has at least one 0 and is as close to 6.8 as possible.

7 Copy the diagram. Write these numbers in the boxes so that all four inequalities are true.
0.940   0.409   0.490   0.904

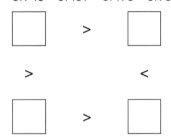

Skills practice B

Reasoning

1 Look at the digit cards

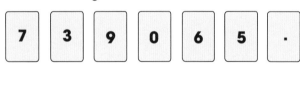

| 7 | 3 | 9 | 0 | 6 | 5 | . |

The largest 3-digit number is 976.

Jack

Use the digit cards to make
  a the largest five-digit number
  b the smallest number using all of the cards
  c six numbers between 60 000 and 70 000 (list them in order from smallest to largest)
  d six five-digit numbers between 6 and 7 (list them in order from smallest to largest).

2 What numbers are shown on the number line below?

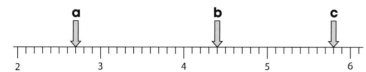

3 What numbers are shown on the number line below?

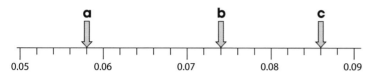

4 Arrange each set of numbers in order of size, smallest first.
   a 0.7, 7, 70, 0.71, 0.07   **b** 36, 0.36, 3.6, 0.036, 0.63
   c 45, 0.45, 0.54, 0.04, 0.005   **d** 1.11, 0.13, 1.3, 1.01, 0.31

5 Copy these strings. Fill in each space with any number between the two either side of it.

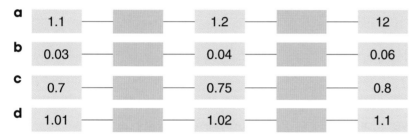

6 a Write down a number between 6.7 and 7.1.
   b Write down a different number between 6.7 and 7.1 that doesn't have a 7 in it.
   c Write down a different number between 6.7 and 7.1 that doesn't have a 7 in it and is five digits long.
   d Write down a different number between 6.7 and 7.1 that doesn't have a 7 in it, is five digits long and has at least one 3.
   e Write down a different number between 6.7 and 7.1 that doesn't have a 7 in it, is five digits long, has at least one 3 and is as close to 6.8 as possible.

7 Harry has tried to put decimals in ascending order. Which of his answers are correct? Explain to Harry what he has done wrong.
   a 0.2, 0.12, 0.21, 0.22   **b** 3.7, 3.73, 3.3, 7.3   **c** 1.06, 1.6, 1.66, 6.1

Wider skills practice

1 Make some cards with the digits 0, 1, 2, 3, 4, 5, 6, 7, 8 and 9 written on them.

   a Place your cards into the boxes to make three 3-digit numbers (you'll have one card left over!) so that the total is
   i as large as you can make it   **ii** as small as you can make it.
   b Explain how you know that your solution is correct without having to work out the calculation.

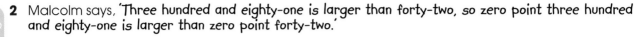

2 Malcolm says, 'Three hundred and eighty-one is larger than forty-two, so zero point three hundred and eighty-one is larger than zero point forty-two.'

What would you say to Malcolm to help him understand his mistakes?

3 The answers to the cross-number puzzle are mixed up in these numbers:

48.96   46.72   44.9   50.91   47.09   40.05   48.35   41.25   59.03   46.78

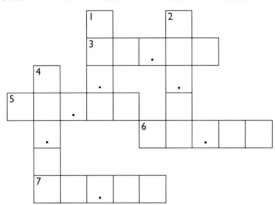

Across

3 The lowest number

5 Higher than 4 down and lower than 2 down

6 A number between 41 and 42

7 The highest number

Down

1 A number with no hundredths

2 The 1 represents one hundredth

4 A number between 48.2 and 48.4

a Use the clues to choose which number goes where.

b There are three numbers remaining.

Write them in the correct positions on a copy of this number line.

46.7   46.8   46.9   47.0   47.1

Applying skills

1 Is it *always* true, *sometimes* true or *never* true that:

the longer a number is, the greater the value of that number?

• If you think *always*, explain how you can be so certain.

• If you think *never*, explain how you can be so certain.

• If you think *sometimes*, explain when it is and when it isn't true.

2 Copy these diagrams. Write digits in the empty boxes so that each statement is true.

a | 0 | | 9 | 0 | | 0 |

b | 0 | | 9 | 0 | | 0 |ᵇ

c | 0 | | 8 | 0 | 0 | |

d | 0 | | 9 | 9 | < | 0 | | 0 |

3 Kelvin writes the number 0.0520
The digit 0 occurs three times.
Discuss why each of them is used in the number.

Reviewing skills

1 Write these fractions as decimals

a $\frac{9}{100}$ b $\frac{21}{100}$ c $\frac{7}{10}$

2 What is the value of the red digit in each of these numbers?

a 35.71   b 215.67   c 1920.04   d 0.009416

3 a Show the number 0.23 on a place-value table.

b Which of the following fractions is the same value as 0.23?

$\frac{23}{1000}$, $2\frac{3}{10}$, $2\frac{3}{100}$, $\frac{23}{100}$

4 a Draw a place-value table, showing the number 9.3

b Draw a place-value table showing 0.093

c Write i 9.3 ii 0.093 as fractions.

Building skills

Example outside the Maths classroom

Mars Climate Orbiter

Toolbox

Remember that multiplying by 10 moves all of the digits left one step while dividing by 10 moves them all right. Only the decimal point is fixed.

Looking at 4.67 multiplied by 10, each digit in 4.67 moves left while the decimal point stays still to give 46.7.

T	U	.	$\frac{1}{10}$	$\frac{1}{100}$
	4	.	6	7
4	6	.	7	

When dividing 4.67 by 10, each digit in 4.67 moves right one step while the decimal point stays still to give 0.467:

T	U	.	$\frac{1}{10}$	$\frac{1}{100}$	$\frac{1}{1000}$
	4	.	6	7	
	0	.	4	6	7

Example – Multiplying and dividing by powers of 10

Work out the answers to these calculations.

a 3.2×100

b 0.32×1000

c $32 \div 10$

d $3.2 \div 100$

Solution

	H	T	U	.	$\frac{1}{10}$	$\frac{1}{100}$	$\frac{1}{1000}$
			3	.	2		
a 3.2 × 100	3	2	0	.	0		
				.	3	2	
b 0.32 × 1000	3	2	0	.	0		
		3	2				
c 32 ÷ 10			3	.	2		
		3		.	2		
d 3.2 ÷ 100				.	0	3	2

> × 100 moves the digits 2 places to the left.

Example – Using powers of 10 in a problem

A length of wood is to be cut into ten equal pieces. The wood is 7.6 m long.
How long is each piece **a** in m **b** in mm?

Solution

a To cut 7.6 m into ten equal pieces, the calculation is 7.6 ÷ 10.
Dividing by 10 moves all of the digits one step to the right.

H	T	U	.	$\frac{1}{10}$	$\frac{1}{100}$	$\frac{1}{1000}$
		7	.	6		
			.	7	6	

So 7.6 ÷ 10 = 0.76
Each piece of wood is 0.76 m long.

b There are 1000 mm in 1 m. To find the length in mm multiply 0.76 by 1000.

	H	T	U	.	$\frac{1}{10}$	$\frac{1}{100}$	$\frac{1}{1000}$
			0	.	7	6	
0.76 × 1000	7	6	0	.			

It is 760 mm long.

Remember:

✦ The decimal point is fixed.
✦ When multiplying by 10, the digits all move one step left.
✦ When dividing by 10, the digits all move one step right.

Skills practice A

1 Copy these place-value tables. Use a calculator to multiply each number by 10, writing the answers below each of the original numbers.

When you have found a rule, write it down.

a

TTh	Th	H	T	U	.	$\frac{1}{10}$	$\frac{1}{100}$	$\frac{1}{1000}$	$\frac{1}{10000}$
			7	6	.				
					.				

b

TTh	Th	H	T	U	.	$\frac{1}{10}$	$\frac{1}{100}$	$\frac{1}{1000}$	$\frac{1}{10000}$
		1	9	2	.	0	2	5	
					.				

c

TTh	Th	H	T	U	.	$\frac{1}{10}$	$\frac{1}{100}$	$\frac{1}{1000}$	$\frac{1}{10000}$
		9	7	0	.				
					.				

2 Copy these place-value tables. Use a calculator to multiply each number by 100, writing the answers below each of the original numbers.

a

TTh	Th	H	T	U	.	$\frac{1}{10}$	$\frac{1}{100}$	$\frac{1}{1000}$	$\frac{1}{10000}$
			2	5	.	3			
					.				

b

TTh	Th	H	T	U	.	$\frac{1}{10}$	$\frac{1}{100}$	$\frac{1}{1000}$	$\frac{1}{10000}$
				6	.	7	2	3	
					.				

3 Copy these place-value tables. Use a calculator to multiply each number by 1000, writing the answers below each of the original numbers.

a

TTh	Th	H	T	U	.	$\frac{1}{10}$	$\frac{1}{100}$	$\frac{1}{1000}$	$\frac{1}{10000}$
				0	.	0	0	2	1
					.				

b

TTh	Th	H	T	U	.	$\frac{1}{10}$	$\frac{1}{100}$	$\frac{1}{1000}$	$\frac{1}{10000}$
			1	8	.	4	2	3	
					.				

4 Repeat question **1** but this time divide by 10.
Do you need to work out the answers on a calculator?

5 Repeat question **2** but this time divide by 100.
Do you need to work out the answers on a calculator?

6 Repeat question **3** but this time divide by 1000.
Do you need to work out the answers on a calculator?

7 Copy and complete these calculations.
   a **i** 5.0 × 10 =   **ii** 6.5 × 10 =   **iii** 7.12 × 10 =
   b **i** 2.5 × 100 =   **ii** 2.03 × 100 =   **iii** 21.4 × 100 =
   c **i** 21 × 1000 =   **ii** 2.14 × 1000 =   **iii** 25.9 × 1000 =

8 Copy and complete these calculations.
   a **i** 2310 ÷ 10 =   **ii** 2310 ÷ 100 =   **iii** 2310 ÷ 1000 =
   b **i** 231 ÷ 10 =   **ii** 231 ÷ 100 =   **iii** 231 ÷ 1000 =
   c **i** 23.1 ÷ 10 =   **ii** 23.1 ÷ 100 =   **iii** 23.1 ÷ 1000 =

Skills practice B

1 Copy the diagram. Fill in each flag to show which operation you need to use.
Choose from × 10, × 100, × 1000, ÷ 10, ÷ 100 and ÷ 1000.

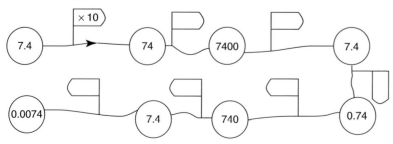

2 Copy the diagram. Fill in the flags and circles to make the diagram correct.
Choose from × 10, × 100, × 1000, ÷ 10, ÷ 100 and ÷ 1000.

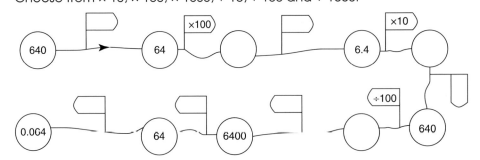

3 Copy the diagram. Fill in the flags and circles to make the diagram correct. This one is more challenging.
Choose from × 10, × 100, × 1000, ÷ 10, ÷ 100 and ÷ 1000.

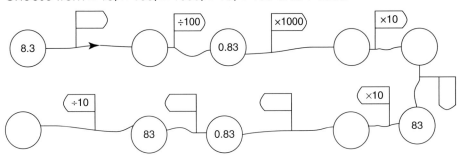

4 A three-digit number is put through this set of steps.

$$ n \longrightarrow \div\ 10 \longrightarrow \times\ 1000 \longrightarrow \div\ 100 \longrightarrow \times\ 100 \longrightarrow \div\ 10 \longrightarrow \text{Output} $$

Which of these could *not* be the output? How do you know?
a 3250 **b** 16 700 **c** 42.5 **d** 0.034 **e** 1.6

5 From the measurements below, match any that are equal in length.

| 200 cm | 5 km | 1.5 m | 2 m | 0.65 m | 5000 m | 1500 cm | 150 cm | 6.5 cm |

| 65 cm | 0.002 km | 500 000 cm | 650 mm | 1500 mm | 65 mm |

6 Matilda wants to change 6.8 into 0.068 using the operation ×10.
Matilda changes 6.8 into 0.068 in two steps as follows:
  6.8 ÷ 10 = 0.68
0.68 ÷ 10 = 0.068
How can Matilda change 6.8 into 0.068 using the operations ×10 and ÷10
a in four steps
b in eight steps?
c Explain why Matilda can't solve the problem using three steps.

Wider skills practice

Reasoning

1 Is it *always* true, *sometimes* true or *never* true that:

when multiplying by 10 you write a 0 onto the end of the number?

- If you think *always*, explain how you can be so certain.
- If you think *never*, explain how you can be so certain.
- If you think *sometimes*, explain when it is and when it isn't true.

2 A record lemon weighs 1130 grams. Write this
  a in milligrams   **b** in kilograms.

Applying skills

1 Fiona and Sam are in charge of stalls at their school fete.

  a Fiona starts with a float of 10p coins. ← A float is money available at the start used for giving change.

  How many 10p coins are needed for a float of
  i £5   **ii** £10   **iii** £12.50   **iv** £19.90?

  b At Sam's stall people throw 1p coins into a bowl of water. His float is in 1p coins.
  How many coins does he need for a float of
  i 50p   **ii** £10.00   **iii** £12.50   **iv** £4.59?

2 Volumes of bottles of liquid are given in litres, centilitres (cl) or millilitres (ml).
From these measurements, select any volumes that are equivalent.

330 ml	70 cl	20 cl	33 cl	200 cl	1.5 litres	50 cl	0.7 litres	2 litres
3300 ml	0.5 litres	1500 ml	3.3 litres	200 ml	500 ml			

Reviewing skills

1 On a copy of this table, fill in the spaces by multiplying or dividing the number shown in the 4th row by 10, 100 or 1000. In some columns you have to work out what the number is.

×1000				4 200 000
×100	2300		46 100	
×10	230		4610	
Number	23	3000		2750
÷10	2.3			
÷100	0.23		4.61	
÷1000		3		

Building skills

Example outside the Maths classroom

Temperature

Toolbox

On a number line, negative numbers are to the left of zero and positive numbers are to the right. Zero itself is neither positive or negative.

Words like 'big' and 'small' can be confusing when thinking about negative numbers. Think about how the number –30 could be considered to be 'bigger' than 10 because it is further from zero on the number line.

```
┌───┬───┬───┬───┬───┐
-30             0   10
```

It is better to use 'higher' and 'lower'. –30 is definitely lower than 10!

Example – Position of numbers

Place each of these numbers in the correct position on a number line.

  –18   18   6   –6   –22   30

Solution

```
-30   -20   -10    0    10    20    30
            ↑  ↑         ↑     ↑     ↑
          -22 -18        6    18    30
```

Example – Ordering numbers

Place these numbers in order, from lowest to highest.

  –10   –17   27   17   7   –7   –27

Solution

  –27   –17   –10   –7   7   17   27

Example – Position of positive and negative numbers

Which of these numbers is furthest from 0?

$$-180 \quad 200 \quad -210 \quad 4 \quad 209 \quad -71 \quad -4$$

Solution

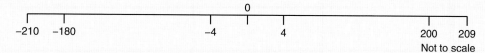

Not to scale

209 is the number that is most positive and −210 is the number that is most negative.
−210 is furthest from 0 on the number line.

Remember:

✦ Always think about a number line when working with negative numbers.

Skills practice A

1 Decide whether to call each of these numbers positive or negative.
- **a** a present of £50
- **b** a speed of 10 mph over the speed limit
- **c** a temperature of 4 °C below freezing
- **d** climbing to a height of 1000 feet
- **e** a National Lottery win of £10
- **f** putting £1 on the lottery but not winning

2 Choose one of these values to go with each description below.

| −36 | +4406 feet | −2286 feet | −10 °C | −55 | +42 |

- **a** the average winter temperature for Moscow
- **b** sea level of the Dead Sea compared with normal sea level
- **c** the goal difference for Premiership champions
- **d** the year Julius Caesar first arrived in Britain
- **e** the goal difference for a relegated team
- **f** the height of Ben Nevis

3 Draw a number line from −10 to 10.
- **a** Place the numbers 9, −8, −7, 3, −5, 5, 0 on the line.
- **b** Which two numbers are the same distance from 0 on your line?

4 Two numbers are placed on a number line.
They are both the same distance from 0 and are 30 apart from each other.
What are the two numbers?

Skills practice B

1 Temperatures are measured above and below zero.
Write down each of these temperatures. Use + or –.

a 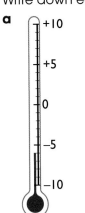   **b** 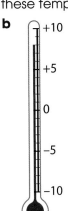   **c** 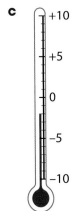   **d**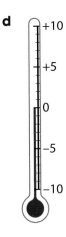

2 Put each set of numbers in order, starting with the lowest.

a 7, 0, 3, 10, –5, 100

b –7, 0, –3, –10, 5, –100

c 7, 0, –3, 10, –5, 100

d –7, 0, 3, –10, 5, –100

3 Hannah is thinking of two numbers.

She says that, when she puts a negative sign in front of each of them, they stay in the same order on the number line.

Is Hannah correct? Use a picture of a number line to explain how you know.

4 These five numbers are all the same distance from one another.

Copy the number line and fill in the gaps.

–32				88

5 Peter is playing snakes and ladders. Copy and complete this table to show his moves.
He starts at 0.

Die	Snake or ladder	Total	Square
3	+12	15	15
4		4	19
1			39
3			24
4			45
5			
3			92
1			75
6			
4			

99 END	98	97	96	95	94	93	92	91	90
80	81	82	83	84	85	86	87	88	89
79	78	77	76	75	74	73	72	71	70
60	61	62	63	64	65	66	67	68	69
59	58	57	56	55	54	53	52	51	50
40	41	42	43	44	45	46	47	48	49
39	38	37	36	35	34	33	32	31	30
20	21	22	23	24	25	26	27	28	29
19	18	17	16	15	14	13	12	11	10
0 START	1	2	3	4	5	6	7	8	9

Reasoning

Wider skills practice

1 **a** Use a copy of the grid below to play a game of 'Boxes' with a partner.

```
•    •    •    •    •    •    •
   +3    0   −1   +1   +2   −2
•    •    •    •    •    •    •
    0   −3   −1   +1    0   −2
•    •    •    •    •    •    •
   −1   −2   +1   −2   +1   −3
•    •    •    •    •    •    •
   +3    0   −3   +5   −1   −2
•    •    •    •    •    •    •
   +1    0   +1   −2   +1   +1
•    •    •    •    •    •    •
   +4   −7   +2   −1    0   +1
•    •    •    •    •    •    •
```

Start with a score of 0.

Take it in turns to join any two adjacent dots with a vertical or horizontal line.

If your line completes a square, then add the number in the square to your score.

The winner is the person with the highest score when all the squares have been completed.

b If one person completed all of the boxes in the grid, what would their score be?

2 A, B, C, D are four different whole numbers.

Use the clues to decide what each number must be.
- Both D and A are the same distance from 0.
- B is 2 more than D.
- C is 4 away from 0.
- Two numbers are above 0.
- The number that is furthest from 0 is 8.
- All of the numbers are different and they are all whole numbers.

Applying skills

1 Wayne's Dad opens his post.

Auntie has sent me a cheque for £60!

Oh dear! Here is the bill from the garage. I must pay £285.

He sorts out his finances on this account sheet.

Credits (+)	Debits (−)	Balance (£)
		503.00
+60.00		
	−285.00	

In this row the balance will be 503.00 + 60.00.

a Copy the account sheet and fill in the two missing balances.

b Extend your copy of the account sheet. Write these items in the correct column.

- Payment for TV licence £9
- Payment for mortgage £250
- Payment for gas bill £70
- Premium Bond win £50
- Salary £1500

Work out the balance each time.

2 Chris is a keen golfer. He visits Hoebridge Manor Golf Course for a game.

On every golf course there is a target score for each hole.

Par 5 means the target for the hole is 5.

Chris scores 4.

He is one less than the target score.

He could write this as (−1).

The next hole is par 3.
He scores 5.

He could write this as (+2).

Write these scores as + or − numbers.

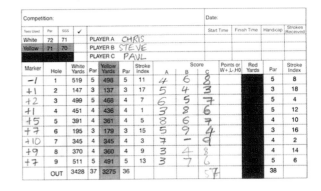

a par 5 / score 4

b par 5 / score 7

c par 4 / score 2

d par 4 / score 3

e par 4 / score 5

f par 3 / score 5

Reviewing skills

1 Write each of these as a positive or negative number.
   a a gift worth £40
   b a diver 60 feet below the surface
   c a bill for £200
   d a temperature of 24 °C
   e 3 °C below freezing
   f a mountaineer 2000 feet up

	Bill of Sale	
Quantity	Description	Goods
1	282 L-G	£88.00
2	606 L-L	£112.00
	TOTAL	£200.00

2 Copy the number line.

```
  -10      -5       0       5      10
```

Mark these numbers on it.
   a −1   b −8   c 6
   d +2   e −6   f 7

3 Put these numbers in order of size, starting with the lowest.
   −1   0   −6   +1   +5   −3

Building skills

Example outside the Maths classroom

Building swimming pools

Toolbox

Thinking of dividing as 'how many are there in...?'

How many 2s are there in 8?

$$2 + 2 + 2 + 2 = 8$$

There are four 2s in 8 so $8 \div 2 = 4$.

How many 0.1s are there in 1.3?

$$0.1 + 0.1 + 0.1 + 0.1 + 0.1 + 0.1 + 0.1 + 0.1 + 0.1 + 0.1 + 0.1 + 0.1 + 0.1 = 1.3$$

There are thirteen 0.1s in 1.3 so $1.3 \div 0.1 = 13$.

This is the same as multiplying 1.3 by 10.

This place-value table shows 4.67 divided by 0.01

H	T	U	.	$\frac{1}{10}$	$\frac{1}{100}$
		4	.	6	7
4	6	7	.		

The place-value table shows that dividing by 0.01 has exactly the same effect as multiplying by 100.

In the same way,

- multiplying by 0.1 is the same as dividing by 10
- multiplying by 0.01 is the same as dividing by 100
- multiplying by 0.001 is the same as dividing by 1000 and so on.

Example – Multiplying and dividing by 0.1 and 0.01

Work out the answers to these calculations.

a 32×0.1

b 320×0.01

c $32 \div 0.1$

d $32 \div 0.01$

Solution

a Using a place-value table to multiply by 0.1, think of 30 lots of 0.1 which makes 3, and 2 lots of 0.1 which makes 0.2.

H	T	U	.	$\frac{1}{10}$	$\frac{1}{100}$	$\frac{1}{1000}$
	3	2	.			
		3	.	2		

> Using a place-value table can help to keep track of the digits when multiplying or dividing by powers of 10.

So 32 lots of 0.1 = 3.2

Using the same idea for the other calculations:

b $320 \times 0.01 = 3.2$

c $32 \div 0.1 = 320$

d $32 \div 0.01 = 3200$

Example – Division using known facts

Use this known fact to work out the calculations below.

$720 \div 0.1 = 7200$

a $7200 \div 0.1$

b $7200 \div 0.01$

c $72 \div 0.1$

d $720 \div 0.01$

e $7200 \div 10$

f $7200 \div 1000$

Solution

a $7200 \div 0.1 = 72\,000$

b $7200 \div 0.01 = 720\,000$

c $72 \div 0.1 = 720$

d $720 \div 0.01 = 72\,000$

e $7200 \div 10 = 720$

f $7200 \div 1000 = 7.2$

Example – Multiplication using known facts

Use this known fact to work out the calculations below.

$720 \times 0.1 = 72$

a 7200×0.1

b 7200×0.01

c 72×0.1

d 720×0.01

e 7200×10

f 7200×1000

Solution

a 7200 × 0.1 = 720
b 7200 × 0.01 = 72
c 72 × 0.1 = 7.2
d 720 × 0.01 = 7.2
e 7200 × 10 = 72 000
f 7200 × 1000 = 7 200 000

Example – Mental calculation using known facts

Work out 5.6 ÷ 0.07 in your head.

Jack

Solution

	56 ÷ 7 = 8
so	5.6 ÷ 7 = 0.8
so	5.6 ÷ 0.7 = 8
and so	5.6 ÷ 0.07 = 80

Ali

Remember:

✦ Think of division as 'how many are there in?' when considering if your answer is reasonable.
✦ There are equivalent calculations to help:
  • Dividing by 0.1 is equivalent to multiplying by 10.
  • Dividing by 0.01 is equivalent to multiplying by 100.
  • Multiplying by 0.1 is equivalent to dividing by 10.
  • Multiplying by 0.01 is equivalent to dividing by 100.

Skills practice A

1 Copy the place-value table. Use a calculator to divide each number by 0.1, writing the answers below each of the original numbers.

When you have a rule, write it down.

a

TTh	Th	H	T	U	.	$\frac{1}{10}$	$\frac{1}{100}$	$\frac{1}{1000}$	$\frac{1}{10000}$
			1	7	.				
					.				

b

TTh	Th	H	T	U	.	$\frac{1}{10}$	$\frac{1}{100}$	$\frac{1}{1000}$	$\frac{1}{10000}$
		3	0	0	.				
					.				

c

TTh	Th	H	T	U	.	$\frac{1}{10}$	$\frac{1}{100}$	$\frac{1}{1000}$	$\frac{1}{10000}$
				4	.	2	8	1	
					.				

d

TTh	Th	H	T	U	.	$\frac{1}{10}$	$\frac{1}{100}$	$\frac{1}{1000}$	$\frac{1}{10000}$
		4	0	2	.	0	7	8	
					.				

e

TTh	Th	H	T	U	.	$\frac{1}{10}$	$\frac{1}{100}$	$\frac{1}{1000}$	$\frac{1}{10000}$
			1	2	.	9			
					.				

f

TTh	Th	H	T	U	.	$\frac{1}{10}$	$\frac{1}{100}$	$\frac{1}{1000}$	$\frac{1}{10000}$
				0	.	0	0	5	3
					.				

g

TTh	Th	H	T	U	.	$\frac{1}{10}$	$\frac{1}{100}$	$\frac{1}{1000}$	$\frac{1}{10000}$
			7	0	.	0	0	9	
					.				

2 Repeat question **1** but this time multiply by 0.1.

Do you need to work out the answers on a calculator?

3 Copy this table and fill in the missing numbers.

Dividing by	is the same as	multiplying by
10	is the same as	
	is the same as	0.01
	is the same as	0.001
0.1	is the same as	
	is the same as	100
0.001	is the same as	

4 Here is Carol's homework.
Mark the homework and correct any answers that are wrong.

> **a** $0.7 \div 10 = 0.07$
> **b** $7 \div 100 = 0.007$
> **c** $5.3 \div 0.1 = 0.53$
> **d** $6.8 \div 0.1 = 68$
> **e** $925 \div 100 = 9.25$
> **f** $654 \times 0.1 = 6.54$
> **g** $9867 \div 0.01 = 986\,700$
> **h** $3.005 \div 0.1 = 3.05$

Skills practice B

1 Write down the answers to these.
  a **i** How many 0.1s are there in 3?
  ii $3 \div 0.1$
  b **i** How many 0.1s are there in 7?
  ii $7 \div 0.1$
  c **i** How many 0.1s are there in 3.2?
  ii $3.2 \div 0.1$
  d **i** How many 0.01s are there in 3?
  ii $3 \div 0.01$
  e **i** How many 0.01s are there in 0.2?
  ii $0.2 \div 0.01$

2 Work out
  a $3.2 \div 0.01$ **b** $4.6 \div 0.01$
  c $19.7 \div 0.1$ **d** $19.7 \div 0.01$

3 Joe has a set of cards like this.

There are lots of each card in the set. Use Joe's cards to fill in the boxes.
You don't have to use each card every time.
  a $5.2 \div \boxed{\ }\boxed{\ } = 0.52$ **b** $70.6 \div \boxed{\ }\boxed{\ }\boxed{\ } = 0.706$
  c $2 \div \boxed{\ }\boxed{\ }\boxed{\ } = 20$ **d** $5.9 \div \boxed{\ }\boxed{\ }\boxed{\ } = 59$
  e $0.7 \div \boxed{\ }\boxed{\ }\boxed{\ } = 7$

4 Using the fact that 354 × 29 = 10 266, find

a 354 × 2.9	**b** 3.54 × 29	**c** 3540 × 290
d 102 660 ÷ 354	**e** 1026.6 ÷ 35.4	**f** 0.354 × 0.29
g 3.54 × 2.9	**h** 10 266 ÷ 0.29	**i** 35.4 × 0.29

5 a Write 2.34 m in **i** cm   **ii** mm.

   b Write 632 cm in **i** m   **ii** km.

6 Write down 6 number sentences based on 9 × 6 = 54 using decimals.
For example, 900 × 0.6 = 540.

7 Copy this number web.

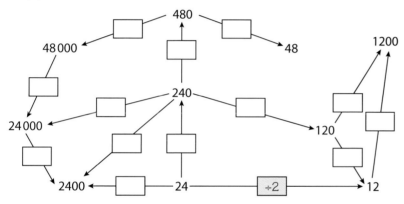

Fill in each of the boxes with one of these:

× 2   ÷ 2   × 10   ÷ 10   × 100   ÷ 100

One has been done for you.

Wider skills practice

1 Each coloured circle represents a different digit.
Write down

a ●●●● × 10	**b** ●●●● ÷ 10	**c** ●●●● ÷ 0.1
d ●●●● ÷ 0.01	**e** ●●●● × 0.1	

   f Write down as many calculations as you can (at least two different ones) that could make
●●● into ●.●●

2 Is it always true, sometimes true or never true that:

dividing a number makes it smaller?

- If you think *always*, explain how you can be so certain.
- If you think *never*, explain how you can be so certain.
- If you think *sometimes*, explain when it is and when it isn't true.

Reasoning

95

Applying skills

1 Alan is making a rabbit hutch.
He needs ten pieces of wood that are 0.3 m long and ten pieces of wood that are 0.9 m long.
He can buy wood in 3 m lengths.
How many of these 3 m lengths of wood does Alan need to buy?

Reviewing skills

1 **a** 3.2 × 10   **b** 3.2 × 100   **c** 4.7 × 1000

2 **a** 4.2 ÷ 0.1   **b** 4.2 ÷ 0.01   **c** 4.2 ÷ 0.001
    d 0.57 ÷ 0.1   **e** 0.63 ÷ 0.01   **f** 0.08 ÷ 0.001
    g 0.46 ÷ 0.01   **h** 3.9 ÷ 0.1

3 **a** Convert 2.3 m into **i** cm   **ii** mm.
    b Convert 6.1 m into **i** cm   **ii** mm.

Building skills

Example outside the Maths classroom

Describing the Universe

Toolbox

Standard form is used to write large numbers and small numbers.

For example, the speed of light is 2.998×10^8 metres per second and the mass of an electron is 9.110×10^{-31} kg.

A number in standard form is

(a number between 1 and 10) × (a power of 10).

So 3.9×10^{-4} is standard form but 39×10^{-5} isn't.

When thinking about numbers in standard form it can be helpful to have a place-value table in mind. The table below shows four million six hundred and seventy thousand (4 670 000), which is sometimes said as 4.67 million.

	M	HTh	TTh	Th	H	T	U	.	$\frac{1}{10}$	$\frac{1}{100}$
							4	.	6	7
4.67×10^6	4	6	7	0	0	0	0	.		

4.67 million is $4.67 \times 1\,000\,000$ or 4.67×10^6. The table shows you that, the $\times 10^6$ moves all of the digits in 4.67 six places to the left; any blanks are filled with zeros.

In 6.8×10^{-3} all of the digits of 6.8 are moved three places to the right and the gaps are filled with zeros.

	H	T	U	.	$\frac{1}{10}$	$\frac{1}{100}$	$\frac{1}{1000}$	$\frac{1}{10000}$
			6	.	8			
6.8×10^{-3}				.	0	0	6	8

Example – Converting small numbers to standard form

A flea weighs around 0.000087kg. Write this number in standard form

Solution

For it to be in standard form, it must start 8.7
$0.000087 = 0.00087 \times 0.1$
$0.000087 = 0.0087 \times 0.01$
$0.000087 = 0.087 \times 0.001$
$0.000087 = 0.87 \times 0.0001$
$0.000087 = 8.7 \times 0.00001$
So
$0.000087 = 8.7 \times 0.00001 = 8.7 \times 10^{-5}$

Example – Converting large numbers from standard form

Convert the standard form number 6.378×10^6 to a normal number.

Solution

M	HTh	TTh	Th	H	T	U	.	$\frac{1}{10}$	$\frac{1}{100}$	$\frac{1}{1000}$
						6	.	3	8	7
6	3	8	7	0	0	0	.			

Using a place-value table the digits will move up 6 columns when multiplied by 10^6
So $6.378 \times 10^6 = 6387000$

Remember:

✦ The decimal part of the number must be 1 or more but less than 10.
✦ To convert from standard form, if the power of 10 is positive, then the digits all move left; if it's negative they all move right.

Skills practice A

1 Write the number in each statement as a power of 10.
   a There are 100 steps to the top of the tower.
   b The winner won by just 0.1 of a second.
   c The car costs £10 000.

2 Write each of these numbers as a power of 10.
   a 1 000 000   b 100 000 000   c 10
   d 0.01   e 0.001   f one hundred thousand
   g one thousand million   h one ten thousandth

3 Write each of these as an ordinary number.

    a 10^5 **b** 10^{10} **c** 10^{-1}

    d 10^{-2} **e** 10^{-3}

4 Work out these multiplications.

    a 4×10^2 **b** 2.6×10^3 **c** 4.8×10^5

    d 1.3×10^4 **e** 2.4×10^7 **f** 3×10^{-1}

    g 4×10^{-2} **h** 5×10^{-3}

5 Copy and complete these. Fill in the missing numbers.

    a $\square \times 10^2 = 500$ **b** $\square \times 10^3 = 3000$ **c** $6 \times 10^{\square} = 6\,000\,000$

    d $\square \times 10^2 = 350$ **e** $4.2 \times 10^{\square} = 42\,000$ **f** $\square \times 10^5 = 450\,000$

    g $4 \times 10^{\square} = 0.4$ **h** $\square \times 10^{-3} = 0.006$ **i** $3 \times 10^{\square} = 0.03$

6 These numbers are in standard form. Write them as ordinary numbers.

    a 2×10^3 **b** 7×10^6 **c** 4.2×10^5

    d 7.1×10^7 **e** 8.6×10^9

7 Write these numbers in standard form.

    a 200   **b** 5000   **c** 7 000 000

    d 3600   **e** 7 200 000

Skills practice B

1 Write these as ordinary numbers,

    a The length of a human chromosome is 5×10^{-6} m

    b The CN tower in Toronto is 5.53×10^2 m tall.

    c The mass of an electron is 9.11×10^{-31} kg.

2 Write these numbers in standard form,

    a The distance between the Earth and the Moon is 239 000 miles.

    b A £5 note is 0.000 22 m thick.

    c Quartz fibre has a diameter of 0.000 001 m.

3 Write down the larger number from each of these pairs.

    a 3×10^4 and 3×10^5 **b** 4.6×10^6 and 5.8×10^6

    c 7×10^9 and 5.3×10^9 **d** 6×10^5 and 1 million

4 Write the numbers in these statements in standard form.

    a There are 1500 pupils in the school.

    b This week's lottery jackpot is worth £3.6 million.

    c The distance from London to New York is about 3000 miles.

5 Write these numbers in order, starting with the smallest.

    3.4×10^4 4.56×10^5 563 000 7.4×10^6 820 000

6 These numbers are all smaller than 1. Write them in order, starting with the smallest.

0.000 004 6.7×10^{-6} 0.000 002 47 3.78×10^{-5}

7 Write down a number that lies between each of these pairs of numbers.

a 2.3×10^4 and 2.3×10^6 **b** 1.2×10^3 and 2.0×10^3

8 In $7000 = 7 \times 10^3$, the power of 10 is 3 and there are 3 zeros in 7000.

Is it *always* true, *sometimes* true or *never* true that the power tells you how many 0s there are in the number?

• If you think *always*, explain how you can be so certain.

• If you think *never*, explain how you can be so certain.

• If you think *sometimes*, explain when it is and when it isn't true.

9 Mark the three pieces of homework below with an appropriate grade.

Give each one a helpful comment on how to improve.

Remember to praise what they're good at too.

Jacqui

Write 3800 in standard form

3.8×10^3

Write 0.000 006 78 in standard form

6.78×10^{-6}

Write 5×10^7 as an ordinary number

50 000 000

Write 9.6 $\times 10^{-5}$ as an ordinary number

0.000 096

Put in order of size, small to big

$2.6 \times 10^4, 2.9 \times 10^2, 2.7 \times 10^{-3}$

$2.7 \times 10^{-3}, 2.9 \times 10^2, 2.5 \times 10^4$

Double 6.7×10^5.

13.4×10^5

Ben

Write 3800 in standard form

3.8×10^3

Write 0.000 006 78 in standard form

6.78×10^{-8}

Write 5×10^7 as an ordinary number

50 000 000

Write 9.6×10^{-5} as an ordinary number

0.000 96

Put in order of size, small to big

$2.6 \times 10^4, 2.9 \times 10^2, 2.7 \times 10^{-3}$

$2.6 \times 10^4, 2.7 \times 10^{-3}, 2.9 \times 10^2$

Double 6.7×10^5.

1.34×10^6

Samuel

Write 3800 in standard form

3.8×10^2

Write 0.000 006 78 in standard form

6.78×10^{-6}

Write 5×10^7 as an ordinary number

50000000

Write 9.6×10^{-5} as an ordinary number

9600000

Put in order of size, small to big

$2.6 \times 10^4, 2.9 \times 10^2, 2.7 \times 10^{-3}$

$2.6 \times 10^4, 2.9 \times 10^2, 2.7 \times 10^{-3}$

Double 6.7×10^5.

1 340 000

Wider skills practice

1 In the number 4.12×10^6, the first digit is worth 4 million or 4 000 000.

The numbers in the table are written in standard form.

Copy the table and fill in the value of the first digit for each number.

Number	Value of first digit		Number	Value of first digit
6.1×10^4			2×10^{-2}	
3.62×10^4			1.46×10^{-2}	
2.9×10^7			3×10^{-4}	
1.352×10^7			6.2×10^{-4}	
4.5×10^9			5×10^{-6}	
1.236×10^9			3.21×10^{-6}	

2 **a i** Explain how to work out 2000×300 in your head.

  ii Now write your answer in standard form.

  b i Write the answer to $(2 \times 10^3) \times (3 \times 10^2)$ in standard form.

  Look carefully at your answer.

  ii How is the number worked out?

  iii How is the power of 10 worked out?

  c Work out

  i $(4 \times 10^2) \times (2 \times 10^3)$ **ii** $(1.2 \times 10^4) \times (3 \times 10^2)$

  d Explain how to multiply numbers when they are written in standard form.

  e Use your method to work out $(3 \times 10^{-2}) \times (4 \times 10^{-3})$.

  Make sure you write your answer in standard form.

Applying skills

1 The problems below can be solved by either multiplying or by dividing.

Choose the correct operation for each one and then answer the question.

  a A mouse weighs 1.5×10^{-2} kg.

  An owl eats 1000 mice in a year.

  What weight is this?

  b The speed of sound is 3.3×10^2 metres per second.

  How far does sound travel in an hour?

  c A grain of salt weighs 2×10^{-5} grams.

  How many grains of salt are there in a 750 gram packet?

  d A packet of 500 sheets of paper is 55 mm thick.

  How thick is each sheet of paper?

  e The average number of clover leaves in a square metre of lawn is 1.5×10^3.

  Estimate the number of clover leaves in a park with 5×10^4 m² of lawns.

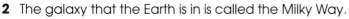

2 The galaxy that the Earth is in is called the Milky Way.

The Milky Way is a disc that is about 120 000 light years across.

The Earth is around 27 000 light years from the centre of the disc.

A light year is the distance that light can travel in a year and it is 9.46×10^{15} metres.

a Imagine a spaceship that can travel at half the speed of light.

It sets off from the Earth towards the centre of the Milky Way. How long would it take?

b How many generations of astronauts do you think it would take?

c Assuming an original crew of 20 people, how many people do you think would arrive at the centre of the Milky Way?

Reviewing skills

1 Write these numbers in standard form.

    a 2000   **b** 32 000   **c** 1450   **d** 36 000 000

    e 0.067   **f** 23   **g** 0.003 41   **h** 0.000 006

2 Write these as ordinary numbers.

    a 2×10^3 **b** 1.4×10^2 **c** 4.56×10^4 **d** 5.6×10^5

    e 3.576×10^{12} **f** 2.7×10^{-3} **g** 8.32×10^{-7} **h** 4.9×10^{-10}

3 Write these numbers in standard form.

    a China has an estimated population of 1 250 000 000.

    b It takes 0.000 000 003 3 seconds for light to travel a distance of 1 metre.

    c The world's longest river, the Nile, is 6695 km long.

    d An amoeba is 0.0005 metres across.

    e Jurassic Park had a UK box office gross of £47 100 000.

4 Write these as ordinary numbers.

    a A red blood cell has a diameter of 7×10^{-3} mm.

    b The Gobi desert covers an area of 1.04×10^6 km^2.

    c The total weight of fish in the world's oceans is estimated at 7.6×10^8 tonnes.

    d The radius of a uranium atom is 8.68×10^{-15} metres.

    e The Nou Camp stadium in Barcelona can hold 1.15×10^5 people.

5 Write these sets of numbers in order of size, starting with the smallest.

    a 2.3×10^4 32 000 5.47×10^3 1.36×10^3 40 thousand

    b 4×10^{-5} 3.7×10^{-4} 1.8×10^{-4} 0.00065   0.00003

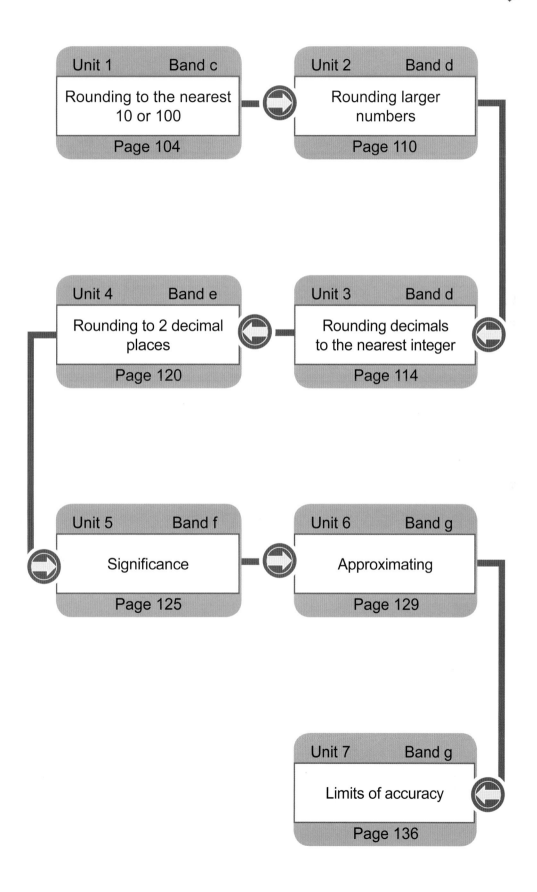

Unit 1   Band c
Rounding to the nearest
10 or 100
Page 104

Unit 2   Band d
Rounding larger
numbers
Page 110

Unit 4   Band e
Rounding to 2 decimal
places
Page 120

Unit 3   Band d
Rounding decimals
to the nearest integer
Page 114

Unit 5   Band f
Significance
Page 125

Unit 6   Band g
Approximating
Page 129

Unit 7   Band g
Limits of accuracy
Page 136

Building skills

Example outside the Maths classroom

Spending within a budget

Toolbox

To round a number to the nearest 10, look at the last digit. If it is 5 or more, round up to the 10 above, if it is less than 5, round down to the 10 below.

- 726 is 730 to the nearest 10.
- 5254 is 5250 to the nearest 10.

To round a number to the nearest 100, look at the tens digit.

- 726 is 700 to the nearest 100.
- 5254 is 5300 to the nearest 100. ← **Remember, 5 rounds up.**

Example – Using an appropriate level of detail

Write an appropriate headline for this newspaper article.

The largest fish caught on a line has been landed off Cuba. It weighed 1208.38 kg.

Solution

The exact weight is not required. The following headlines would be appropriate:

- Shark weighing over 1000 kg landed in Cuba.
- Angler struggles to land world-record fish weighing 1200 kg.

Example – Reading a scale to the nearest rounded number

The speedometer shows 62 mph.
What is this speed in mph to the nearest 10 mph?

Solution

The arrow points to 62 mph.
Decide whether 60 or 70 would be nearer.
62 is nearer to 60.
62 mph is 60 mph to the nearest 10 mph.

Example – Identifying the range of a rounded number

Here is a number line.

150 151 152 153 154 155 156 157 158 159 160 161 162 163 164 165 166 167 168 169 170

Circle the whole numbers that round to 160 to the nearest 10.

Solution

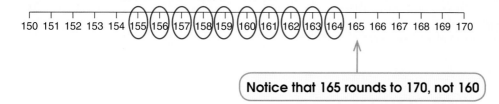

150 151 152 153 154 (155) (156) (157) (158) (159) (160) (161) (162) (163) (164) 165 166 167 168 169 170

Notice that 165 rounds to 170, not 160

Remember:

✦ A number ending in 5, such as 215, is half way between two 10s.
It is rounded up to the nearest 10. So 215 rounds to 220.

✦ A number ending with 50, such as 250, is half way between two 100s.
It is rounded up to the nearest 100. So 250 rounds to 300.

Skills practice A

1 Round these numbers to the nearest 10.
  a 69   **b** 121   **c** 9980   **d** 1324 175

2 Round these numbers to the nearest 100.
  a 169   **b** 121   **c** 9990   **d** 1001

3 Copy this number line from 300 to 1200

| | | | | | | | | | |
|300|400|500|600|700|800|900|1000|1100|1200|

  a Mark each of these numbers on it:
     524   620   902   982   1120
  b Round each number to the nearest 100.

4 600 is the next largest whole 'hundred' to 555.
  a Which whole 'hundred' is the next largest to 774?
  b Which whole 'hundred' is the next smallest to 774?
  c Which whole 'hundred' is closest to 774?

5 600 is the next largest 'ten' to 596.
  a Which 'ten' is the next largest to 478?
  b Which 'ten' is the next smallest to 478?
  c Which 'ten' is closest to 478?

6 Draw a number line showing which whole numbers round to
  a 290, to the nearest 10
  b 400, to the nearest 100.

7 a Change the order of the digits 3, 7 and 9
    to make six different three-digit numbers. ← **For example, 379 or 793.**
  b Use your numbers to fill in a table like the
    one below.

Number	Nearest 100	Nearest 10
379	400	380
793	800	790

  c Repeat parts **a** and **b** using the digits 8, 1 and 5.

8 Copy and complete this table for the remaining five numbers.

Number	Nearest 100	Nearest 10
5760	5800	5760
7603	7600	7610
6507		
6750		
7056		
7065		
7650		

Reasoning

Skills practice B

1 Round these lengths to the nearest 10 m.

a 31 m	**b** 48 m	**c** 56 m	**d** 82 m
e 25 m	**f** 98 m	**g** 164 m	**h** 201 m
i 195 m	**j** 649 m	**k** 5 m	**i** 399 m
m 2 m	**n** 855 m		

2 Round these weights to the nearest 100 kg.

a 345 kg	**b** 408 kg	**c** 633 kg	**d** 755 kg
e 50 kg	**f** 849 kg	**g** 234 kg	**h** 1098 kg
i 78 kg	**j** 3499 kg	**k** 5067 kg	**l** 4610 kg

3 Round these amounts to the nearest £10.

| **a** £299 | **b** £309 | **c** £303 |
| **d** £295 | **e** £305 | |

4 Look at these rounded numbers.

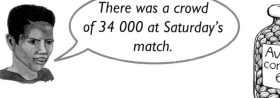 

There was a crowd of 34 000 at Saturday's match.

Average contents 600

Rockville population 19 700

There were actually 34 217 people at the football match, 612 nuts in the jar and 19 652 people living in Rockville. Are the rounded numbers correct or not? Explain your answers.

5 Round each measurement **a** to **f** to the nearest 10 mm.

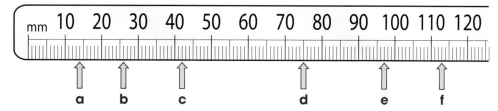

6 30 is the nearest 10 to 27.

a Write four more whole numbers that will round to 30 when rounded to the nearest 10.

b Mark them on a copy of this number line.

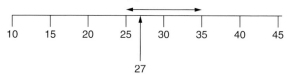

c Write down the smallest and the largest number you can choose.
Mark these on your number line.

d The double-arrowed line stretches across all the numbers that round to 30.
This is called the range of 30 (to the nearest 10).
Draw diagrams to show the range of each of these.

    i 60 (to the nearest 10)   **ii** 90 (to the nearest 10)

Reasoning

7 Newspapers often contain big numbers.

Sometimes they seem unrealistically accurate.

In each of the headlines below suggest a better way of giving the number.

a   **b**   **c**

Sports Daily

5879 at local football match

Evening News

Mum wins £ 7226 in lottery

local Echo

Man walks 1783 miles, 465 yards for charity

Wider skills practice

Reasoning

1 Write newspaper headlines for each of these facts.

You will need to decide a suitable style of reporting and the level of rounding that you use.

a The AA reported that 312 cars were heading to Scarborough every 5 minutes.

b A Greek island fire burns 297 acres of trees, bush and wasteland.

c 217 people are injured in an explosion at a power station.

d Scientists discover 367 bacteria present in one tablespoon of water.

e New transatlantic air service will take passengers to New York in 6 hours 57 minutes and 12 seconds.

Applying skills

Reasoning

1 Snacks can contain a lot of calories, fat and sugar.

  a Write this table with

- calories rounded to the nearest 100
- fat rounded to the nearest 10 g
- sugar rounded to the nearest 10 g

  b During one week, Leroy has one of each item every day.

Work out the total calories he has in two different ways.

    i use your rounded figures from part **a**

    ii use the unrounded figures in the table, then round your total to the nearest 100.

    iii Is your answer to **i** or **ii** more accurate?

Snack	Calories	Fat	Sugar
Can of cola (330 ml can)	135	none	36 g
Crisps (30 g packet)	159	10.3 g	0.2 g
Half a pizza (130 g)	360	13.4 g	2.9 g
Portion of oven chips (110 g)	178	4.6 g	0.8 g
Bar of chocolate (50 g)	260	15.4 g	28.5 g
Beefburger, no bun (90 g)	284	22 g	none

2 The United Kingdom's tallest mountain is Ben Nevis. It is 1343 metres high.

  a Find the heights of six more mountains. Round each height to the nearest 100 m.

  b Make a table like this one to show your results.

Mountain	Exact number	Rounded number
Ben Nevis	1343 m	1300 m

Reviewing skills

1   Round these amounts to the nearest 10p.

   a 42p   b 67p   c 8p   d 96p

   e 55p   f 123p   g 479p

2   Copy this table and round these numbers.

Number	Nearest 100	Nearest 10
371		
402		
6399		
1045		

3   This table shows the number of kilometres between some cities.

	London	Birmingham	Cardiff
Birmingham	175		
Cardiff	244	163	
Glasgow	629	459	592

   a How far is it from Cardiff to Birmingham to the nearest 10 kilometres?

   b How far is it from Glasgow to London to the nearest 10 kilometres?

   c How far is it from Glasgow to Cardiff to the nearest 100 kilometres?

Building skills

Example outside the Maths classroom

Buying a house

Toolbox

The larger the number, the greater the degree of rounding that is needed for us to make sense of it.

To round to the nearest million ...

24 850 175

decide whether the next digit indicates that you should round up ... or round down.

When you round to the nearest million (1,000,000) decide whether the million below or the million above is nearer to the number.

24,850,175 is between 24 million and 25 million.
25 million is nearer, so round 24,850,175 to 25 million.
Sometimes the context determines that it is better to always round up or always round down, so read the question carefully.

Example – Rounding to the nearest 1000 or 10 000

A water testing laboratory reports that the number of bacteria in a litre of water is 44 659.
Round this number

a to the nearest 1000.

b to the nearest 10 000.

Solution

a 44 659 is between 44 000 and 45 000. It is nearer to 45 000, so the number rounds up to 45 000.

b 44 659 is between 40 000 and 50 000. It is nearer to 40 000, so the number rounds down to 40 000

Remember:

✦ When a number is exactly half way between two numbers, round up.

Skills practice A

1 Write each of these numbers to the nearest thousand.

   a 2135   **b** 4697   **c** 8052

   d 7904   **e** 87 241   **f** 43 278

   g 45 649   **h** 145 625

2 Estimate the positions of the arrows on this number line and round the numbers to the nearest 1000.

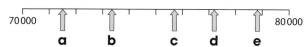

3 The map shows the area (in square kilometres) of some European countries.

Write each area correct to the nearest thousand square kilometres and list the countries in order of size.

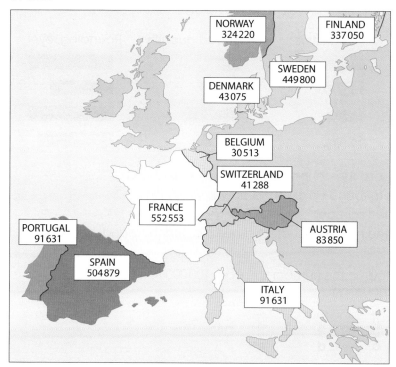

Skills practice B

1 Write each of these numbers to the nearest million.

| **a** 2 718 355 | **b** 1 425 197 | **c** 6 804 452 | **d** 7 956 604 |
| **e** 18 447 241 | **f** 18 743 278 | **g** 45 649 | **h** 145 625 333 |

2 Write newspaper headlines for each of these facts.
You will need to decide a suitable style of reporting and the level of rounding that you use.

a Police reported that 4285 cars per hour were heading to Brighton.

b Bush fire in California spreads across 2197 acres of land.

c Cyclist takes 14 days to cover 1407 km from Land's End to John O'Groats.

d Scientists say that our solar system is located 26 835 light years from the centre of the Milky Way.

3 Round the distances of these planets from the Sun to the nearest ten million kilometres.

a Mercury: 57 910 000 km

b Venus: 108 200 000 km

c Earth: 149 600 000 km

d Mars: 227 940 000 km

4 Round the distances of these planets from the Sun to the nearest hundred million kilometres.

a Jupiter: 778 330 000 km

b Saturn: 1 429 400 000 km

c Uranus: 2 870 990 000 km

d Neptune: 4 504 300 000 km

5 Match these items, quantities and rounded numbers to the level of rounding given.

Items	Quantities	Rounded quantity	Rounding level
Cost of sports pavilion	£3 628 216	360	nearest 10 000
Population of Liechtenstein	£362 821	36 000	nearest 10
Distance of space station from Earth	36 282	4 000 000	nearest million
Lottery prize win	362 km	360 000	nearest 1000

6 Using the number 25 832 500 investigate the connection between **A**, **B** and **C**.

A The digits which tell you whether to round up or round down

B The number of zeros in the rounded number

C The degree of rounding (e.g. to the nearest hundred, thousand, ten thousand, hundred thousand, million)

7 Estimate the numbers being indicated on this number line from 100 000 to 110 000.
Write each number to the nearest thousand.

Wider skills practice

1 Give a sensible approximation to the number in each of the following statements.
In each case, state the level of rounding you are using.

a The pathologist's sample indicated that there were 42 675 755 bacteria in the swimming pool.

b The orchard packed 1 972 355 grams of apples for the drinks company.

c The vineyard produced 6720 bottles of its best wine.

Applying skills

1 The average speed of the Apollo spacecraft was 39 896 kilometres per hour.

a Round this speed to the nearest 10 000 kilometres per hour.

b Estimate how far the spacecraft travelled in one day.
Round your answer to the nearest million kilometres.

c The spacecraft took 2 years to reach Mars. Estimate how for it travelled.

Reviewing skills

1 On a copy of this table, round each number to the nearest 1000, 10 000 and 100 000.

Number	Nearest 1000	Nearest 10000	Nearest 100000
2587	2590	2600	
9449			
16 508			
12 473			
47 900			

2 One of the following statements is wrong. Which one?

a 83 860, rounded to the nearest 1000, is 84 000.

b 8386, rounded to the nearest 100, is 8400.

c 8 386 500, rounded to the nearest million is 8 000 000.

d 8 386 500, rounded to the nearest ten thousand is 8 380 000.

Building skills

Supermarket shopping

Toolbox

- If the decimal part of the number is 0.5 or greater, round up to the next whole number.
- If the decimal part of the number is less than 0.5, round down to the next whole number.

Example – Rounding numbers with one decimal place to the nearest whole number

On a motorway, there is an emergency telephone every kilometre.

There are marker posts every 100 metres, so a car's location can be identified to the nearest tenth of a kilometre.

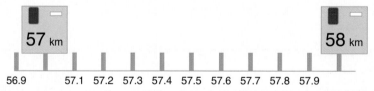

a A car breaks down at the 57.6 km marker. Which telephone is closer – the one at 57 km or the one at 58 km?

b For which marker posts on the motorway is the 57 km telephone the closest?

Solution

a The 57.5 marker post is exactly half way, so the 57.6 marker is closer to the 58 km telephone.

b The telephone at 57 km is the closest for all the posts from 56.6 to 57.4.

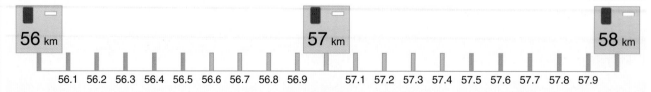

Example – Rounding numbers with two decimal places to the nearest whole number

Passengers' bags are weighed at an airport check-in.

The weights are rounded to the nearest kilogram.

Each passenger is allowed 23 kg free of charge.

a Round the weight of each of these bags to the nearest kilogram.

Are any of them overweight?

b What is the largest actual weight of suitcase that the check-in will allow to pass as 23 kg?

Solution

a The large blue suitcase is 24 kg and the light blue holdall is 26 kg – they are both overweight. The other three are 21 kg (black suitcase), 23 kg (green holdall) and 19 kg (small blue case).

b 23.5 kg will be rounded to 24 and so will be liable to an extra charge.

23.49 kg will be rounded down to 23 and will be accepted.

Remember:

✦ To round a decimal number to the nearest whole number, check the tenths (the first decimal place) to know if you will round up or round down.

Skills practice A

1 Round these to the nearest whole number.

   a 4.3   **b** 1.5   **c** 2.9

2 Round these to the nearest whole number.

   a 27.5   **b** 108.1   **c** 0.2   **d** 9.9

3 Round these to the nearest whole number.

   a 7.45   **b** 8.15   **c** 9.26   **d** 9.89

4 Write each of these numbers to the nearest whole number.

a 2.8	**b** 5.9	**c** 63.5	**d** 56.4
e 404.6	**f** 9.9	**g** 20.7	**h** 4.5
i 1.4	**j** 99.9		

5 Round these amounts to the nearest pound (£).

a £1.18	**b** £4.27	**c** £6.72	**d** £9.88
e £10.32	**f** £12.47	**g** £19.12	**h** £22.83

6 Write these costs and measurements to the nearest whole unit.

a €24.25	**b** 16.85 kg	**c** 5.91 metres	**d** £6.40
e £4.85	**f** 6.87 g	**g** 55.55 miles	**h** 9.66 litres

Skills practice B

1 The numbers indicated by the arrows **a** to **e** are all between 10 and 20.
Write each of the numbers to the nearest whole number.

2 The number shown by arrow **a** is 14.8.

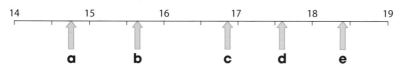

The nearest whole number is 15. Estimate each of the numbers shown by the arrows **b** to **e** to 1 decimal place and round each of them to the nearest whole number.

3 Write the costs of these shoes to the nearest £1.

£ 46.60

£36.50

£ 62.80

£40.99

£26.75

£32.25

4 Here are four smartphones.

£74.15

£57.42

£57.75

£74.75

The prices of the smart phones have been rounded to the nearest 10p and also to the nearest £1.
Match the three sets of numbers.

Prices to the nearest 10p: £74.80, £74.20, £57.40, £57.80

Prices to the nearest £1: £57, £58, £74, £75

5 Here is some information about British coins.

Value	Weight	Thickness
1p	3.6 g	1.6 mm
2p	7.1 g	2.0 mm
10p	6.5 g	1.9 mm
20p	5.0 g	1.7 mm
50p	8.0 g	1.8 mm
£1	9.5 g	3.2 mm
£2	12.0 g	2.5 mm

a Round the weight of each coin to the nearest gram.

b Round the thickness of each coin to the nearest millimetre.

6 Complete the table.

Amount £	Round to nearest £ 1	Round to nearest £ 10
18.88		
52.09		
109.82		
0.81		
1.18		

Wider skills practice

1 Salome wants to find the perimeter of this quadrilateral.

She uses her calculator to add the length of the four sides together. Her answer is 48.97 cm

Salome thinks it looks wrong. Follow these steps to check.

a Write down the length of each side to the nearest whole number.

b Add the four whole numbers together without using a calculator.

c How does this tell you that Salome's answer was wrong?

Salome made a mistake with one of the + signs. She pressed the × key instead.

d Find out which step Salome mis-keyed.

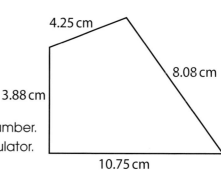

4.25 cm

8.08 cm

3.88 cm

10.75 cm

Applying skills

1 Lucy and John are planning a disco in their village hall.
Each ticket holder will get a beefburger, a packet of crisps and a can of cola.

How much do we charge per ticket?

Lucy

We need to work out roughly how much the disco will cost first.

John

Village Hall
Booking Form
£30.25 per evening

Zamba Disco
All the latest music
£44.75
+ £24.50 per hour

Avonford Party Caterers

Beefburgers	85p each
Crisps	28p per packet
Cola	47p per can

The disco will be from 7 pm to 11 pm. The price for a ticket must be a whole number of £s. John and Lucy must cover their costs. Use the table to help them decide the cost of tickets.

	Costs for 50 people	Costs for 80 people	Costs for 100 people
Beefburger			
Crisps			
Cola			
Hall			
Disco			
Total			
Cost for 1 person			

2 Stella has 175 megabytes (MB) of free storage space on her computer memory stick.
She wants to load these folders.
- Sketchpad folder 34.78 MB
- Music folder 54.81 MB
- Photo folder 80.62 MB
- Drawing template 0.91 MB
- Design template 3.67 MB

a Round each folder size to the nearest whole number.

b Use the rounded numbers to estimate whether Stella's memory stick has space for them all.

c Do you get the same result using the unrounded folder sizes?

Reviewing skills

1　Copy this number line.

```
  0  1  2  3  4  5  6  7  8  9  10
```

a　Mark these numbers on your copy of the number line.

　　i　3.2　　　　　　ii　7.8　　　　　　iii　9.1　　　　　iv　1.9　　　　　v　0.2

b　Round each number to the nearest whole number.

2　Which of the numbers on this number line round to 6? Which round to 7?

```
6.0  6.1  6.2  6.3  6.4  6.5  6.6  6.7  6.8  6.9  7.0  7.1  7.2  7.3  7.4  7.5
```

3　Round these numbers to the nearest whole number.

　　a　14.7　　　　　b　19.1　　　　　c　49.9　　　　　d　106.5　　　　e　28.3

Building skills

 Example outside the Maths classroom

Sharing a bill

Toolbox

To round a number to 1 decimal place, look at the $\frac{1}{100}$ digit.
In 1.642 the $\frac{1}{100}$ digit is 4, so 1.642 rounds down to 1.6 ← | **1.642 is nearer 1.6 than 1.7** |

To round a number to 2 decimal places, look at the $\frac{1}{1000}$ digit.
In 1.642 this is the 2, so 1.642 rounds down to 1.64 ← | **1.642 is nearer 1.64 than 1.65** |

Example – Rounding to 1 decimal place

Look at the numbers **a** = 2.127, **b** = 2.4736 and **c** = 3.0491758 on this number line.

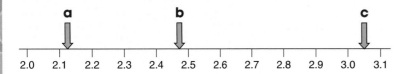

Round each number to 1 decimal place.

Solution

- **a** rounds down to 2.1 (because of the 2). ← | **Look at the second decimal place.** |
- **b** rounds up to 2.5 (because of the 7).
- **c** rounds down to 3.0 (because of the 4).

Example – Rounding calculator answers to 3 decimal places

Write the number on each of these calculator displays to 3 decimal places.

a
65.9083461

b
108.275621

c
0.94860321

Solution

a 65.908   65.9083461   → The 3 tells you the number is closer to 65.908

b 108.276   108.275621   → The 6 tells you the number is closer to 108.276

c 0.949   0.94860321   → The 6 tells you the number is closer to 0.949

Remember:

✦ The first of the decimal digits that you don't need is the digit which tells you whether to round up or round down.

Skills practice A

1 Look at the numbers in this table.

1.7	0.111	5.5	23.23
2.006	0.4	0.04	236.809
23.8	115.66	10.1	700.09
0.40	2.021	1.99	468.9

a Find the numbers with 1 decimal place and write them in order of size, smallest first.
b Find the numbers with 2 decimal places and write them in order of size, smallest first.
c Find the numbers with 3 decimal places and write them in order of size, smallest first.

2 a Add 0.1 to
  i 4   **ii** 7.6   **iii** 10   **iv** 2.9   **v** 9.9
 b Subtract 0.1 from
  i 8.4   **ii** 0.6   **iii** 0.12   **iv** 10   **v** 100
 c Write down the number that is 0.01 more than
  i 6.48   **ii** 12.33   **iii** 0.02   **iv** 0.09   **v** 9.99
 d Write down the number that is 0.01 less than
  i 7.56   **ii** 0.04   **iii** 3.452   **iv** 0.1   **v** 1

3 Write down a number that is

   a more than 10, and is given to 2 decimal places

   b between 6 and 7, and is given to 1 decimal place

   c between 100 and 101, and is given to 1 decimal place

   d between 10 and 10.1, and is given to 3 decimal places.

4 **a** Draw a number line starting 6.9, 7.0, 7.1 and continuing every 0.1 up to 8.1

   b Round these numbers to 1 decimal place and circle your answers on your number line.

      i 6.91   **ii** 7.236   **iii** 7.462   **iv** 8.04   **v** 8.051

5 **a** Continue this sequence until you reach 2.32.

    2.20, 2.21, 2.22, 2.23,…

   b Round these numbers to 2 decimal places (the answers are all in the sequence in part **a**).

      i 2.213   **ii** 2.294   **iii** 2.301   **iv** 2.207   **v** 2.3156

6 Copy this number line.

    4.55 4.56 4.57 4.58 4.59 4.60 4.61 4.62 4.63 4.64 4.65

   a Put these numbers in the correct place on your line.

      i 4.632   **ii** 4.576   **iii** 4.645   **iv** 4.602

   b Round each of the numbers in part **a** to 2 decimal places and circle the rounded numbers on your number line.

   c Write the numbers in part **a** in order, starting with the smallest.

7 Write these numbers to 1 decimal place and to 2 decimal places.

   a 0.333   **b** 1.333   **c** 5.333   **d** 5.033   **e** 5.066

   f 0.066   **g** 10.066   **h** 5.366   **i** 5.336   **j** 5.666

8 Write this list of 12 numbers in order of size.

    4.6285 4.7 4.6825 4.6528 4.8625 4.8265

    4.6 4.85 4.65 4.685 4.268 4.526

> You can copy the numbers onto 12 pieces of paper to help you sort them.

9 Write each of these numbers to 1 decimal place and to 2 decimal places.

   a 12.6723   **b** 1.438   **c** 0.6951   **d** 0.076

   e 1.0359   **f** 4.0032   **g** 9.951   **h** 0.9999

Skills practice B

1 Find a number that lies between

   a 2.95 and 2.96   **b** 3.99 and 4.01   **c** 0.23 and 0.37

   d Find the number that is exactly half way between each pair of numbers in parts **a, b, c**.

2 Copy the table. Fill in the missing numbers.

Number	Rounded to nearest 1	Rounded to nearest 10	Rounded to nearest 100	Rounded to 1 decimal place	Rounded to 2 decimal places
110.178					
84.9222					
4506.467					

3 Round the numbers on these calculator displays to the nearest whole number.

a

354.67299

b

127.94535

c

4367.8437

4 Round the numbers on these calculator displays to 1 decimal place.

a

56.489243

b

21.874399

c

7.8945265

5 Round the numbers on these calculator displays to 2 decimal places.

a

1.8745597

b

0.476589324

c

0.87587587

6 Write each of these sets of numbers in order, smallest first.

a 1.345, 1.4, 1.38, 1.045   **b** 0.2956, 0.3, 0.29, 0.29513   **c** 0.0657, 0.06612, 0.06571

7 Copy this number line.

3.60	3.61	3.62	3.63	3.64	3.65	3.66	3.67	3.68	3.69	3.70	3.71

a Place these numbers on your number line.

A = 3.614   B = 3.6472   C = 3.705

b Round each of the numbers to 2 decimal places.

c Circle the rounded numbers on your number line.

8 Rewrite these sentences using suitably rounded numbers.

a The batting average of a top Avonsford batsman is 41.64.

b The average gate at Avonford Town's football league matches is 2788.37.

c In a typical year, Avonford Council spends £89 187 on games fields.

d In a typical year, Avonford Cricket Club teams score 15 893 runs.

Reasoning

Wider skills practice

Problem solving

1 Investigate how to format cells on a spreadsheet to a given number of decimal places.

	A	B	C	D	E
1		1 d.p.	2 d.p.	3 d.p.	4 d.p.
2	1.316779	1.3	1.32	1.317	1.3168
3	15.90557	15.9	15.91	15.906	15.9056
4	230.8964	230.9	230.90	230.896	230.8964
5	4509.556	4509.6	4509.56	4509.556	4509.5560

Applying skills

1 These are the numbers with 2 decimal places that are nearest to 72.3586:

72.35 < 72.3586 < 72.36

72.3586 = 72.36, correct to 2 decimal places.

a Complete the inequalities below to show the numbers with 2 decimal places that are nearest to each number.

i ☐ < 13.24379 < ☐   **ii** ☐ < 0.19632 < ☐   **iii** ☐ < 0.0614 < ☐

iv ☐ < 6.3257 < ☐   **v** ☐ < 0.092 < ☐   **vi** ☐ < 0.0962 < ☐

b Round each of the numbers given in part **a i** and **vi** to two decimal places.

2 This question is about two different ways of rounding 8.446

a Directly: Round 8.446 to the nearest whole number.

b In stages:

i Round 8.446 to 2 decimal places

ii round your answer to part **i** to 1 decimal place

iii Round your answer to part **ii** to the nearest whole number.

c The two ways above give different answers. Which one is correct?

Reviewing skills

1 Write these numbers correct to the number of decimal places shown in brackets.

a 34.34 (1)   **b** 14.45 (1)   **c** 1.646 (1)   **d** 1.646 (2)

e 0.137 (2)   **f** 0.95 (1)   **g** 0.4962 (2)   **h** 0.998 (2)

2 a Round 8.156 to the nearest whole number.

b Round 8.156 to 1 decimal place.

c Round 8.156 to 2 decimal places.

3 Write the numbers on these calculator displays to 3 decimal places.

a 37.964375   **b** 8.6749523   **c** 90.090909   **d** 0.6666666

Building skills

Example outside the Maths classroom

Precision engineering

Toolbox

The length of one year is 365.2422 days. This is 365 when rounded to the nearest whole number. This is the same as saying it has been rounded to 3 **significant figures** (s.f.).

365.2422 is also

400 to 1 significant figure

370 to 2 significant figures

365.2 to 4 significant figures

365.24 to 5 significant figures

The first non-zero digit is always the first significant figure.

Example – Rounding very small numbers

The answer 0.000 253 745 was given on a calculator. Write the number to 2 significant figures.

Solution

| These 3 zeros are place holders. | | 2 is the first significant digit. |

0.000 253 745

The answer is 0.000 25 (to 2 significant figures).

| | 3 is smaller than 5 so the number rounds down. |

Remember:

✦ The first significant figure is the first non-zero digit.

✦ After the first significant figure, all digits are significant figures.

Skills practice A

1 Round these numbers to the nearest 10.

   a 254 **b** 1785 **c** 21.35 **d** 103.67 **e** 458 361

2 Write these numbers correct to 1 decimal place.

   a 34.43 **b** 12.372 **c** 1.567 **d** 0.432 **e** 0.2561

3 The first significant figure is red in each of these numbers.

   4136   12.8   0.523   0.000 063 2   4 200 000

   Is the first significant figure always the first figure? Explain your answer.

4 **a** Copy these numbers and underline the first 3 significant figures in each of them.

   i 45.3 **ii** 12 706 **iii** 0.6351 **iv** 0.000 845 **v** 587 210

   b Use your answers to part **a** to write each number correct to 2 significant figures.

5 **a** Copy these numbers and underline the first 4 significant figures in each of them.

   i 2745.3 **ii** 127 453 **iii** 0.647 135 1 **iv** 0.000 845 12 **v** 50 087 210

   b Write each of the numbers correct to 3 significant figures.

6 Write these numbers correct to 1 significant figure.

   a 43.34 **b** 372.12 **c** 1.765 **d** 0.0234 **e** 0.256 821

7 Write the number 324 860 correct to

   a 1 s.f. **b** 2 s.f. **c** 3 s.f. **d** 4 s.f. **e** 5 s.f.

8 Write these numbers correct to the number of significant figures shown in brackets.

   a 18.34 (2) **b** 41.359 (3) **c** 1246 (3) **d** 0.015 (1)

   e 460 (1) **f** 4986 (2) **g** 0.0204 (2) **h** 0.1096 (3)

Skills practice B

1 Write the numbers on these calculator displays to 3 significant figures.

   a   **b**   **c**

   65.9083461   108.275621   0.94860321

2 Write the number 17 032.9 correct to

   a 1 significant figure **b** 2 significant figures

   c 3 significant figures **d** 4 significant figures.

Reasoning

3 A teacher writes the number 1 000 000 on the board and asks the class to say how many significant figures it has.

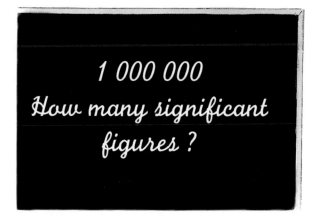

1 000 000
How many significant figures?

Amrit says 1, Ben says 2, Claire says 3, Danny says 4, Elaine says 5, Fatima says 6 and Gajan says 7. Who is correct?

Reasoning

4 Each of the statements **a** to **e** contains a mistake.
Rewrite the statements correctly and explain the mistakes.

   a 354 = 35 correct to 2 significant figures.

   b The digit 4 is the second significant figure in the number 20 453.

   c 2135 = 2130 correct to 3 significant figures.

   d 0.4196 = 0.42 correct to 3 significant figures.

   e 0.23 is exactly the same as 0.230.

5 Peter rounds a number to 2 significant figures and gets 41.45. Explain his mistake.

6 Use your calculator to do these calculations.
Give your answers correct to 3 significant figures.

   a $56 \times 112 \div 37$ **b** $5.6 \times 11.2 \div 3.7$ **c** $0.56 \times 1.12 \div 37$

7 The answers below were found using a calculator. Write each of the answers

   i correct to 2 significant figures

   ii correct to 3 significant figures.

   a 49.737 cm^2 **b** £283 721   **c** 7.8241 cm

   d 0.067 36 m   **e** 0.000 484 2   **f** 8.937 kg

   g 10.785 m   **h** £37 694   **i** 40.038 cm^3

   j 0.706 83 m^2 **k** 40.96 kg   **l** 20.81 litres

   m 0.9008 km   **n** 5.942 m   **o** 10.94 cm^2

> **Putting your answers in a table might help.**

8 Use your calculator to do these calculations.
Give your answers to the degree of accuracy shown in brackets.

   a $(11.47 - 3.56)^2$ (3 s.f.)   **b** 3.7^2 (3 s.f.)   **c** $\pi \times 20.8^2$ (2 s.f.)

   d $(9.56 + 3.37)^2 \times (9.56 + 3.37)^2 \div 0.0102$ (2 s.f.)

   e 0.025^2 (2 s.f.)

9 Write the number 0.999 999 correct to

   a 1 s.f.   **b** 2 s.f.   **c** 3 s.f.   **d** 4 s.f.   **e** 5 s.f.

10 Here are five answers from calculator displays.

| 3.4457982 | 3.4561207 | 3.5471035 | 3.5568156 | 3.4672331 |

  i Match each of them to three of the answers below.

    a 3.45 to 2 d.p.   **b** 3.6 to 1 d.p.   **c** 3.456 to 3 d.p.

    d 3.5 to 1 d.p.   **e** 3.557 to 3 d.p.   **f** 3.47 to 2 d.p.

    g 3.46 to 2 d.p.   **h** 3.547 to 3 d.p.   **i** 3.4 to 1 d.p.

    j 3.446 to 3 d.p.   **k** 3.56 to 2 d.p.   **l** 3.467 to 3 d.p.

    m 3.55 to 2 d.p.

> d.p. means decimal places.

  ii Now write each of the calculator answers to 3 significant figures.

Wider skills practice

1 Some fractions and their equivalent decimal values are given below. Write each decimal correct to 3 significant figures.

> A dot over a digit shows that the digit recurs, e.g. $0.8\dot{3} = 0.833\,33....$

a $\dfrac{2}{3} = 0.\dot{6}$ **b** $\dfrac{5}{6} = 0.8\dot{3}$ **c** $\dfrac{5}{11} = 0.\dot{4}\dot{5}$

> Two dots show that the digits between the dots recur, e.g. $0.\dot{8}3\dot{5} = 0.835\,835\,835....$

d $\dfrac{7}{80} = 0.0875$ **e** $\dfrac{5}{12} = 0.416\dot{6}$ **f** $\dfrac{5}{7} = 0.\dot{7}1428\dot{5}$

g $\dfrac{11}{12} = 0.91\dot{6}$ **h** $\dfrac{7}{13} = 0.\dot{5}3846\dot{1}$ **i** $\dfrac{5}{13} = 0.\dot{3}8461\dot{5}$

j $\dfrac{1}{7} = 0.\dot{1}42857$

Applying skills

1 This question is about the numbers 123.5678 and 0.1235678

  a Round these numbers to **i** 3 decimal places **ii** 3 significant figures.

  b In part **a** which of the numbers gives the same answer?

  c Write down another number which is the same when rounded to 3 decimal places and 3 significant figures.

Reviewing skills

1 a Copy these numbers and underline the third significant figure in each of them.

    i 23.7   **ii** 1056   **iii** 0.437   **iv** 0.002 57   **v** 759 218

  b Write each of the numbers in part **a** to 2 significant figures.

2 Write these numbers correct to the number of significant figures shown in brackets:

  a 26.45 (2)   **b** 89.149 (3)   **c** 56.257 (3)   **d** 1766 (3)

  e 0.0276 (2)   **f** 7121.9 (1)   **g** 0.002 17 (1)   **h** 0.0305 (2)

Building skills

Example outside the Maths classroom

Costing jobs

Toolbox

Approximating is about:
- rounding numbers for a calculation so that you can do it in your head
- making a rough calculation to anticipate what sort of answer to expect.
- recognising when an error has been made
- giving a number to the level of detail that suits the context.

Example – Rounding numbers to make a calculation easier

Mo and Sahar are buying a new radiator for their bedroom.

To choose the right radiator they first need to know the volume of the room.
Mo measures the room in metres. It is 3.8 m long, 3.2 m wide and 2.7 m high.
Use rounded numbers to find the approximate volume of the room.

Solution

- Volume = 3.2 × 2.7 × 3.8
- Approximate values 3 × 3 × 4

The approximate volume is 36 m³.

Example – Rounding to recognise when an error has been made

Pete's dog is 7 years 10 months old.
Pete says that this is equivalent to a human aged 70 because 1 dog year is like 7 human years.
Is he correct?

Solution

7 years 10 months is nearly 8 years.
7 × 8 = 56 Pete's dog would be less than 56, not 70.

You could also use an inverse argument to say that, to get a result of 70 when multiplying by 7, you would need to start with 10 (Pete's dog is not yet 10 years old).

Remember:

✦ An approximate answer is often found by rounding numbers to 1 significant figure.
✦ It is always useful to check calculated answers by approximating.

Skills practice A

1 Give a sensible answer to each of these questions.

a
6 eggs

*I need 15 eggs.
How many boxes should I buy?*

b 42 lb

How many 5 lb bags of potatoes can be filled?

c
Cola 330ml

The Cola is to be shared between 4 glasses. How much Cola in each glass?

2 Is each of these true or false? Explain your answer.
   a 76.3 is about 76.
   b 457.8 is about 48.
   c 141.2 is about 141.
   d 9607 is about 9600.
   e 47 132 is about 4713.
   f 191 is about 200.

3 Jan and her friends want to buy three bars of chocolate and four drinks. They have £5.
Use approximate costs to find if they have enough money.

96p

68p

4 Write a mental calculation to estimate the answer to each of these.

   a $\dfrac{92 \times 46}{5}$
   b $\dfrac{381 + 227}{3.2}$
   c $(28.4 + 8.7)^2$

5

Avonford Fisheries

Fish and chips £3.25

Pie and chips £2.55

Sausage and chips £1.90

Three portions of fish and chips, two pie and chips and a sausage and chips please.

John

a Round each price to the nearest pound.

b Use your answers to estimate the cost of John's order.

c John has £20. Is this enough?

6 One of the four numbers below is the correct answer for 59 × 122.

7205   7817   7198   7216

An approximate answer is 60 × 120 = 7200.

Without using a calculator, choose the correct answer and explain your choice.

7 For each of these calculations, there is a choice of answers.

Use an approximation to help you select the correct answer.

a 3.2 × 8.9

   i 284.8   **ii** 28.48   **iii** 54.8

b 72 ÷ 12.5

   i 9.45   **ii** 3.76   **iii** 5.76

c $\dfrac{110 \times 94}{55}$

   i 188   **ii** 1880   **iii** 18.8

8 Des does several calculations. For each one, he estimates the answer then uses his calculator to do the calculation accurately. Here are his results.

a Rough 6, calculator 7.162   **b** Rough 0.1, calculator 10.29

c Rough 450, calculator 489.2   **d** Rough 24, calculator 2.414

e Rough 0.048, calculator 0.0511   **f** Rough 17.5, calculator 84.23

Which estimates suggest that an error has been made in using the calculator?

9 For each of the calculations below

   i estimate the answer

   ii work out the correct answer on your calculator

   iii compare your estimate with the correct answer.

a 134 ÷ 8.9   **b** 79 × 8.31   **c** 2.3 + 45.9 + 123.7

d $\dfrac{47.6 + 16.87}{6.9}$ **e** 897 ÷ 19.25   **f** 56 × 72 × 12

g 21.3 × 47.2   **h** 634 ÷ 3.9

10 Quick checks by rounding the numbers will tell you that three of these answers are wrong.

Which three?

a 9.2 × 17.5 = 161   **b** 45.8 ÷ 17 = 2.694...   **c** 28.9 × 11.2 = 40.1

d 3.2 × 2.9 × 19.1 = 177.2...   **e** $\dfrac{29}{14.7}$ = 14.3   **f** $\dfrac{13.2 \times 21.6}{4.9}$ = 58.18...

Reasoning

Reasoning

Reasoning

Skills practice B

1 Kelly is reading a book that has 217 pages. She reads about 40 pages each evening. Roughly how many days will it take Kelly to read the book?

2 Ari saved regularly every week so that he had £189.50 in a year.

Approximately how much did he save each week?

3 Estimate the volume of this room.

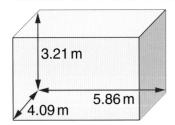

3.21 m

5.86 m

4.09 m

4 Here is a problem and some calculations.

There are 1170 pupils in the school. There are 42 tutor rooms. Approximately how many pupils are in each tutor group?

1170 × 42

1170 ÷ 42

1200 ÷ 40

1200 × 40

1100 ÷ 44

a Which two calculations will not help to solve the problem?

b Which two calculations give approximate solutions to the problem?

c Which calculation would you use?

5 Emma is on holiday in Spain. She has ten things in her shopping basket.

Round the cost of each item to the nearest euro and estimate the total cost.

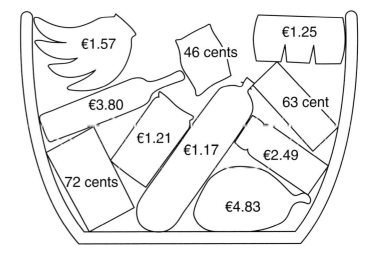

€1.57

46 cents

€1.25

€3.80

63 cent

€1.21

€1.17

€2.49

72 cents

€4.83

Reasoning

6 At a Flower Show, 1794 entrance tickets were sold. The total amount of money made was £8232.

   a Estimate the average amount each person spent.

   b At last year's Flower Show, they sold 2057 tickets and made £7483.
     Did people spend more money this year or last year?

7 Jenny and her father are disagreeing over the volume of a box.
  Who is correct?

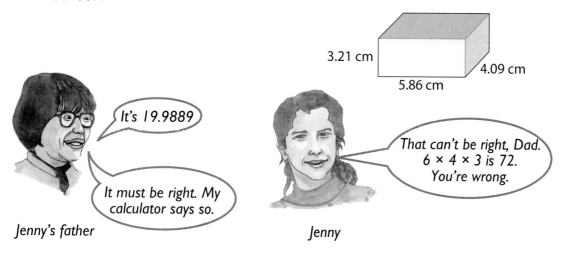

3.21 cm   4.09 cm   5.86 cm

It's 19.9889

That can't be right, Dad. 6 × 4 × 3 is 72. You're wrong.

It must be right. My calculator says so.

Jenny's father   *Jenny*

8 Estimate the cost of

   a 48 litres of petrol at 148.99p per litre

   b a phone call lasting 14 minutes 51 seconds at 9p per minute

   c 9.2 metres of curtain tape at 80p per metre.

9 a There are 36 eggs in a tray. A box of eggs contains 12 trays of eggs.
     Approximately how many eggs are in a box?

   b Approximately how many 62-seater coaches are needed to take a school of 1796 students on
     a trip?

   c A bottle of cola contains 1950 ml. Approximately how many millilitres are there in 11 bottles?

   d A bottle of cola contains 1950 ml. 205 ml are needed to fill a cup.
     Approximately how many cups can be filled from one bottle?

   e A job pays £214 per week. Approximately how much is this in one year (52 weeks)?

   f One pint of milk is sufficient for 22 cups of tea.
     Approximately how many pints are needed for 485 cups of tea?

10 For each of the calculations in parts **a**, **b**, **c** and **d** use approximation to identify the correct one
    from the four possible answers given. Explain your choice.

   a 385^2

     i 164 025   **ii** 148 225   **iii** 1425   **iv** 1615

   b 45.6×8.1

     i 412.36   **ii** 305.26   **iii** 369.36   **iv** 402.46

   c $3.9^2 + 2.1^2$

     i 17.52   **ii** 36.3   **iii** 12.44   **iv** 19.62

   d $\dfrac{12.3 + 18.9}{7.2}$

     i 4.33   **ii** 6.33   **iii** 15.33   **iv** 20.33

Wider skills practice

1 Give an approximate answer for each of these.

a $\sqrt{35}$ **b** $\sqrt{119}$ **c** $\sqrt{340}$

d $\sqrt{52 \times 1.9}$ **e** $2.8^2 + 7.13^2$ **f** $\sqrt{4^2 \times 5^2}$

g $\dfrac{12.7 + 108}{8.7}$ **h** $\pi \times 4.8$ **i** $\pi \times 2.7^2$

> Use a calculator and your judgement to find which operations to use.

2 In these calculations, each box represents an operation (+, −, × or ÷). Copy and complete the calculations.

a (37 ☐ 21) ☐ 223 = 1000   **b** (756 ☐ 18) ☐ 29 = 1218

c 27 ☐ (36 ☐ 18) = 675   **d** 31 ☐ (87 ☐ 19) = 2108

e 476 ☐ (2040 ☐ 24) = 391   **f** (3461 ☐ 276) ☐ 101 = 37

g (967 ☐ 34) ☐ (1023 ☐ 654) = 369 369   **h** (29 ☐ 8²) ☐ 9 = 84

i (619 ☐ 316) ☐ 425 ☐ 196 = 924   **j** 6975 ☐ (36 ☐ 39) = 93

3 Give an approximate answer to each of these problems.

a Rashide cycles 45 km at an average speed of 11 km per hour. How long does this take?

b Vera is paid £35 for working 9 hours. How much is this per hour?

c Weldon takes 20 strides to walk 18 metres. How long is each stride?

d Alex collected £115 after doing a 35 km sponsored walk.
How much money is this per kilometre?

e A lift can carry a maximum of 8 people or 650 kilograms.
What does this give as the average weight of a person?

f A garden bench 2 m long seats three people. How much room does each person have?

Applying skills

1 The Bonzo Children's Charity is organising a competition to guess how many balloons can be put inside a saloon car. The best estimate wins the car (which has been donated by the manufacturer)! What is your estimate?

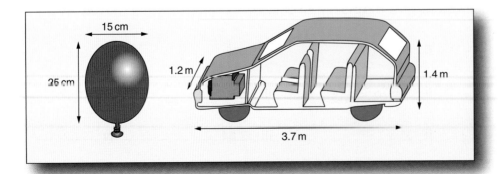

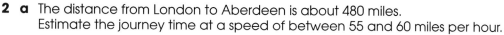

Problem solving

2 **a** The distance from London to Aberdeen is about 480 miles.
Estimate the journey time at a speed of between 55 and 60 miles per hour.

   b Estimate the number of seconds you sleep in one day.

   c Estimate the weight of a box of 12 books which each weigh 1.75 kg.

   d Estimate the number of jelly men in the jar. Show all your working.

A jelly
man is
I cm thick.

1 cm

2 cm

20 cm

Jelly
Men

35 cm

3 The table shows how long Jane worked at different rates of pay last week.

	Hours worked	Rate of pay
Normal pay	25 hours 45 mins	£7.90 per hour
Overtime	5 hours 20 mins	£9.95 per hour
Sunday	2 hours 40 mins	£12.75 per hour

Which four of these calculations help to estimate Jane's earnings for the week?

a $3 \times 13 = 39$ **b** $25 \times 8 = 200$ **c** $10 \times 13 = 130$

d $5 \times 10 = 50$ **e** $8 \times 10 = 80$ **f** $26 + 5 + 3 = 33$

g $40 + 200 + 50 = 290$

Reviewing skills

1 You are told that $T = \dfrac{7.8^2 + 5.79^2}{17.67}$

   a Estimate an approximate value for T by rounding all the numbers to 1 significant figure.

   b Use your calculator to find the true value of T correct to 3 significant figures.

2 A flight from Edinburgh Airport to London Gatwick takes $1\frac{1}{2}$ hours. The distance is 432 miles.
Estimate the speed of the plane.

3 Estimate the number of minutes in a year. Give your answer to 1 significant figure.

4 Alan works five days every week.
In a typical day he spends about 1 hour 40 minutes travelling to and from work.

   a Estimate the number of hours Alan spends travelling in a full working year of 48 weeks.

   b Approximately how many days does he spend travelling?

5 Here are six calculations:

   a $(49.7 \times 43) \div (12.6 - 7.4)$ **b** $\sqrt{(8.7^2 + 7.8^2)}$ **c** $(675.6 - 123.2) \div (17.8 + 12.3)$

   d $\sqrt[3]{(1.2^2 + 2.8^2 + 3.9^2)}$ **e** $\pi \times 5.2^2$ **f** $\sqrt{\dfrac{314.16}{\pi}}$

   The correct answers, to 1 decimal place, are given below but they have been mixed up.

   2.9   18.4   411.0   84.9   10.0   11.7

Use estimation to match each answer to the correct calculation.

Building skills

Buying in bulk

Toolbox

- To say how accurate a measurement is, give its lower and upper bounds.

The length of a line is l, recorded as 36 cm to the nearest centimetre.

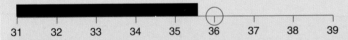

All lines between 35.5 cm and 36.499999... cm are rounded to 36 cm.

35.5 cm is called the **lower bound.**

36.499999 is effectively 36.5 cm so 36.5 cm is called the **upper bound**.

This is written as

$$35.5 \leqslant l < 36.5$$

Another way of writing it is

$$l = 35 \pm 0.5 \text{ cm}$$

Example – Recognising the effect of bounds on a result

Stella draws a square with a side length of 21 cm to the nearest centimetre.

a What are the upper and lower bounds of the side length of the square?

b What are the upper and lower bounds of the perimeter of the square she has drawn?

Solution

a Upper bound is 21.5 cm
   Lower bound is 20.5 cm

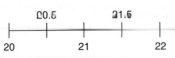

b Upper bound of perimeter = 4 × 21.5 = 86 cm
   Lower bound of perimeter = 4 × 20.5 = 82 cm

Remember:

✦ Always be aware of the lower and upper bounds when you are working with measurements.

Skills practice A

1 Write the number 1030 correct to
   a 1 significant figure
   b 2 significant figures
   c 3 significant figures
   d 4 significant figures.
   e Explain your answers to parts **c** and **d**.

2 How many significant figures might the number 100 have?

3 350 is accurate to 2 significant figures.
   a Explain why John rounded 349 to 350 to 2 s.f.
   b Write down two other numbers smaller than 349 which will round to 350 to 2 s.f.

4 2.56 is correct to 2 decimal places.
   a Explain why Mary wrote 2.563 as 2.56 to 2 decimal places.
   b Write down two more numbers bigger than 2.563 that Mary would still round to 2.56 to 2 decimal places.
   c Write down two numbers less than 2.56 which will round up to 2.56 to 2 decimal places.
   d What are the biggest and the smallest numbers that can round to 2.56 to 2 decimal places?

5 **a** Write these numbers correct to 2 significant figures.
   i 1.24   **ii** 1.237   **iii** 1.1652
   iv 1.151   **v** 1.249   **vi** 1.249 99
   b The number 1.2 is given correct to 2 significant figures. Write this as a range of numbers.

6 All of these numbers have been rounded.
   Write down lower and upper bounds for each of them.
   a 123   **b** 1.044   **c** 3.333
   d 3.1416   **e** 0.0589   **f** 1.50
   g 8.005   **h** 107.05
   i 0.004 07   **j** 4125

7 All of these numbers have been rounded. Write down lower and upper bounds for each of them.
   a 510 correct to the nearest 10
   b 2600 correct to the nearest 100
   c 23.5 correct to 3 significant figures
   d 21.15 correct to 2 decimal places
   e 440 correct to 2 significant figures

8 Write each of these as an inequality.

    a 230 (correct to the nearest 10)

    b 5.62 (correct to 2 decimal places)

    c 200 (correct to 1 s.f.)

    d 200 (correct to 2 s.f.)

    e 0.4 (correct to 1 s.f.)

    f 0.40 (correct to 2 s.f.)

Skills practice B

1 Ari buys a box of matches and notices that the small print says 'Contents 45 (±5) matchsticks'. What is the minimum number of matches that he can expect in the box?

2 750 g is a measurement accurate to 2 significant figures.

    a Explain why 750 is 746 correct to 2 significant figures.

    b What is the smallest number that will give 750 when rounded to 2 significant figures?

    c Write down the largest number that will give 750 when rounded to 2 significant figures.

3 Brian weighs 67 kg to the nearest kilogram.

    a Round these weights to the nearest kilogram.

        67.4 kg, 66.97 kg, 66.52 kg, 67.499 9 kg

    b Write down the smallest possible value for Brian's weight.

    c Write down the largest possible value for Brian's weight.

    d Write Brian's weight as an inequality.

4 Write each of these measurements as an inequality.

    a 45 cm to the nearest cm

    b 124 litres to the nearest litre

    c 58 grams to the nearest gram

    d 4.1 cm to the nearest mm   ←   (Change 4.1 cm to mm first.)

    e 2.5 km to the nearest metre.   ←   (Change 2.5 km to metres first.)

5 A bottle of apple juice holds 75 cl to the nearest centilitre.

    a What is the largest possible error when measuring to the nearest centilitre?

    b Write down the smallest possible value for the volume of apple juice.

    c Write down the largest possible value for the volume of apple juice.

    d Write the volume of apple juice as an inequality.

6 10 Swiss francs are worth £4.30 to the nearest 10 pence.

    a What is the largest possible error when measuring to the nearest 10 pence?

    b Write down the smallest possible value for 10 Swiss francs.

    c Write down the largest possible value for 10 Swiss francs.

    d Write the value of 10 Swiss francs in pounds as an inequality.

7 The diameter of a roundabout is given as 6 m to 1 significant figure.

   a What are the maximum and minimum possible lengths of the roundabout's diameter?

   b What is the maximum possible length of the roundabout's radius?

   c Write an inequality giving the upper and lower bounds of the radius r of the roundabout.

8 A box of soap powder is labelled 4 kg.

   a If this labelling is correct to the nearest kilogram, what are the minimum and the maximum amounts of soap powder in the box?

   b Write this as an inequality.

9 Explain why it might not be safe for these people to travel together in the lift.

   • David 65 kg

   • Brian 92 kg

   • Bronwen 74 kg

   • Pat 54 kg

   • Peter 86 kg

   • Bruce 95 kg

   • Ahmed 89 kg

   • Mark 93 kg

Lift
Maximum safe load
8 persons or
650 kg

10 A paperback book is 2.6 cm thick, measured to the nearest $\frac{1}{10}$ of a centimetre and contains 378 numbered pages.

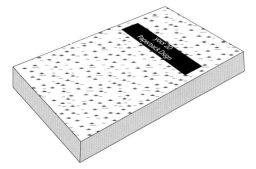

   a What is the maximum thickness of the book?

   b What is the maximum thickness of one sheet of paper in millimetres?

     Give your answer to 2 significant figures. ◄─── **Note: sheets are not the same as pages.**

Reasoning

Reasoning

11 Look at this diagram. The lengths have been rounded.

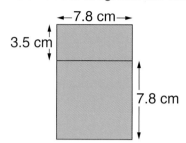

    a How accurately are the measurements given?

    b Write the upper and lower bounds for each measurement.

    c These measurements are used to calculate the perimeter of the combined shape. What are the upper and lower bounds for the answer?

Wider skills practice

1 The angles a and b are 100° and 140° (to the nearest degree).

    a Find the upper and lower bounds of a and b

    b What is the smallest angle c can be?

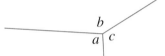

2 The measurements of this photograph are accurate to the nearest millimetre.

    a Write the upper and lower bounds of each measurement.

    b Work out the smallest possible measurement for the perimeter of the photograph.

    c Work out the largest possible value for the perimeter.

    d Work out the smallest and largest values for the area of the photograph.

3 The side of a piece of square card is 21 cm to the nearest centimetre. This means that the side length could be anywhere between 20.5 cm and 21.5 cm. The area of the square could be

- largest possible area = $21.5 \times 21.5 = 462.25 \text{ cm}^2$
- smallest possible area = $20.5 \times 20.5 = 420.25 \text{ cm}^2$

So the range of area for this square is $462.25 - 420.25 = 42 \text{ cm}^2$.

    a Another square has sides 16 cm to the nearest cm.

        Find the range of possible values for the area of this square.

    b Can you find a connection between the length of the side of a square and the possible range for its area?

    c Prove that your result is true for any square.

Reasoning

Applying skills

1 Mary has 64 CDs. Each CD is 1 cm wide (to the nearest mm). She needs a shelf to store her CDs. How long should she make her shelf?

2 Stella is designing a central heating flue duct to take waste fumes out through the wall.
The hole for the duct has to be sealed.
There is a 16.5 cm square plate with a 4.5 cm radius circle removed from it.
The measurements are given accurate to 1 decimal place.

   a Calculate the maximum and minimum areas of the square sheet of metal needed.

   b Calculate the maximum and minimum areas of the circle to be removed.

   c Calculate the maximum area of the metal seal (the metal remaining after the circle has been cut out).

   d Write an inequality to show the upper and lower bounds of the area of the metal seal.

Reviewing skills

1 Gary's height is being measured. He is 178 cm tall to the nearest centimetre.

   a What is the largest possible error when measuring to the nearest centimetre?

   b Write down the smallest possible value for Gary's height.

   c Write down the largest possible value for Gary's height.

   d Write Gary's height as an inequality.

2 Write each of these measurements as an inequality.

   a 23 cm to the nearest centimetre   **b** 61 litres to the nearest litre

   c 690 mm to the nearest millimetre   **d** 43 km to the nearest kilometre

   e 29 kg to the nearest kilogram   **f** 541 kg to the nearest gram

3 Apple juice is sold in cuboidal cartons.
The measurements shown are correct to the nearest centimetre.

19 cm

9 cm   6 cm

What are the upper and lower bounds of each measurement?

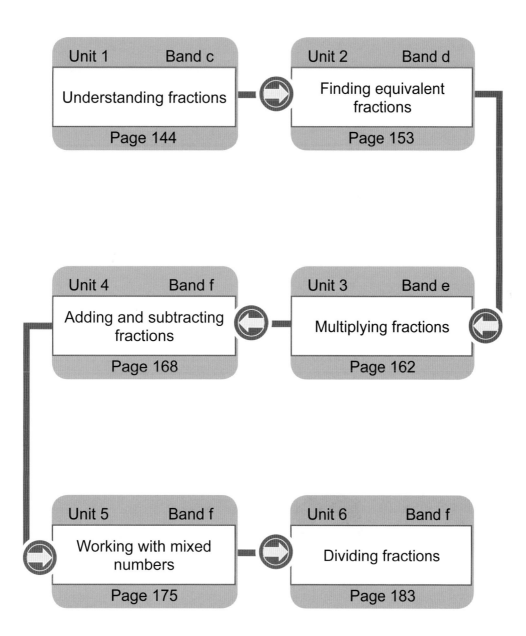

Unit 1   Band c

Understanding fractions

Page 144

Unit 2   Band d

Finding equivalent fractions

Page 153

Unit 4   Band f

Adding and subtracting fractions

Page 168

Unit 3   Band e

Multiplying fractions

Page 162

Unit 5   Band f

Working with mixed numbers

Page 175

Unit 6   Band f

Dividing fractions

Page 183

Building skills

 Example outside the Maths classroom

Cloud cover

 Toolbox

A fraction is a number that has a top (the numerator) and a bottom (the denominator).

For example, $\frac{3}{6}$

The top line tells you the number of parts you have.

The bottom line tells you the total number of equal parts.

Here are six equal parts.
Three of those parts are red.

I can write this as a fraction.
$\frac{3}{6}$ of the badge is red.

Meena

Here, four out of seven rectangles are red.
$\frac{4}{7}$ are red.

Now, two more rectangles are red.

$\frac{6}{7}$ is now red.

To find a fraction of an amount you first divide the amount into a number of equal parts.
The bottom line of the fraction tells you how many parts.

Then you multiply by the number of parts you want.
The top line of the fraction tells you how many parts you want.

So, to find $\frac{2}{5}$ of 60

60

12	12	12	12	12

Divide 60 into 5 equal parts, Each part represents $\frac{1}{5}$.

12	12	12	12	12

Two pieces will give you $\frac{2}{5}$.

So $\frac{2}{5}$ of 60 = 2 × 12

= 24

Example – Finding a fraction of an amount

Find $\frac{7}{10}$ of £80.

Solution

The amount is £80.

80 ÷ 10 = 8

First divide the amount into the number of equal parts given, in this case 10.

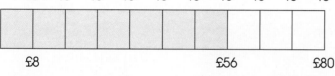

So each part is £8

You want 7 parts.

8 × 7 = £56

Then multiply the number in each part by the number of parts needed, given by the numerator.

$\frac{7}{10}$ of £80 = £56

Remember:

✦ Fractions are always about **equal** parts.
✦ Thinking about fractions as pictures will help you understand what you are doing.

Skills practice A

1 What fraction of each of these flags is red?

a

France

b

Germany

c

Italy

d

Greenland

e

Thailand

f

Austria

2 What fraction of each of these flags is
  i white
  ii green?

a

Ireland

b

Nigeria

3 What fraction of each of these flags is blue?

a

b

c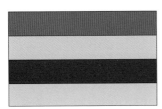

d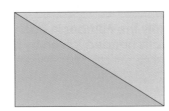

4 Match each of these patterns to a fraction from the box.

a 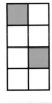 **b** 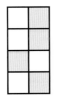 **c**   **d**   **e**   **f**

$\dfrac{7}{8}$ $\dfrac{1}{4}$ $\dfrac{3}{4}$ $\dfrac{5}{8}$ 1 $\dfrac{1}{2}$

5 Draw eight circles like these.

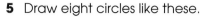

Colour $\frac{1}{2}$ of the circles red.

Colour $\frac{1}{4}$ of the circles blue.

Colour the rest in yellow.

What fraction of the circles are yellow?

6 a $\frac{1}{2}$ of a flag is blue. The rest is green.

What fraction is green?

b $\frac{1}{4}$ of a flag is red. The rest is yellow.

What fraction is yellow?

c $\frac{1}{3}$ of a flag is orange. The rest is green.

What fraction is green?

d $\frac{3}{5}$ of a flag is white. The rest is red.

What fraction is red?

7 Draw 12 circles like these.

a Show how 12 sweets can be shared equally between four people.
b A group of people share out the 12 sweets equally.
They get two each.
How many people are there?

8 Copy and complete these statements.

a $\frac{1}{2}$ of 12 = ☐   **b** $\frac{1}{3}$ of 12 = ☐   **c** $\frac{2}{3}$ of 12 = ☐

d $\frac{1}{4}$ of 12 = ☐   **e** $\frac{1}{6}$ of 12 = ☐

9 For each of the numbers below find

a $\frac{1}{2}$ of it   **b** $\frac{1}{4}$ of it   **c** $\frac{3}{4}$ of it

i 8   **ii** 16   **iii** 20   **vi** 100   **v** 10

10 Work out these.

   a $\frac{3}{4}$ of 24   **b** $\frac{2}{5}$ of 20   **c** $\frac{5}{9}$ of 27   **d** $\frac{2}{15}$ of 30

   e $\frac{4}{7}$ of 28   **f** $\frac{3}{10}$ of £2.50   **g** $\frac{2}{3}$ of £3.99   **h** $\frac{4}{5}$ of £3.60

Skills practice B

1 Write each of these fractions.
   a 30 seconds as a fraction of a minute
   b 5 minutes as a fraction of an hour
   c 2 days as a fraction of a week
   d 35 days as a fraction of a year
   e 25 years as a fraction of a century

2 Which of these badges are coloured correctly?

   a $\frac{1}{2}$ pink   **b** $\frac{1}{2}$ green   **c** $\frac{1}{4}$ white   **d** $\frac{1}{3}$ white

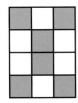 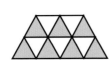

3 A packet containing 18 sweets is emptied.
   a Copy and complete this table.

Colour	Red	Blue	Brown	Yellow	Pink	Green
Number						

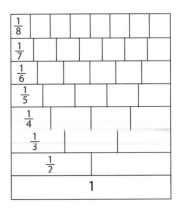

   b What fraction is
     i blue   **ii** brown   **iii** pink
     iv red or green   **v** blue or yellow **vi** not red?

4 Use this diagram to write these fractions in order of size, smallest first.

   $\frac{2}{5}$ $\frac{1}{2}$ $\frac{1}{8}$ $\frac{3}{7}$ $\frac{5}{6}$ $\frac{2}{3}$ $\frac{3}{4}$

$\frac{1}{8}$							
$\frac{1}{7}$						
$\frac{1}{6}$					
$\frac{1}{5}$				
$\frac{1}{4}$			
$\frac{1}{3}$		
$\frac{1}{2}$	
1

5 The table shows the points scored by the football teams in the Premier League one year.

Team	Number of points scored	Team	Number of points scored
Manchester United	83	Middlesbrough	49
Arsenal	78	Charlton	49
Newcastle	69	Birmingham	48
Chelsea	67	Fulham	48
Liverpool	64	Leeds	47
Blackburn	60	Aston Villa	45
Everton	59	Bolton	44
Southampton	52	West Ham	42
Manchester City	51	West Bromwich	26
Tottenham	50	Sunderland	19

a How many teams are there?

b How many teams scored more than 60 points?

c What fraction is this?

6 Copy and complete this statement.

$$\frac{1}{2} \text{ of } 100 = \frac{1}{4} \text{ of } \boxed{}$$

Reasoning

7 Work out these.

a i $\frac{1}{3}$ of 60 minutes

ii $\frac{2}{3}$ of 60 minutes

b i $\frac{1}{4}$ of 28 days

ii $\frac{3}{4}$ of 28 days

c i $\frac{1}{7}$ of £56

ii $\frac{2}{7}$ of £56

8 Calculate the reduced prices.

a   **b**

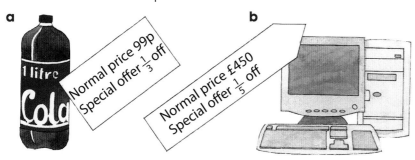

1 litre Cola — Normal price 99p. Special offer $\frac{1}{3}$ off

Normal price £450. Special offer $\frac{1}{5}$ off

9 Work out these.

a $\frac{1}{4}$ of 100 cm

b $\frac{1}{3}$ of 45 minutes

c $\frac{2}{5}$ of 60 minutes

d $\frac{3}{4}$ of 64 kg

e $\frac{2}{3}$ of 18 kg

f $\frac{5}{16}$ of 32 ounces

g $\frac{3}{7}$ of 28 days

h $\frac{4}{9}$ of 360°

10 Work out these.

    a $\frac{4}{7}$ of $42   **b** $\frac{6}{11}$ of £33   **c** $\frac{3}{10}$ of 1000 m   **d** $\frac{4}{9}$ of 63 km

    e $\frac{11}{25}$ of 100 kg   **f** $\frac{3}{20}$ of £40   **g** $\frac{7}{12}$ of 132 g

11 Half of Melissa's sweets were red.
Wayne had 12 sweets.
A third of Wayne's sweets were red.
He gave half of his red sweets to Melissa.
She now has 11 red sweets.
How many sweets does Melissa now have altogether?

Wider skills practice

1 Jo, Sophie and Meena share £60 between them.

Jo gets $\frac{1}{2}$.

Sophie gets $\frac{1}{3}$.

    a How much money do Jo and Sophie each get?
    b **i** How much is left for Meena?
        ii What fraction does Meena get?

2 There are 12 inches in 1 foot, 3 feet in 1 yard and 1760 yards in 1 mile.
    a Work out how many **i** feet **ii** inches there are in 1 mile

    b Which is greater, $\frac{1}{4}$ of a mile or 1800 inches?

    c Which is greater, $\frac{1}{110}$ of a mile or 48 feet?

3 Tim, Humza and Mark share £30 between them.

Tim gets $\frac{1}{3}$.

Humza gets $\frac{1}{6}$.

Mark gets $\frac{2}{5}$.

    a How much money does each person get?
    b **i** How much is left over?
        ii What fraction is left over?

4 Jeremy has drawn this pie chart to show how he spends his pocket money.

Jeremy

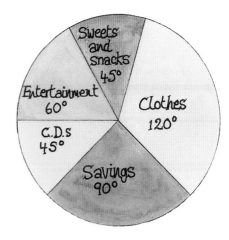

a What fraction of his money does he spend on

   i entertainment

   ii sweets and snacks

   iii clothes?

b He gets a total of £600 pocket money each year. (£50 each month.)

   Work out how much he spends on each category in a year.

Applying skills

1 A dartboard is a circle divided into 20 sectors numbered 1 to 20.

a Work out the angle for each number.

b **i** What fraction of the board is even numbers?

   ii What fraction is odd numbers?

c What fraction of the sectors are black?

d **i** What fraction of the black sectors are even numbers?

   ii What fraction of the black sectors are odd numbers?

e Add the black numbers and the white numbers.

   What fraction of the total is black?

Reviewing skills

1 What fraction of each of these shapes is coloured?

a

b

c

d

e

f

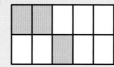

2 What fraction of this square is
   a blue
   b green
   c red
   d white?

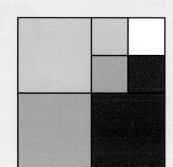

3 There are 16 coloured sweets.
   How many of the sweets are red when

   a $\frac{1}{2}$ are red   b $\frac{1}{4}$ are red   c $\frac{3}{4}$ are red?

4 Work out these.

   a $\frac{1}{3}$ of £24   b $\frac{3}{4}$ of 84 people   c $\frac{5}{8}$ of 16 ounces   d $\frac{1}{4}$ of £16

5 By how much is each of these items reduced?

Building skills

Example outside the Maths classroom

Risk

Toolbox

Look at Meena's badge.

Three out of the six rectangles are red.

Three is half of six.
$\frac{1}{2}$ *of the badge is red.*

Meena

You can say that $\frac{3}{6}$ may be **simplified** or **cancelled down** or **reduced** to give $\frac{1}{2}$.

$$\frac{3}{6} = \frac{1}{2}$$

÷3 ... ÷3

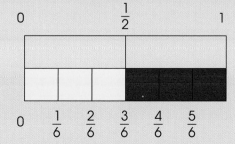

Look at Jack's badge.

Two out of the six rectangles are green.

$\frac{2}{6}$ of the badge is green.

$\frac{2}{6}$ can be simplified or cancelled down or reduced to give $\frac{1}{3}$.

To simplify a fraction, you divide the top and bottom by the same number.

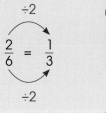

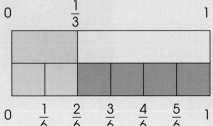

Sometimes there is more than one way to get to the simplest form.

$$\overset{\div 2}{\frac{54}{60}} = \overset{\div 3}{\frac{27}{30}} = \frac{9}{10} \qquad \overset{\div 6}{\frac{54}{60}} = \frac{9}{10}$$

$$\underset{\div 2}{} \qquad \underset{\div 3}{} \qquad \underset{\div 6}{}$$

When you cannot cancel any further, the fraction is in its **simplest form**.

$\frac{54}{60}, \frac{27}{30}$ and $\frac{9}{10}$ are called **equivalent fractions**.

Equivalent fractions are found by dividing the top and bottom by the same number *or* by multiplying the top and bottom by the same number.

Here are some fractions which are equivalent to $\frac{3}{5}$.

$$\overset{\times 2}{\frac{3}{5} = \frac{6}{10}} \qquad \overset{\times 3}{\frac{3}{5} = \frac{9}{15}} \qquad \overset{\times 7}{\frac{3}{5} = \frac{21}{35}}$$

$$\underset{\times 2}{} \qquad \underset{\times 3}{} \qquad \underset{\times 7}{}$$

So $\frac{3}{5} = \frac{6}{10} = \frac{9}{15} = \frac{21}{35}$.

Example – Comparing fractions

Harry ran $\frac{3}{5}$ of a mile and Anna ran $\frac{4}{7}$ of a mile.

Who ran further?

Solution

To compare the fractions, write them as equivalent fractions with the same bottom lines (a common denominator).

$$\frac{3}{5} = \frac{21}{35} \qquad \frac{4}{7} = \frac{20}{35}$$

×7   ×5

×7   ×5

The numbers on the bottom must be the same.

When the fractions have a common denominator, they can be compared directly.

$\frac{21}{35}$ is bigger than $\frac{20}{35}$, so Harry ran further.

Remember:

✦ Thinking about a fraction bar can help.
✦ The value of a fraction doesn't change if you multiply the top and bottom of the fraction by the same amount.

Skills practice A

1 Copy and complete the statements for these badges.

a

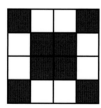

b

c

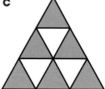

Blue: $\frac{\square}{16} = \frac{\square}{\square}$

White: $\frac{\square}{16} = \frac{\square}{\square}$

Red: $\frac{\square}{6} = \frac{1}{\square}$

White: $\frac{\square}{6} = \frac{2}{\square}$

White: $\frac{\square}{9} = \frac{\square}{3}$

Purple: $\frac{\square}{9} = \frac{2}{\square}$

2 Write down the fractions of these badges in each colour.
Then give your answers in their simplest form.

a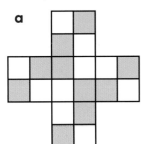

b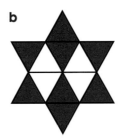

c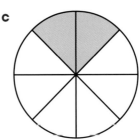

3 Copy and complete these statements.

a $\dfrac{1}{10} = \dfrac{\square}{20}$ **b** $\dfrac{2}{5} = \dfrac{\square}{20}$ **c** $\dfrac{1}{4} = \dfrac{\square}{20}$

d $\dfrac{3}{5} = \dfrac{\square}{20}$ **e** $\dfrac{3}{4} = \dfrac{\square}{20}$ **f** $\dfrac{3}{10} = \dfrac{\square}{20}$

4 Match the fractions in the red box to equivalent fractions in the blue box.

$$\dfrac{4}{8} \qquad \dfrac{4}{6} \qquad \dfrac{2}{6} \qquad \dfrac{6}{8} \qquad \dfrac{3}{12}$$

$$\dfrac{1}{4} \qquad \dfrac{1}{3} \qquad \dfrac{1}{2} \qquad \dfrac{2}{3} \qquad \dfrac{3}{4}$$

5 a Write $\dfrac{5}{6}$ and $\dfrac{3}{4}$ as equivalent fractions with a denominator of 12.

← **The denominator is the number on the bottom line of a fraction.**

b Which fraction is bigger, $\dfrac{5}{6}$ or $\dfrac{3}{4}$?

6 Which of these fractions are equivalent to two-thirds $\left(\dfrac{2}{3}\right)$?

$$\dfrac{4}{6} \quad \dfrac{15}{25} \quad \dfrac{12}{18} \quad \dfrac{14}{20} \quad \dfrac{8}{10} \quad \dfrac{16}{24} \quad \dfrac{20}{30} \quad \dfrac{10}{20} \quad \dfrac{12}{16} \quad \dfrac{16}{20} \quad \dfrac{14}{21} \quad \dfrac{24}{30} \quad \dfrac{34}{51} \quad \dfrac{24}{28} \quad \dfrac{32}{48}$$

7 Write down three fractions that are equivalent to $\dfrac{5}{7}$.

8 Write these fractions in their simplest form.

a $\dfrac{5}{10}$ **b** $\dfrac{3}{12}$ **c** $\dfrac{2}{16}$

d $\dfrac{4}{20}$ **e** $\dfrac{6}{12}$

9 a Write these fractions as equivalent fractions with a denominator of 50.

$$\dfrac{2}{5} \qquad \dfrac{3}{10} \qquad \dfrac{1}{2} \qquad \dfrac{7}{25}$$

b Now write the fractions in order of size, starting with the smallest.

10 For each pair of fractions
  i write the fractions with a common denominator
  ii write down the smaller fraction from the pair.

  a $\frac{1}{2}$ and $\frac{1}{3}$ **b** $\frac{3}{4}$ and $\frac{5}{7}$ **c** $\frac{4}{5}$ and $\frac{5}{6}$ **d** $\frac{1}{3}$ and $\frac{5}{12}$

  e $\frac{1}{4}$ and $\frac{3}{10}$ **f** $\frac{2}{5}$ and $\frac{13}{30}$ **g** $\frac{5}{8}$ and $\frac{2}{3}$ **h** $\frac{2}{9}$ and $\frac{5}{18}$

11 Write these fractions in their simplest form.

  a $\frac{4}{16}$ **b** $\frac{6}{8}$ **c** $\frac{9}{12}$ **d** $\frac{12}{18}$

  e $\frac{14}{21}$ **f** $\frac{4}{6}$ **g** $\frac{10}{30}$ **h** $\frac{7}{21}$

  i $\frac{12}{40}$ **j** $\frac{18}{24}$ **k** $\frac{36}{60}$ **l** $\frac{68}{80}$

12 Which of these fractions are equivalent to $\frac{9}{12}$?

  $\frac{18}{24}$ $\frac{6}{9}$ $\frac{12}{15}$ $\frac{12}{16}$ $\frac{15}{20}$ $\frac{30}{40}$

13 Match these into pairs of equivalent fractions.

  $\frac{4}{9}$ $\frac{5}{8}$ $\frac{10}{12}$ $\frac{8}{18}$ $\frac{12}{20}$ $\frac{35}{56}$ $\frac{15}{18}$ $\frac{9}{15}$

Skills practice B

1 Copy this table.

$\frac{2}{4}$	$\frac{8}{12}$	$\frac{9}{27}$	$\frac{5}{10}$
$\frac{2}{6}$	$\frac{15}{20}$	$\frac{6}{8}$	$\frac{3}{12}$
$\frac{6}{10}$	$\frac{9}{12}$	$\frac{12}{16}$	$\frac{3}{9}$
$\frac{7}{14}$	$\frac{11}{33}$	$\frac{4}{16}$	$\frac{14}{28}$

Colour all the fractions that are equivalent to $\frac{1}{2}$ in red.

Colour all the fractions that are equivalent to $\frac{1}{3}$ in blue.

Colour all the fractions that are equivalent to $\frac{3}{4}$ in yellow.

Write the other fractions in their simplest form.

2 Copy and complete these sets of equivalent fractions.

a $\dfrac{1}{2} = \dfrac{3}{\square} = \dfrac{\square}{14}$ **b** $\dfrac{1}{3} = \dfrac{\square}{9} = \dfrac{5}{\square}$ **c** $\dfrac{1}{4} = \dfrac{\square}{8} = \dfrac{6}{\square}$

d $\dfrac{2}{3} = \dfrac{4}{\square} = \dfrac{\square}{12}$ **e** $\dfrac{3}{4} = \dfrac{\square}{16} = \dfrac{24}{\square}$ **f** $\dfrac{2}{5} = \dfrac{8}{\square} = \dfrac{\square}{15}$

3 Which of these fractions are equivalent to the shaded fraction of this circle?

$\dfrac{10}{16}$ $\dfrac{8}{11}$ $\dfrac{50}{80}$ $\dfrac{25}{40}$ $\dfrac{25}{64}$ $\dfrac{15}{18}$

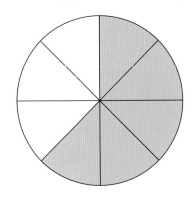

4 Which of these fractions are equivalent to the shaded fraction of this rectangle?

$\dfrac{8}{10}$ $\dfrac{5}{6}$ $\dfrac{12}{15}$ $\dfrac{8}{9}$ $\dfrac{40}{50}$ $\dfrac{80}{100}$ $\dfrac{16}{25}$ $\dfrac{44}{55}$ $\dfrac{14}{15}$ $\dfrac{34}{36}$ $\dfrac{404}{505}$ $\dfrac{5}{4}$

5 Write down the larger fraction from each pair.

a $\dfrac{3}{4}$ and $\dfrac{7}{8}$ **b** $\dfrac{2}{3}$ and $\dfrac{5}{6}$ **c** $\dfrac{3}{7}$ and $\dfrac{2}{5}$ **d** $\dfrac{4}{9}$ and $\dfrac{2}{5}$

6 Lucy, Michelle and Ali share £36 between them.
Lucy gets £18, Michelle gets £12 and Ali gets £6.
What fraction does each get?
Write the fractions in their simplest form.

7 Find a fraction that lies between each of these pairs of fractions.
The first one has been done for you.

a $\dfrac{1}{2}$ and $\dfrac{3}{4}$

$\dfrac{1}{2} = \dfrac{4}{8}$ and $\dfrac{3}{4} = \dfrac{6}{8}$ so $\dfrac{5}{8}$ lies between $\dfrac{1}{2}$ and $\dfrac{3}{4}$.

b $\dfrac{1}{2}$ and $\dfrac{1}{4}$

c $\dfrac{1}{2}$ and $\dfrac{1}{3}$ $\longleftarrow$ Write each fraction as twelfths this time.

d $\dfrac{1}{2}$ and $\dfrac{2}{3}$

e $\dfrac{1}{4}$ and $\dfrac{2}{5}$

f $\dfrac{3}{8}$ and $\dfrac{3}{4}$

Reasoning

8 Rachel scores 3 out of 7.

Charles scores 4 out of 9.

Whose score is better? Explain your answer.

9 Michela gets €5 pocket money.

This is how she spends it.

a What fraction does she spend on

i sweets

ii magazines

iii make-up?

Michela saves any money she has left.

b What fraction does she save?

Magazines   €1·50

Sweets   50 cent

Make-up   €2

10 Write each of these sets of fractions in order of size, starting with the smallest.

a $\dfrac{3}{4}$ $\dfrac{5}{6}$ $\dfrac{3}{7}$ $\dfrac{7}{10}$ $\dfrac{4}{5}$ $\dfrac{9}{10}$

b $\dfrac{9}{21}$ $\dfrac{40}{50}$ $\dfrac{1}{3}$ $\dfrac{2}{4}$ $\dfrac{15}{18}$

c $\dfrac{4}{8}$ $\dfrac{6}{10}$ $\dfrac{50}{60}$ $\dfrac{13}{39}$ $\dfrac{16}{20}$

11 a Write each of these fractions with a denominator of 100.

i $\dfrac{4}{5}$ **ii** $\dfrac{7}{10}$ **iii** $\dfrac{3}{4}$

iv $\dfrac{11}{20}$ **v** $\dfrac{9}{50}$ **vi** $\dfrac{3}{25}$

b Write each of the fractions in part **a** as a percentage.

c Place them in order, starting with the largest.

12 Say whether these statements are true or false.

If false, change it to make a true statement.

a 20 minutes is $\dfrac{1}{3}$ of an hour

b 10 grams are $\dfrac{1}{10}$ of a kilogram

c 20 pence are $\dfrac{1}{5}$ of £1

d 3 millimetres are $\dfrac{3}{10}$ of a centimetre.

e 5 weeks are $\dfrac{1}{10}$ of a year.

Wider skills practice

1 Here are Ellie's exam marks.

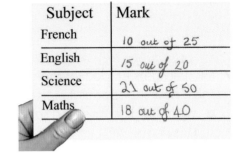

Subject	Mark
French	10 out of 25
English	15 out of 20
Science	21 out of 50
Maths	18 out of 40

a Copy and complete this statement.

$$\frac{10}{25} = \frac{\square}{100}$$

b Write $\frac{10}{25}$ as a percentage.

c Write the rest of Ellie's marks as percentages.

d Which is Ellie's
i best subject
ii worst subject?

2 Look at this claim.

8 out of 10 cats prefer Kati-kins

a Write it as
i a fraction   ii a percentage.

b Jane's granny has 30 cats.
How many would you expect to prefer Kati-kins?

Applying skills

1 The pie chart shows the fish in an aquarium.
An angle of 30° is used for the perch.

This shows that the fraction of perch is $\frac{30}{360} = \frac{1}{12}$.

a What fraction of the fish are
i roach
ii minnows
iii carp?

b There are 120 fish in the aquarium.
There are 10 perch. ◄——

$\frac{30}{360}$ **is equivalent to** $\frac{10}{120}$.

Work out the number of each type of fish in the aquarium, showing your working in the same way as given above.

Pie chart labels: Roach, Minnows, Carp, Perch, Tench, Sticklebacks. Angles: 30°, 15°, 90°, 75°, 120°, 30°.

2 Here are Brian's end-of-term test results.

a Which is Brian's best subject?

b Which is his least good subject?

School Report

Pupil – *Brian Jones*

Test Results

French $\frac{15}{20}$

English $\frac{25}{50}$

Geography $\frac{44}{80}$

Maths $\frac{48}{60}$

Reviewing skills

1 Write the fractions in order of size, starting with the smallest.

$\frac{2}{3}$ $\frac{3}{4}$ $\frac{5}{12}$ $\frac{5}{6}$ $\frac{1}{2}$

2 Write these fractions in their simplest form.

a $\frac{4}{8}$ **b** $\frac{12}{16}$ **c** $\frac{25}{30}$ **d** $\frac{12}{18}$

e $\frac{21}{35}$ **f** $\frac{24}{32}$ **g** $\frac{12}{20}$ **h** $\frac{240}{360}$

3 Which is the larger fraction in each pair?

a $\frac{1}{4}$ and $\frac{3}{8}$ **b** $\frac{3}{5}$ and $\frac{4}{7}$ **c** $\frac{3}{4}$ and $\frac{5}{6}$

d $\frac{5}{9}$ and $\frac{2}{3}$ **e** $\frac{2}{5}$ and $\frac{4}{15}$ **f** $\frac{2}{3}$ and $\frac{4}{5}$

g $\frac{4}{12}$ and $\frac{7}{18}$ **h** $\frac{1}{6}$ and $\frac{2}{15}$

4 Wayne, Andy and John share £48 between them.

Wayne gets £16, Andy gets £12 and John gets the rest.

What fraction does each get?

Write the fractions in their simplest form.

Building skills

Genetics

Toolbox

Sally's mother cuts a pizza into two halves.
She then cuts each half into three slices.
She has cut the whole pizza into six pieces, so each slice is

one-sixth, or $\frac{1}{6}$.

In fact she did $\frac{1}{3}$ of $\frac{1}{2}$ = $\frac{1}{3} \times \frac{1}{2}$

$$= \frac{1}{6}$$

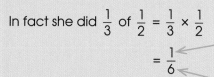

> **Multiply the numbers on the top together: 1 × 1 = 1**

> **Multiply the numbers on the bottom together: 3 × 2 = 6**

The word '**of**' when using fractions means ×.

What is $\frac{1}{4}$ of $\frac{1}{4}$?

$$\frac{1}{4} \times \frac{1}{4} = \frac{1 \times 1}{4 \times 4} = \frac{1}{16}$$

> $\frac{1}{4}$ of the square

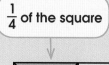

> $\frac{1}{4}$ of $\frac{1}{4}$ of the square

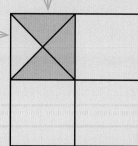

Sometimes cancelling down can be done before multiplying the
top and bottom lines.

For example, when working out $\frac{5}{8}$ of $\frac{16}{19}$:

$$\frac{5}{\overset{}{\underset{1}{8}}} \times \frac{\overset{2}{16}}{19} = \frac{5 \times 2}{1 \times 19} = \frac{10}{19}$$

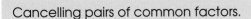

Cancelling pairs of common factors.

$$\frac{6}{7} \times \frac{14}{27} \times \frac{3}{4} = \frac{6 \times \overset{2}{\cancel{14}} \times 3}{\underset{1}{\cancel{7}} \times 27 \times 4}$$ ← Cancel by 7.

$$= \frac{6 \times 2 \times \overset{1}{\cancel{3}}}{1 \times \underset{9}{\cancel{27}} \times 4}$$ ← Cancel by 3.

$$= \frac{\overset{2}{\cancel{6}} \times 2 \times 1}{1 \times \underset{3}{\cancel{9}} \times 4}$$ ← Cancel by 3 again.

$$= \frac{\overset{1}{\cancel{2}} \times \overset{1}{\cancel{2}} \times 1}{1 \times 3 \times \underset{1}{\cancel{4}}}$$ ← Cancel twice by 2.

$$= \frac{1}{3}$$

Example – Solving fraction problems

David has $\frac{1}{5}$ of his book left to read over the weekend.

He reads $\frac{2}{3}$ of it on Saturday.

What fraction of the book does he read on Saturday?

David has $\frac{1}{5}$ of his book left to read.

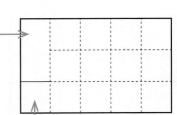

Solution

This is $\frac{2}{3} \times \frac{1}{5} = \frac{2}{15}$. So David reads $\frac{2}{15}$ on Saturday.

He reads $\frac{2}{3}$ on Saturday.

He still has $\frac{1}{15}$ of the book to read.

Example – Multiplying fractions

Work out $\frac{5}{6}$ of $\frac{3}{10}$

Solution

$$\frac{5}{6} \times \frac{3}{10} = \frac{15}{60} = \frac{1}{4}$$

or $\frac{\overset{1}{\cancel{5}}}{\underset{2}{\cancel{6}}} \times \frac{\overset{1}{\cancel{3}}}{\underset{2}{\cancel{10}}} = \frac{1}{4}$

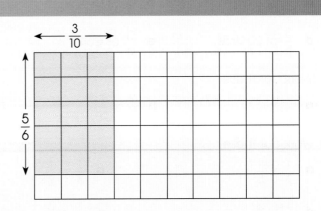

Remember:

✦ When you are working with fractions, the word 'of' means 'times'.
✦ Multiply fractions to find a fraction of a fraction,
✦ A whole number is a fraction: $20 = \frac{20}{1}$.

Skills practice A

1

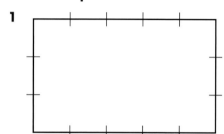

Copy this diagram. Shade in $\frac{1}{3}$ of $\frac{4}{5}$ of the rectangle.

2

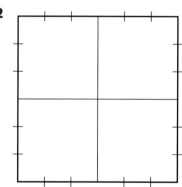

Copy this square. Shade in $\frac{2}{3}$ of $\frac{1}{4}$ of the square.

3 Find

  a $\frac{1}{2}$ of 6 km   **b** $\frac{2}{3}$ of £60   **c** $\frac{1}{4}$ of 12 kg

  d $\frac{3}{5}$ of 20 litres   **e** $\frac{3}{4}$ of €640   **f** $\frac{3}{10}$ of kilobytes

4 Work out these.

  a $\frac{1}{2} \times \frac{1}{4}$ **b** $\frac{2}{3} \times \frac{1}{5}$ **c** $\frac{3}{8} \times \frac{2}{5}$ **d** $\frac{4}{9} \times \frac{7}{10}$

5 Work out these.

  a $\frac{1}{2} \times \frac{1}{5}$ **b** $\frac{1}{3} \times \frac{1}{7}$ **c** $\frac{1}{6} \times \frac{1}{4}$

  d $\frac{1}{3} \times \frac{2}{5}$ **e** $\frac{1}{4} \times \frac{3}{5}$ **f** $\frac{3}{7} \times \frac{5}{8}$

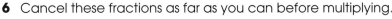

6 Cancel these fractions as far as you can before multiplying.

a $\dfrac{2}{5} \times \dfrac{1}{4}$ **b** $\dfrac{3}{8} \times \dfrac{4}{9}$ **c** $\dfrac{3}{10} \times \dfrac{5}{12}$

d $\dfrac{7}{9} \times \dfrac{3}{14}$ **e** $\dfrac{5}{18} \times \dfrac{6}{25}$ **f** $\dfrac{8}{27} \times \dfrac{9}{32}$

7 Cancel these fractions as far as you can before multiplying.

a $\dfrac{5}{8} \times \dfrac{2}{3}$ **b** $\dfrac{3}{16} \times \dfrac{4}{5}$ **c** $\dfrac{7}{9} \times \dfrac{6}{14}$

d $\dfrac{11}{12} \times \dfrac{2}{9}$ **e** $\dfrac{5}{14} \times \dfrac{7}{8}$ **f** $\dfrac{2}{30} \times \dfrac{13}{14}$

8 Work out these.

a $\dfrac{2}{15} \times \dfrac{5}{12} \times \dfrac{8}{9}$ **b** $\dfrac{3}{8} \times \dfrac{5}{9} \times \dfrac{16}{25}$ **c** $\dfrac{7}{8} \times \dfrac{12}{21} \times \dfrac{16}{20}$

d $\dfrac{15}{33} \times \dfrac{14}{25} \times \dfrac{11}{21}$ **e** $\dfrac{12}{45} \times \dfrac{15}{81} \times \dfrac{27}{30}$ **f** $\dfrac{54}{33} \times \dfrac{49}{56} \times \dfrac{11}{63}$

Skills practice B

1 Work out these.

a $\dfrac{1}{4}$ of $\dfrac{1}{5}$ of a tin of 120 sweets.   **b** $\dfrac{2}{3}$ of $\dfrac{2}{5}$ of a lottery win of £3 million.

c $\dfrac{2}{3}$ of $\dfrac{2}{7}$ of 28 tonnes of sand.   **d** $\dfrac{5}{6}$ of $\dfrac{5}{8}$ of a 96 hectare field of wheat.

2 Delroy has a market garden. It is 12 acres.

He grows potatoes on $\dfrac{2}{3}$ of it.

He grows peas on $\dfrac{3}{4}$ of the rest and asparagus on the remaining area.

a Draw a diagram showing this information.

b What is $\dfrac{3}{4} \times \dfrac{1}{3}$ of 12?

c What area does Delroy use for asparagus?

3 Hamish is a fisherman. One day he lands 600 kg of fish. $\dfrac{2}{3}$ of this is flat fish. $\dfrac{3}{4}$ of the rest is codling. The remainder is a variety of other species.

a Draw a diagram showing this information.

b What is $\dfrac{3}{4} \times \dfrac{1}{3}$ of 600? What does this represent in this case?

c What weight of Hamish's fish were neither flatfish nor codling?

4 Wai Peng is reading a book 400 pages long. On Monday he reads $\dfrac{1}{2}$ of it.

On Wednesday he reads $\dfrac{1}{2}$ of what remains. On Thursday he reads $\dfrac{1}{2}$ of what remains.

a How many pages has he still to read on Friday?

b What fraction is this of the pages in the book?

c What is $\dfrac{1}{2} \times \dfrac{1}{2} \times \dfrac{1}{2} \times \dfrac{1}{2}$?

Reasoning

Reasoning

Reasoning

5 John gave Peter $\frac{2}{5}$ of his CDs.

Peter gave a quarter of these CDs to his sister, Nina.

What fraction did each person get?

6 Paul ordered a lorry load of sand.

Nadir took $\frac{3}{4}$ of it.

Paul used $\frac{1}{3}$ of what was left to build his patio.

The rest was used to build a wall.

What fraction of the lorry load was used to build the wall?

Reasoning

7 Wine growers harvested a field of grapes.

$\frac{1}{8}$ of the crop was ruined by the rain.

They sell $\frac{3}{5}$ of the rest to a large wine producer.

What fraction of the crop was sold?

Reasoning

8 A wholesaler sold 5000 bottles of vinegar to a distributor.

The distributor sold $\frac{3}{4}$ of the bottles to Mr Patel.

Mr Patel sold $\frac{3}{5}$ of these bottles within the first week.

How many bottles did Mr Patel have left?

Reasoning

9 A car has two-thirds of a tank of petrol.

A quarter of this amount of petrol is used on a journey.

What fraction was used on the journey?

Wider skills practice

1 Calculate the area of these rectangles.

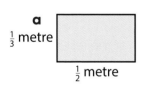
a $\frac{1}{3}$ metre — $\frac{1}{2}$ metre

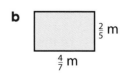
b $\frac{2}{5}$ m — $\frac{4}{7}$ m

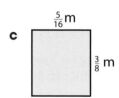
c $\frac{5}{16}$ m — $\frac{3}{8}$ m

2 Work out these. Simplify if possible.

a $\frac{m}{4} \times \frac{n}{2}$

b $\frac{w}{5} \times \frac{t}{4}$

c $\frac{m}{3} \times \frac{m}{4}$

d $\frac{4}{c} \times \frac{8}{d}$

e $\frac{5}{y} \times \frac{y}{7}$

f $\frac{2}{x} \times \frac{x}{8}$

g $\frac{m}{3} \times \frac{15}{m}$

h $\frac{d}{24} \times \frac{4}{e}$

Applying skills

1 Tabby is a cat. On Sunday a dog chased her a long way from her home.

The dog bit her leg but she escaped up a tree.

On Monday she walked half the way home but her leg was sore.

On each day after that she walked half of the distance remaining at the start of the day but her leg got worse.

a Copy and complete this table showing Tabby's progress as a fraction of the total distance Tabby had to walk.

Day	Sunday	Mon	Tues	Wed	Thurs	Fri	Sat
Distance travelled this day		$\frac{1}{2}$					
Total distance travelled so far		$\frac{1}{2}$	$\frac{3}{4}$				
Distance still to go	1	$\frac{1}{2}$	$\frac{1}{4}$				

b Tabby was chased 2560 metres.

On Saturday evening her family found her.

How far from home was she then?

c If Tabby's family had not found her, when would she have reached home?

Reviewing skills

1 Work out these.

a $\frac{3}{4} \times \frac{5}{7}$

b $\frac{2}{5} \times \frac{4}{11}$

c $\frac{5}{9} \times \frac{4}{7}$

2 Work out these.

a $\frac{11}{12}$ of $\frac{3}{7}$

b $\frac{2}{3}$ of $\frac{9}{10}$

c $\frac{5}{9}$ of 180

3 Work out these.

a $\frac{7}{8} \times \frac{4}{7}$

b $\frac{2}{9} \times \frac{9}{10}$

c $\frac{2}{5} \times \frac{5}{8} \times \frac{4}{7}$

d $\frac{5}{6} \times \frac{8}{7} \times \frac{14}{15}$

e $\frac{6}{11} \times \frac{7}{30} \times \frac{22}{35}$

f $\frac{11}{28} \times \frac{15}{33} \times \frac{21}{25}$

4 Four-fifths of the trees in a park are deciduous.

A third of these deciduous trees are oak trees.

What fraction of the trees in the park are oak trees?

Building skills

Example outside the Maths classroom

Building tolerences

Toolbox

Jack cuts a pizza into eight equal slices.
Jack eats a slice and Christina eats two slices.

Jack eats $\frac{1}{8}$ of the pizza and Christina eats $\frac{2}{8}$.

Altogether they eat $\frac{1}{8} + \frac{2}{8} = \frac{3}{8}$.

The fractions already have the same bottom lines. You only need to add the top lines.

You often have to use equivalent fractions to make the bottom lines the same. This is called the common denominator.

Jared eats $\frac{1}{4}$ of a cake.

He then goes back for 'seconds' and eats another $\frac{1}{6}$ of the cake.

I have eaten $\frac{1}{4} + \frac{1}{6}$, but what is that as a single fraction?

Jared

The bottom lines are, 4 and 6. They are both factors of 12.

Change each fraction to an equivalent fraction with 12 as the denominator.

$$\frac{1}{4} = \frac{3}{12}$$

$$\frac{1}{6} = \frac{2}{12}$$

$\frac{1}{4}$

$\frac{3}{12}$

$\frac{1}{6}$

$\frac{2}{12}$

> Once the denominators are the same, you can add the top lines.

$$\frac{1}{4} + \frac{1}{6} = \frac{3}{12} + \frac{2}{12} = \frac{5}{12}$$

$\frac{5}{12}$

$\frac{3}{12}$ $\frac{2}{12}$

Jared has eaten $\frac{5}{12}$ of the cake.

Example – Subtracting fractions

Jared has $\frac{7}{12}$ of his cake left.

He gives $\frac{1}{2}$ of the cake to his sister.

How much is left now?

Solution

Jared has $\frac{7}{12} - \frac{1}{2}$ left.

$$\frac{1}{2} = \frac{6}{12}$$

> $\frac{1}{2}$ and $\frac{6}{12}$ are equivalent fractions.

$$\frac{7}{12} - \frac{1}{2} = \frac{7}{12} - \frac{6}{12} = \frac{1}{12}$$

> Once the denominators are the same, you can subtract the top lines.

> 12 is the lowest common denominator of 12 and 2.

$\frac{1}{12}$ of the cake is left.

Remember:

✦ To add or subtract fractions, the fractions must have the same denominators.
✦ If necessary, change the fractions to equivalent fractions with a common denominator.
✦ You can think of subtracting a fraction as adding a negative fraction.

Skills practice A

1 Add these fractions.

a $\frac{1}{3} + \frac{1}{3}$ **b** $\frac{1}{5} + \frac{2}{5}$ **c** $\frac{2}{7} + \frac{4}{7}$ **d** $\frac{2}{9} + \frac{5}{9}$

2 Subtract these fractions.

a $\frac{5}{8} - \frac{3}{8}$ **b** $\frac{5}{7} - \frac{2}{7}$ **c** $\frac{3}{4} - \frac{1}{4}$ **d** $\frac{5}{9} - \frac{2}{9}$

3 Work out these.

a $\frac{1}{7} + \frac{2}{7}$ **b** $\frac{1}{4} + \frac{3}{4}$ **c** $\frac{4}{5} - \frac{3}{5}$ **d** $\frac{7}{8} - \frac{5}{8}$

4 These fraction bars represent additions or subtractions of fractions.
In each case write down the calculation and the answer.

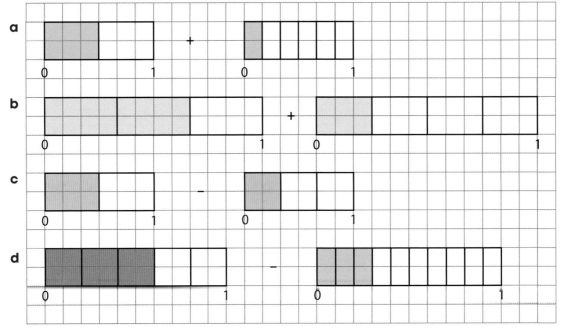

5 Use fraction bars to represent these additions and subtractions.
Use them to work out the answers.

a $\frac{1}{2} + \frac{1}{3}$ **b** $\frac{1}{3} + \frac{1}{4}$ **c** $\frac{2}{3} - \frac{1}{4}$ **d** $\frac{5}{6} - \frac{1}{3}$

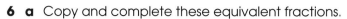

6 a Copy and complete these equivalent fractions.

i $\quad \dfrac{1}{5} = \dfrac{\square}{10} = \dfrac{\square}{20}$

ii $\quad \dfrac{2}{5} = \dfrac{\square}{10} = \dfrac{\square}{20}$

b Use your answers to part **a** to work out these.

i $\quad \dfrac{3}{10} - \dfrac{1}{5}$ ii $\quad \dfrac{3}{10} + \dfrac{2}{5}$ iii $\quad \dfrac{1}{5} - \dfrac{1}{20}$ iv $\quad \dfrac{7}{20} + \dfrac{2}{5}$ v $\quad \dfrac{2}{5} - \dfrac{7}{20}$

7 Look at these pairs of fractions.
Find the lowest common denominator for each pair.
Add up each pair.

a $\dfrac{1}{4} + \dfrac{1}{6}$ **b** $\dfrac{3}{4} + \dfrac{1}{8}$ **c** $\dfrac{1}{3} + \dfrac{1}{5}$ **d** $\dfrac{1}{6} + \dfrac{3}{8}$

8 Copy and complete these calculations.

a $\dfrac{1}{2} + \dfrac{1}{4} + \dfrac{1}{8} = \dfrac{\square}{8}$ **b** $\dfrac{1}{2} + \dfrac{\square}{\square} = \dfrac{3}{4}$ **c** $\dfrac{\square}{\square} + \dfrac{5}{7} = \dfrac{13}{14}$ **d** $\dfrac{1}{6} + \dfrac{\square}{8} = \dfrac{13}{\square}$

9 Copy and complete these.

a $\dfrac{1}{2} + \dfrac{\square}{\square} = 1$ **b** $\dfrac{3}{4} + \dfrac{\square}{\square} = 1$ **c** $\dfrac{1}{3} + \dfrac{\square}{\square} = 1$ **d** $\dfrac{2}{5} + \dfrac{1}{5} + \dfrac{\square}{\square} = 1$

10 Work out these.

a $\dfrac{5}{12} + \dfrac{7}{12}$ **b** $\dfrac{3}{7} + \left(-\dfrac{2}{7}\right)$ **c** $\dfrac{10}{19} + \left(-\dfrac{3}{19}\right)$ **d** $\dfrac{2}{5} - \dfrac{1}{10}$

e $\dfrac{2}{5} + \dfrac{3}{10}$ **f** $\dfrac{3}{4} + \left(-\dfrac{5}{12}\right)$ **g** $1 - \dfrac{2}{5}$ **h** $\dfrac{1}{3} + \dfrac{1}{4} + \dfrac{1}{5}$

Skills practice B

1 Work out these.

a $\dfrac{2}{3} + \left(-\dfrac{1}{3}\right)$ **b** $\dfrac{5}{6} + \left(-\dfrac{1}{2}\right)$ **c** $\dfrac{11}{12} + \left(-\dfrac{1}{3}\right)$

d $\left(-\dfrac{1}{4}\right) + \left(-\dfrac{1}{4}\right)$ **e** $\left(-\dfrac{1}{2}\right) + \dfrac{1}{2}$ **f** $\left(-\dfrac{3}{4}\right) + \left(-\dfrac{1}{4}\right)$

2 This diagram represents six fractions added together.
Write down the calculation and the answer.

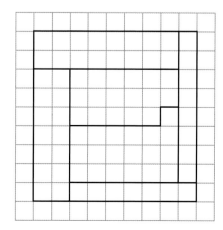

3 Matt paints his bathroom and hall blue.

The bathroom takes $\frac{1}{3}$ of a tin of paint.

The hall takes $\frac{1}{5}$ of the tin of paint.

What fraction of the tin of paint is left?

4 Darren, Paul and Bill are standing for team captain.

$\frac{3}{10}$ of the votes are for Darren.

Paul gets $\frac{3}{8}$ of the votes.

a What fraction vote for Bill?
b Which is the larger fraction?
c Who is chosen as team captain?

5 Can all the shampoo in the three bottles below be put into one bottle?

6 David receives money for his birthday.

He spends $\frac{3}{7}$ of his money on a sweatshirt and $\frac{5}{14}$ of his money on some T-shirts.

He saves the rest of the money.
What fraction does he save?

7 $\frac{3}{5}$ of a garden is lawn.

$\frac{2}{9}$ is used for growing vegetables.

What fraction is left for other uses?

8 A painter uses $\frac{3}{8}$ of a tin of paint on Monday and $\frac{2}{5}$ of the tin of paint on Tuesday.

What fraction of the tin has he used altogether?

9 A cook has $\frac{5}{8}$ of a litre of buttermilk left after cooking on Wednesday.

She uses $\frac{2}{5}$ of a litre of buttermilk on Thursday.

How much is left?

Wider skills practice

1 Pete can buy two different tins of sweets. He likes toffees best.

  a In Tin A, he finds that $\frac{1}{5}$ are soft toffees and $\frac{1}{4}$ are hard toffees.
  What fraction of Tin A is toffees?

  b In Tin B, $\frac{3}{10}$ are truffles and $\frac{1}{4}$ are plain chocolate, the rest are toffees.
  What fraction of Tin B is toffees?

  c Tin A costs £5 and holds approximately 20 sweets, Tin B costs £3 and holds approximately 15 sweets. Which tin would you buy?

2 Simplify these algebraic expressions.

  a $\frac{x}{3} + \frac{x}{2}$

  b $\frac{m}{4} + \frac{m}{5}$

  c $\frac{d}{2} + \frac{3d}{7}$

  d $\frac{x}{5} + \frac{2x}{9}$

  e $\frac{e}{3} - \frac{e}{5}$

  f $\frac{5h}{6} - \frac{h}{4}$

Applying skills

Problem solving

1 a When the number 5 bus leaves the terminus it is $\frac{1}{4}$ full.

  At the first stop, $\frac{1}{8}$ of a bus load get on.

  How full is the bus now?

b At the second stop, $\frac{1}{16}$ of a bus load get off and $\frac{1}{2}$ of a bus load get on.

  What fraction of the bus is full now?

c Nobody gets off at the next stop and the bus is full when it leaves.
  What fraction of a bus load got on?

d The bus remains full until eight people get off.

  It is then $\frac{7}{8}$ full.

  How many people does the bus hold?

e At the next stop $\frac{5}{16}$ of a bus load get off.

  How many people is this?

2 Corina is driving to Milan.

a At the start of her journey she has $\frac{3}{4}$ of a tank of petrol.

At the end of her journey she has $\frac{1}{8}$ of a tank.

What fraction of a tank of petrol has she used?

b At Milan she puts $\frac{3}{4}$ of a tank of petrol in.

How full is her tank now?

c On the way home she only uses $\frac{1}{2}$ of a tank.

i How full is the tank at the end of the journey?

ii What fraction is needed to fill the tank?

Reviewing skills

1 Work out these.

a $\frac{3}{7} + \frac{4}{9}$

b $\frac{5}{6} - \frac{2}{3}$

c $\frac{1}{4} + \frac{1}{5} + \frac{1}{10}$

d $\frac{7}{9} - \frac{5}{18}$

e $\frac{1}{6} + \frac{1}{4}$

f $\frac{3}{8} + \frac{5}{12}$

g $\frac{2}{3} - \frac{2}{7}$

h $\frac{7}{12} - \frac{3}{8}$

i $\frac{1}{2} + \frac{1}{4} - \frac{5}{8}$

j $\frac{1}{4} - \frac{9}{16} + \frac{3}{8}$

k $\frac{1}{6} - \frac{1}{3} + \frac{1}{2}$

l $\frac{3}{10} - \frac{1}{2} + \frac{2}{5}$

2 Mr Brown starts his journey with $\frac{1}{2}$ of a tank of petrol.

He uses $\frac{1}{3}$ of a tank.

a How much petrol does he have left?

b What fraction must he put in his tank to fill it up?

Building skills

 Example outside the Maths classroom

Recipes

Toolbox

To find out if all the sand can be placed in one bucket:

$$\frac{1}{2} + \frac{2}{5} + \frac{1}{3} = \frac{15 + 12 + 10}{30} = \frac{37}{30}$$

$\frac{30}{30}$ is one whole.

$\frac{37}{30}$ is one whole and $\frac{7}{30}$. That is $1\frac{7}{30}$.

So the sand takes up one whole bucket and $\frac{7}{30}$ of a second one.

$\frac{37}{30}$ is called a **top-heavy fraction** or an **improper fraction**.

$1\frac{7}{30}$ is called a **mixed number**.

Every improper fraction can be written as a mixed number.

Example – Converting between improper fractions and mixed numbers

a Express $\frac{19}{5}$ as a mixed number.

b Express $2\frac{7}{8}$ as an improper fraction.

Solution

a You change $\frac{19}{5}$ to a mixed number by dividing 19 by 5.

$19 \div 5 = 3$ remainder 4

So $\frac{19}{5} = 3\frac{4}{5}$

b To find how many eighths there are in $2\frac{7}{8}$, you multiply 2 by 8 and then add 7.

$$2\frac{7}{8} = \frac{16}{8} + \frac{7}{8} = \frac{23}{8}$$

So $2\frac{7}{8} = \frac{23}{8}$

Example – Multiplying, adding and subtracting mixed numbers

Work out

a $2\frac{1}{3} \times 1\frac{4}{5}$ **b** $2\frac{1}{3} + 1\frac{4}{5}$ **c** $2\frac{1}{3} - 1\frac{4}{5}$

Solution

a Start by writing $2\frac{1}{3}$ and $1\frac{4}{5}$ as top-heavy fractions.

$$2\frac{1}{3} = \frac{7}{3} , \quad 1\frac{4}{5} = \frac{9}{5}$$

So $2\frac{1}{3} \times 1\frac{4}{5} = \frac{7}{3} \times \frac{\cancel{9}^{3}}{5}$ ← **Cancel using a common factor.**

$$= \frac{21}{5}$$

$$= 4\frac{1}{5}$$

b $2\frac{1}{3} + 1\frac{4}{5}$ Add the whole numbers and the fractions separately.

$$= (2+1) + \left(\frac{1}{3} + \frac{4}{5}\right)$$

$$= 3 + \left(\frac{5}{15} + \frac{12}{15}\right) \leftarrow \boxed{\text{15 is the common denominator.}}$$

$$= 3 + \frac{17}{15} \leftarrow \boxed{\begin{array}{c}\text{Make this top-heavy fraction}\\\text{into a mixed number.}\end{array}}$$

$$= 3 + 1\frac{2}{15}$$

$$= 4\frac{2}{15}$$

c $2\frac{1}{3} - 1\frac{4}{5} = \frac{7}{3} - \frac{9}{5}$

Convert the top-heavy fractions to equivalent fractions with a common denominator.

$\boxed{\begin{array}{c}\text{You can also use a method}\\\text{like that in part b.}\end{array}}$

$$\overset{\times 5}{\frac{7}{3}} = \frac{35}{15} \qquad \overset{\times 3}{\frac{9}{5}} = \frac{27}{15}$$

$$\underset{\times 5}{} \qquad \underset{\times 3}{}$$

$$\frac{7}{3} - \frac{9}{5} = \frac{35}{15} - \frac{27}{15} = \frac{8}{15}$$

Remember:

✦ When adding and subtracting mixed numbers you can work with them as top-heavy fractions. Alternatively, you can work with the whole numbers and fractions separately and bring then together at the end.

✦ When multiplying mixed numbers, you must change them into top-heavy fractions first.

Skills practice A

1 The diagram shows the mixed number $1\frac{5}{6}$.

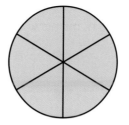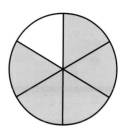

   a How many sixths are there in the diagram?

   b Write $1\frac{5}{6}$ as a top-heavy fraction.

2 a Colour a copy of this diagram to show the mixed number $1\frac{3}{4}$.

   b Write $1\frac{3}{4}$ as a top-heavy fraction.

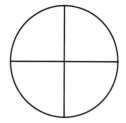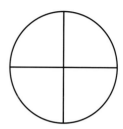

3 Colour a copy of these diagrams to show these fractions.

   a $\frac{11}{8}$
     b $\frac{16}{6}$

4 Change these mixed numbers to top-heavy fractions.

   a $1\frac{1}{2}$ **b** $1\frac{1}{4}$ **c** $1\frac{2}{3}$

   d $1\frac{4}{5}$ **e** $1\frac{2}{7}$ **f** $2\frac{1}{2}$

   g $2\frac{1}{3}$ **h** $3\frac{1}{2}$ **i** $4\frac{1}{2}$

5 Change these top-heavy fractions to mixed numbers.

   a $\frac{3}{2}$ **b** $\frac{5}{3}$ **c** $\frac{5}{2}$

   d $\frac{7}{3}$ **e** $\frac{7}{4}$ **f** $\frac{9}{5}$

   g $\frac{11}{5}$ **h** $\frac{22}{3}$ **i** $\frac{38}{5}$

6 Work out these.

   Give your answers as mixed numbers.

   a $\frac{2}{5} + \frac{4}{5}$ **b** $\frac{4}{5} + \frac{7}{10}$ **c** $\frac{1}{2} + \frac{2}{3} + \frac{3}{4}$

   d $\frac{13}{4} + \frac{15}{7}$ **e** $\frac{15}{8} + \frac{5}{3}$ **f** $\frac{17}{6} + \frac{7}{4}$

   g $\frac{39}{10} + \frac{13}{8}$ **h** $\frac{8}{3} + \frac{19}{5}$ **i** $\frac{19}{7} + \frac{13}{5}$

7 Work out these.
Give your answers as mixed numbers where appropriate.

a $\dfrac{7}{4} - \dfrac{7}{8}$

b $\dfrac{5}{3} - \dfrac{5}{6}$

c $\dfrac{13}{8} - \dfrac{9}{16}$

d $\dfrac{5}{2} - \dfrac{5}{3}$

e $\dfrac{10}{3} - \dfrac{15}{8}$

f $\dfrac{13}{4} - \dfrac{19}{10}$

g $\dfrac{17}{8} - \dfrac{11}{6}$

h $\dfrac{9}{2} - \dfrac{16}{9}$

i $\dfrac{27}{5} - \dfrac{19}{7}$

8 Work out these.
Give your answers as mixed numbers.

a $1\dfrac{1}{2} + 1\dfrac{7}{10}$

b $2\dfrac{1}{3} + 1\dfrac{7}{9}$

c $5\dfrac{1}{4} + 2\dfrac{7}{8}$

d $1\dfrac{9}{10} + 2\dfrac{5}{6}$

e $3\dfrac{5}{8} + 2\dfrac{3}{4}$

f $6\dfrac{6}{7} + 3\dfrac{7}{10}$

g $2\dfrac{7}{9} + 2\dfrac{5}{6}$

9 Work out these.
Give your answers as mixed numbers where appropriate.

a $1\dfrac{1}{2} - \dfrac{9}{10}$

b $2\dfrac{1}{3} - \dfrac{7}{8}$

c $8 - 5\dfrac{1}{3}$

d $2\dfrac{1}{3} - 1\dfrac{4}{5}$

e $2\dfrac{1}{4} - 1\dfrac{5}{6}$

f $3\dfrac{2}{5} - 2\dfrac{7}{8}$

g $4\dfrac{1}{2} - 1\dfrac{9}{10}$

h $6\dfrac{2}{3} - 2\dfrac{7}{9}$

i $5\dfrac{2}{7} - 2\dfrac{6}{11}$

10 Work out these.
Give your answers as mixed numbers.

a $5 \times 1\dfrac{1}{2}$

b $6 \times 2\dfrac{2}{3}$

c $2\dfrac{1}{5} \times \dfrac{1}{3}$

d $1\dfrac{1}{4} \times \dfrac{4}{7}$

e $1\dfrac{4}{5} \times 1\dfrac{2}{3}$

f $2\dfrac{1}{7} \times 1\dfrac{3}{8}$

g $3\dfrac{7}{10} \times 2\dfrac{1}{2}$

h $5\dfrac{1}{4} \times 1\dfrac{1}{3}$

i $1\dfrac{7}{8} \times 3\dfrac{4}{5}$

Skills practice B

1 Write these as mixed numbers.

a 80 minutes in hours

b 2325 grams in kilograms

c 24 days in weeks

d 420 centimetres in metres

e 500 seconds in minutes

2 Work out these.

Give your answers as mixed numbers.

a $1\frac{3}{4} + 3\frac{1}{2} - \frac{1}{4}$

b $5\frac{1}{3} - 1\frac{1}{5} + \frac{13}{15}$

c $2\frac{1}{4} \times 3\frac{2}{5} \times \frac{2}{17}$

d $3\frac{5}{6} + 4\frac{7}{8} - 1\frac{2}{3}$

e $4\frac{4}{5} - 1\frac{8}{9} - 1\frac{1}{9}$

f $2\frac{3}{5} \times 2\frac{2}{3} \times 1\frac{2}{13}$

g $1\frac{3}{4} + 2\frac{1}{5} \times 3\frac{2}{3}$

h $8\frac{1}{2} - 4\frac{1}{3} \times 1\frac{7}{8}$

i $2\frac{1}{4} \times 1\frac{1}{5} + 2\frac{3}{10}$

j $3\frac{2}{3} + 1\frac{4}{5} + 2\frac{1}{2}$

k $2\frac{5}{8} + 3\frac{6}{7} - 4\frac{1}{2}$

l $2\frac{2}{3} \times 1\frac{3}{4} \times 2\frac{1}{2}$

3 Give your answers to these questions as mixed numbers.

a A glass contains 200 ml. How many glasses amount to 750 ml?

b Jennie earns £9 per hour. How many hours would she need to work to make £100?

c Abdul takes 4 minutes to read one page. How many pages does he read in 15 minutes?

d A bag of sugar weighs 250 grams. How many bags are needed to get 1300 grams?

4 The map shows the distances in miles along a footpath.
Find the total length of the path.

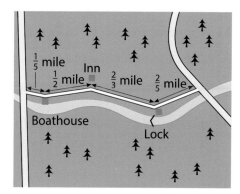

5 Yaya is a long distance runner. She runs a steady $7\frac{1}{2}$ miles each hour. How far does she travel in

a $2\frac{1}{2}$ hours

b 3 hours 20 minutes?

6 Jenny is trying to limit her screen time to 3 hours a day.

One day she uses her screen time like this.

a How much screen time has she spent?

b How much screen time does she have left?

Computer games	$\frac{1}{2}$ hr
Watching videos on the internet	$\frac{3}{4}$ hr
TV	$\frac{1}{2}$ hr
Social media	$\frac{5}{6}$ hr

7 To get to school, John walks $\frac{3}{4}$ km to the bus stop.

He catches the bus to the station, a distance of $5\frac{1}{2}$ km.

His train journey is $23\frac{2}{3}$ km.

Finally he walks $\frac{1}{5}$ km to school.

What is the total length of John's journey to school?

8 A cross country race circuit is 2500 metres.

   a On Monday Ailsa runs 7000 metres.

      How many circuits is this? (Give your answer as a mixed number.)

   b On Tuesday Ailsa runs 9000 metres. How many circuits is this?

   c Add your answers to parts **a** and **b**.

   d How many metres does Ailsa run on Monday and Tuesday together? Convert your answer to a number of circuits.

9 Erica is preparing a party for 30 people.
She estimates the amount of food each person will eat.
How much of each type of food should Erica buy?

Pizza	$\frac{1}{4}$
Garlic bread	$\frac{1}{3}$ loaf
Lettuce	$\frac{1}{6}$
Tomato	$\frac{3}{4}$
Salad cream	$\frac{1}{12}$ bottle
Coleslaw	$\frac{1}{8}$ tub

10 A bus arrives at a bus stop.

It is already $\frac{3}{4}$ full.

The number of people standing at the stop could fill $\frac{1}{3}$ of the bus.

What fraction of a bus load are left at the bus stop?

11 A sponsored walk for charity is 15 miles long.

Checkpoint A is $6\frac{2}{3}$ miles from the start.

Checkpoint B is $4\frac{1}{4}$ miles from the finish.

   a How far is checkpoint B from the start?

   b What is the distance between checkpoints?

Wider skills practice

1 Calculate the area of each of these shapes.

   a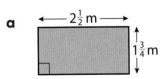

   b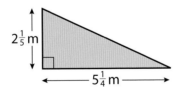

   c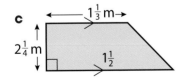

   d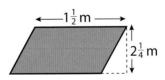

2 Sometimes the mixed number $3\frac{1}{7}$ is used as an approximation to π.

Use this value to work out the circumference and area of these circles without a calculator.

   a

   b

   c

Reasoning

3 Ben eats $\frac{3}{4}$ of a tin of dog food each day.

  a How long will $1\frac{1}{2}$ tins last?

  b How long will 6 tins last?

  c How many tins will Ben eat in

   i 12 days   **ii** 5 days   **iii** 7 days?

Applying skills

1 A rug measures 9 feet 6 inches by 12 feet 4 inches.

This is $9\frac{1}{2}$ feet by $12\frac{1}{3}$ feet.

  a Calculate the area of the rug by
   i changing the measurements to inches then converting your answer to square feet and square inches
   ii working with the measurements as fractions, in feet.
  b Compare your methods.

There are 144 square inches in a square foot.

Problem solving

2 a Emily fills both cups with milk and empties them into the bowl. How much milk is in the bowl?
  b She adds another $\frac{1}{3}$ litre.

   How much is in the bowl now?
  c Explain how Emily can measure 1 litre of milk.
  d She needs to measure $\frac{1}{6}$ litre of cream.

   Explain how she can do this.
  e Write down three more exact measurements that she can measure with the cups.
   Explain how each measurement is made.

Reviewing skills

1 Work out these. Give your answers as mixed numbers.

a $3 \times 2\frac{1}{2}$

b $7 \times 1\frac{1}{4}$

c $1\frac{1}{5} - \frac{2}{3}$

d $2\frac{1}{8} + \frac{1}{2}$

e $1\frac{2}{3} \times 1\frac{1}{4}$

f $2\frac{1}{2} - 1\frac{3}{5}$

g $1\frac{9}{10} + 1\frac{1}{2}$

h $2\frac{7}{8} \times 2\frac{1}{3}$

i $3\frac{1}{4} - 1\frac{2}{7}$

2 Tom needs $3\frac{1}{2}$ cups of dried fruit for a cake recipe. He only has $\frac{3}{4}$ cup of sultanas and $1\frac{1}{3}$ cups of raisins. He has plenty of currants.

How many currants does he need to use?

Building skills

Organising time

Toolbox

Reciprocals

$\frac{1}{4}$ is known as the **reciprocal** of 4.

The fraction $\frac{1}{3}$ is the reciprocal of 3.

You can write the whole number 3 as $\frac{3}{1}$.

You turn a fraction upside down to find its reciprocal.

$\frac{5}{2}$ is the reciprocal of $\frac{2}{5}$. In the same way $\frac{2}{5}$ is the reciprocal of $\frac{5}{2}$.

Division problems

Each glass holds $\frac{1}{4}$ of a bottle of lemonade.

How many glasses can be filled from three bottles?

The problem can be solved by finding how many quarters in 3.

$$3 \div \frac{1}{4} = 12$$

It can also be solved as a multiplication.

One bottle can fill 4 glasses. How many glasses can three bottles fill?

So dividing by a fraction is the same as multiplying by its reciprocal.

$3 \times 4 = 12$

Example – Dividing a fraction by a fraction

Work out $\dfrac{5}{4} \div \dfrac{2}{3}$.

Solution

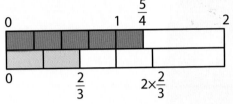

> The bar diagram shows the answer will be just less than 2.

You find the answer by multiplying by the reciprocal.

> The reciprocal of $\dfrac{2}{3}$ is $\dfrac{3}{2}$.

$$\dfrac{5}{4} \div \dfrac{2}{3} = \dfrac{5}{4} \times \dfrac{3}{2}$$

$$= \dfrac{15}{8}$$

Remember:

Change mixed numbers into improper fractions before dividing.

Skills practice A

1 Write down the reciprocals of these numbers.

a 4   **b** $\dfrac{1}{5}$ **c** $\dfrac{3}{4}$ **d** $\dfrac{2}{7}$

e $2\dfrac{1}{2}$ **f** $1\dfrac{3}{4}$ **g** $5\dfrac{2}{3}$ **h** $1\dfrac{7}{8}$ **i** $6\dfrac{4}{5}$

2 This bar diagram illustrates

$4 \div \dfrac{1}{2} = 8$

State the division represented by each of the following bar diagrams.

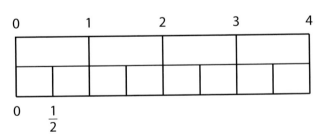

a

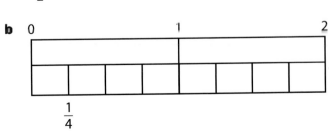

b

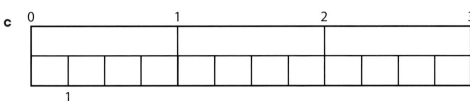

c

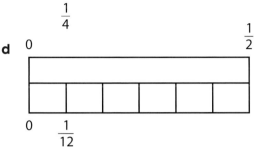

d

3 a Represent each of the division sums on a bar diagram. Use it to estimate the answer as accurately as possible.

i $4 \div \dfrac{1}{3}$ **ii** $5 \div \dfrac{1}{4}$ **iii** $6 \div \dfrac{2}{3}$

iv $\dfrac{1}{2} \div \dfrac{1}{4}$ **v** $\dfrac{2}{3} \div \dfrac{1}{3}$ **vi** $\dfrac{3}{4} \div \dfrac{1}{4}$

b Use reciprocals to calculate the exact answer. Check by comparing with your answers in part **a**.

4 Change each of these into a multiplication and then work out the answer.

a $\dfrac{1}{6} \div 3$ **b** $\dfrac{1}{4} \div 5$ **c** $\dfrac{2}{5} \div 5$

d $\dfrac{3}{5} \div 3$ **e** $\dfrac{4}{7} \div 2$ **f** $\dfrac{6}{7} \div 3$

g $\dfrac{4}{5} \div 6$ **h** $\dfrac{2}{9} \div 8$ **i** $\dfrac{7}{8} \div 10$

5 Work out

a $\dfrac{1}{3} \div \dfrac{1}{5}$ **b** $\dfrac{1}{2} \div \dfrac{1}{7}$ **c** $\dfrac{1}{4} \div \dfrac{2}{3}$

d $\dfrac{1}{6} \div \dfrac{3}{5}$ **e** $\dfrac{2}{3} \div \dfrac{4}{5}$ **f** $\dfrac{5}{6} \div \dfrac{3}{8}$

g $\dfrac{7}{9} \div \dfrac{4}{5}$ **h** $\dfrac{3}{10} \div \dfrac{5}{6}$ **i** $\dfrac{7}{8} \div \dfrac{7}{9}$

6 Work out

a $\dfrac{1}{4} \div 3$ **b** $\dfrac{1}{6} \div 4$ **c** $\dfrac{2}{3} \div 5$

d $\dfrac{3}{4} \div 7$ **e** $\dfrac{7}{10} \div 6$ **f** $5 \div \dfrac{1}{2}$

g $3 \div \dfrac{1}{4}$ **h** $2 \div \dfrac{2}{3}$ **i** $5 \div \dfrac{3}{4}$

7 Work out

a $15 \div \dfrac{1}{3}$ **b** $\dfrac{1}{4} \div 3$ **c** $2 \div \dfrac{3}{5}$ **d** $10 \div \dfrac{2}{7}$

e $\dfrac{1}{4} \div \dfrac{1}{5}$ **f** $\dfrac{1}{2} \div \dfrac{1}{9}$ **g** $\dfrac{2}{3} \div \dfrac{5}{7}$ **h** $\dfrac{4}{5} \div \dfrac{9}{11}$

i $\dfrac{7}{8} \div \dfrac{3}{5}$ **j** $\dfrac{5}{6} \div \dfrac{3}{4}$

Skills practice B

1 Work out

a $1\frac{3}{4} \div 2$ **b** $2\frac{1}{8} \div 3$ **c** $4 \div 1\frac{1}{2}$

d $5 \div 2\frac{2}{3}$ **e** $1\frac{1}{4} \div 1\frac{1}{2}$ **f** $2\frac{3}{5} \div 1\frac{1}{3}$

g $3\frac{3}{7} \div 1\frac{3}{4}$ **h** $5\frac{4}{9} \div 2\frac{5}{6}$ **i** $6\frac{1}{2} \div 8\frac{2}{3}$

2 Jane eats $\frac{2}{5}$ of a bar of chocolate.

She divides the rest between her three friends.

What fraction of the bar does each friend have?

3 Jack is preparing for a party.

He estimates that each person will eat $\frac{1}{4}$ of a pizza.

How many people can he feed with five pizzas?

4 Anna shares $\frac{1}{4}$ of her birthday cake between five people.

What fraction of the cake does each person get?

5 George has read $\frac{1}{5}$ of his book in two days.

a What fraction is this per day?

b What fraction has he still not read?

c He must return the book to the library in six days' time.
What fraction must he now read each day?

6 Work out the speed of an object that travels ⟵ $\boxed{\textbf{Speed = Distance ÷ Time taken}}$

a $\frac{4}{5}$ of a kilometre in $\frac{3}{4}$ of an hour **b** $\frac{3}{10}$ of a kilometre in $\frac{4}{5}$ of an hour

c $\frac{5}{8}$ of a mile in $\frac{1}{3}$ of an hour **d** 6 miles in $\frac{1}{10}$ of an hour

7 Work out these.

a $\frac{2}{3} \times \frac{1}{2} \div 4$ **b** $\frac{2}{7} \times 14 \div \frac{1}{2}$ **c** $\frac{1}{3} \times \frac{1}{4} \div \frac{1}{2}$

d $\frac{4}{9} \div \frac{2}{3} \times 3$ **e** $\frac{4}{7} \div \frac{3}{7} \times \frac{3}{4}$ **f** $\frac{5}{8} \div \frac{5}{16} \times \frac{1}{4}$

g $\frac{3}{10} \div \frac{3}{20} \div 2$ **h** $\frac{7}{12} \div \frac{1}{6} \div \frac{1}{2}$

8 Richard walks $\frac{2}{5}$ of a kilometre to school each day.

It takes him 10 minutes.

Work out Richard's speed in kilometres per hour, giving your answer as a mixed number.

Reasoning

9 The area of each of the shapes below is given.
For each shape find the missing length.

a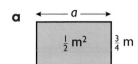

b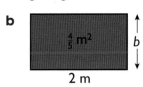

c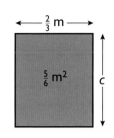

d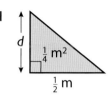

e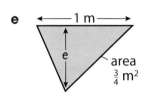

f

Wider skills practice

1 Work out.

a $\dfrac{5}{6} + \dfrac{1}{4} \div 7$ **b** $\dfrac{6}{7} \div \dfrac{1}{2} + \dfrac{9}{10}$ **c** $2\dfrac{1}{2} + 1\dfrac{7}{8} \div 3\dfrac{1}{2}$ **d** $2\dfrac{3}{4} - 1\dfrac{5}{6} \div 2\dfrac{1}{3}$

2 Copy and complete this multiplication grid.

×	$\dfrac{1}{2}$	$\dfrac{3}{7}$	$\dfrac{7}{9}$		$\dfrac{1}{5}$		$\dfrac{1}{3}$
$\dfrac{1}{2}$							
$\dfrac{3}{4}$							
$\dfrac{2}{5}$							
$\dfrac{5}{8}$							
			$\dfrac{2}{3}$				
$\dfrac{5}{16}$			$\dfrac{3}{16}$				
					$\dfrac{1}{15}$	$\dfrac{1}{4}$	$\dfrac{1}{9}$

3 George paints $\dfrac{2}{5}$ of his garage in $1\dfrac{1}{2}$ hours.
How long would he take to paint

a $\dfrac{1}{5}$ **b** $\dfrac{3}{5}$ **c** all of the garage?

4 Work out these.

a $\dfrac{x}{4} \div 3$ **b** $\dfrac{d}{6} \div \dfrac{1}{2}$ **c** $\dfrac{m}{4} \div \dfrac{3}{8}$

d $\dfrac{e}{d} \div \dfrac{e}{d}$ **e** $\dfrac{3c}{4} \div \dfrac{c}{8}$ **f** $\dfrac{x^2}{5} \div \dfrac{x}{5}$

Applying skills

1 Martin Miller the Millionaire left his fortune to be divided between his children and his grandchildren.

  a A quarter of his money is to be divided equally between his three children.
What fraction does each receive?

  b The remainder is to be divided equally between his ten grandchildren.
What fraction is this for each grandchild?

  c His fortune was worth £4 million.
Calculate the amount that each of his children and each of his grandchildren received.

2 **i** For each situation, write down the calculation that needs to be done to find the answer.
Explain how you decided.

  ii Calculate the answer.

    a A rectangle has a width of $2\dfrac{1}{4}$ m and a length of $3\dfrac{1}{3}$ m. What is its area?

    b Alex has 84 metres of ribbon and wants ribbons of $\dfrac{4}{5}$ m in length to make choclate box bows.
How many will he make?

    c Donna has 27 buckets each with a capacity of $1\dfrac{1}{4}$ gallons. What is the total capacity?

    d Sarah has $3\dfrac{1}{2}$ kg of chocolate to share equally with her seven friends. She wants to know
how much each will get.

    e Gordon has 12 litres of orange juice and some glasses, each with a volume of $\dfrac{3}{5}$ litre.
How many glasses can he fill?

Reviewing skills

1 Work out these.

  a $7 \div \dfrac{1}{5}$ **b** $\dfrac{6}{7} \div 3$ **c** $5 \div \dfrac{2}{7}$

  d $\dfrac{3}{4} \div \dfrac{1}{5}$ **e** $\dfrac{2}{9} \div \dfrac{3}{4}$ **f** $3\dfrac{1}{3} \div 2\dfrac{1}{4}$

  g $\dfrac{7}{10} \div \dfrac{3}{5}$ **h** $8\dfrac{2}{3} \div 2\dfrac{5}{6}$ **i** $6\dfrac{4}{5} \div 2\dfrac{3}{4}$

2 Write down the reciprocals of these numbers.

  a 12   **b** $\dfrac{4}{5}$ **c** $\dfrac{7}{3}$ **d** $1\dfrac{2}{3}$ **e** $3\dfrac{1}{2}$

3 A box contains 3 kg of washing powder.
One machine wash uses $\dfrac{1}{8}$ kg of powder.
How many washes will you get from a full box?

4 A farmer has a field with an area of $7\dfrac{3}{4}$ acres.
Each day he uses $1\dfrac{1}{2}$ acres to graze his cows.
For how many days can he graze his cows in this field?

Strand 5 • Percentages

Unit 1	Band d
Understanding and using percentages	
Page 190	

Unit 2	Band e
Calculating percentages of quantities	
Page 197	

Unit 4	Band f
Applying percentage increases and decreases to amounts	
Page 212	

Unit 3	Band e
Converting fractions and decimals to and from percentages	
Page 205	

Unit 5	Band g
Finding the percentage change from one amount to another	
Page 221	

Unit 6	Band h
Reverse percentages	
Page 226	

Building skills

Example outside the Maths classroom

Money lenders

Toolbox

Percentage means "out of 100" or "parts per hundred".

A percentage is the top line of a fraction with bottom line 100.

$\frac{35}{100}$ is 35%

When you write a fraction as a percentage you want the equivalent fraction with 100 on the bottom line.

$$\frac{7}{20} \overset{\times 5}{\underset{\times 5}{=}} \frac{35}{100} = 35\%$$

It is often helpful to start by writing a fraction as a decimal.

$$\frac{7}{20} = 0.35$$
$$= 0.35 \times \frac{100}{100}$$
$$= \frac{35}{100}$$
$$= 35\%$$

> Then multiply top and bottom by 100, which is the same as multiplying by 1.

It helps to have some mental methods, like a ratio table and a percentage bar chart.

A ratio table

Think of $\frac{7}{20}$ as a mark of 7 out of 20.

Mark	7	14	21	35
Out of	20	40	60	100

The table shows this is equivalent to 35 out of 100, or 35%.

A percentage bar chart

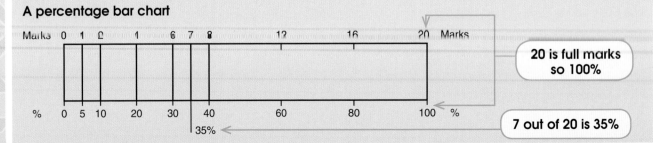

> 20 is full marks so 100%

> 7 out of 20 is 35%

Example – Finding Percentages

a One season, a football club wins 35% and draws 25% of its games.
What percentage of its games does it lose?

b Next season, the football club wins 24 out of the 40 games it plays.
What percentage is this?

Solution

a Percentage lost = 100 − 35 − 25 = 40%

b Percentage won = $\frac{24}{40} \times \frac{100}{100} = 0.6 \times \frac{100}{100} = \frac{60}{100} = 60\%$

Remember:

✦ 100% represents $\frac{100}{100}$ or 1. It is the whole amount.

Skills practice A

1 Class 8E did a survey. They found that 15% of the students are vegetarians.
What percentage of the students are not vegetarians?

2 75% of a class caught a cold last year. What percentage did not catch a cold?

3 A sweater is made from 70% acrylic. The rest is wool. What percentage is wool?

4 A skirt is 60% lambswool, 20% angora and the rest is polyamide. What percentage is polyamide?

5 In an election, 33% voted for Bill Bloor, 27% voted for Sarah Vaughan and 36% voted for Terry Kenwright.
The rest voted for Neil Leach. What percentage voted for Neil Leach?

6 a Draw percentage bars like the ones shown below for each of Dani's school subjects.
  b Complete the bars to convert Dani's test marks to percentages.
  c Has Dani improved her marks since last year?
   i History: Last year's test mark: 20 out of 80.
        This year's test mark: 15 out of 50.

```
                                                    100%
┌──────────────────────────────────────────────────┐
│                                                    │
└──────────────────────────────────────────────────┘
                                                    80

                                                    100%
┌──────────────────────────────────────────────────┐
│                                                    │
└──────────────────────────────────────────────────┘
                                                    50
```

   ii Maths: Last year's test mark: 24 out of 60.
         This year's test mark: 50 out of 80.
   iii English: Last year's test mark: 14 out of 24.
          This year's test mark: 36 out of 60.

7 **a** Draw ratio tables like these ones for each of Dani's school subjects below.

   b Complete the tables to convert Dani's test marks to percentages.

   c Has Dani improved her marks since last year?

     i RS: Last year's test mark: 50 out of 80.

            This year's test mark: 42 out of 70.

Mark	50					
Out of	80					

Mark	42					
Out of	70					

     ii Business studies: Last year's test mark: 18 out of 24.

                        This year's test mark: 36 out of 60.

Mark	18					
Out of	24					

Mark	36					
Out of	60					

8 John achieved 45 out of a possible 50 points in an archery competition. What is this as a percentage?

9 Write these as percentages.

   a 24 out of 75   **b** 144 out of 150   **c** 15 out of 40

10 Janice enters a driving competition. There are three sections.
Convert each mark into a percentage.

   a Parking 6 out of 10   **b** Hill starts 15 out of 20   **c** Car control 35 out of 40   **d** Overall Mark

Skills practice B

1 **a** On one trawler, the fishermen throw back 4% of the fish caught because they are too small. What percentage of the fish caught do they keep?

   b On another trawler, the fishermen reject 0.36 tonnes of fish out of a catch of 72 tonnes. What percentage do they reject?

2 Eva keeps a record of the number of sunny days on her holidays. She writes them as fractions. Write them in order, highest first.

   Isle of Man $\frac{15}{20}$ Cornwall $\frac{20}{25}$ Florida $\frac{6}{10}$ Mallorca $\frac{36}{40}$ Home $\frac{39}{50}$

3 Brass is made up of $66\frac{2}{3}\%$ copper. The rest is zinc. What percentage is zinc?

4 Wai Peng has 2.5 square kilometres of rice fields. He has planted 1.7 square kilometres. What percentage has he planted?

5 Ahmed has saved up £48 towards a bike. His parents are paying the rest.
The bike costs £120. What percentage of the cost is Ahmed paying?

6 Freddy plants 75 seeds. 66 grow.
What percentage of his seeds doesn't grow?

7 Suzie earns £600 per month. Her rent is £180 per month.
What percentage of her income is spent on rent?

8 There are 140 students in Year 8 at Avonford High School. 21 of them are left-handed.
What percentage of the students are not left-handed?

9 a 35 of the 500 people on a train travel first class.
What percentage don't travel first class?

 b 44 people out of 80 buy a programme at a rugby match.
What percentage of the people buy a programme?

10 6 out of 30 pupils in one class play cricket for a local club.
What percentage of the pupils is this?

11 These pie charts show the constituents of cheese and eggs.

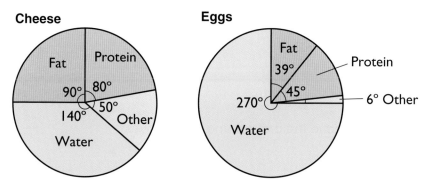

Cheese

Eggs

 a Write a comparison of these constituents of cheese and eggs, giving your numbers as percentages.

 b Which has more fat, 200 g of cheese or 200 g of eggs?

12 In Year 9 at Avonford High School, students can choose to take Spanish, German or neither language. The table shows what they choose.

	Spanish	German	Neither
Boys	12	18	30
Girls	22	11	22

 a How many girls are there in Year 9?

 b What percentage of the girls chose Spanish?

 c What percentage of the boys chose German?

 d What percentage of the Year 9 students chose neither Spanish nor German?

13 2250 people went to a concert. 1890 were female.
What percentage were male?

Wider skills practice

1 The list below shows the number of eggs laid by a flock of 30 hens in a 100-day period. (A hen never lays more than one egg in a day.) The numbers are given as percentages.

19, 22, 32, 39, 39, 43, 45, 45, 46, 52, 54, 56, 59, 61, 64, 64, 64, 64, 67, 68, 68, 74, 77, 80, 81, 85, 85, 91, 93

   a Hens laying on at least 80% of days are graded "top layers". What percentage of the hens is this?

   b The hens laying the fewest eggs are graded "unproductive". What was the lowest percentage gained by one of these hens?

   c What percentage of the hens achieved between 50% and 70%?

2 In a TV competition there were 300 000 votes.
   Sui Lin received 14% of the votes. Clare had 75 000 votes. Mike had 96 000 votes. Simon had the rest.

   a What percentage did each person get?

   b Copy and complete this bar chart to show the voting.

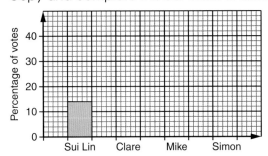

   c The person with the lowest vote has to leave the programme. Who leaves?

Applying skills

1 Any country's land use can be split into four categories:
   • arable – growing food, e.g. rice
   • pasture – growing grass to feed animals
   • forest – trees
   • other – desert, towns, mountains, etc.

   a Norfolk Island is a small island off the east coast of Australia. The pie chart shows land use in Norfolk Island.
   25% of the land is used for pasture. Norfolk Island has a total area of 40 km².
   What percentage of the land is not pasture?

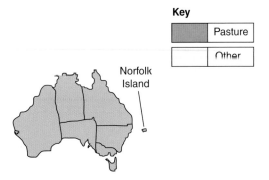

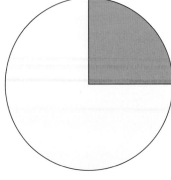

Key

| | Pasture |
| | Other |

b Liechtenstein is a country in central Europe with a total area of 160 km². What percentage of land is arable?

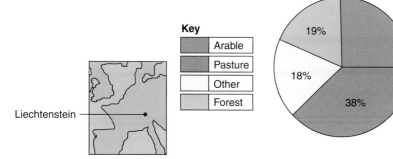

c Sierra Leone is a country in West Africa with a total area of 71 740 km². What area of land is arable?

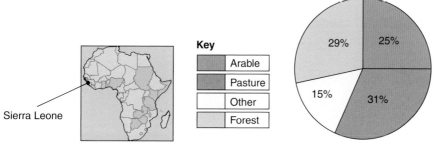

d Portugal is a country in southern Europe with a total area of 92 390 km². One land use accounts for 27 717 km² of the country. Which is it?

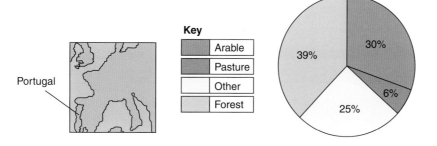

Reasoning

Reviewing skills

1 'Silver' coins actually contain no silver. They are, in fact, made of cupro-nickel, which contains 76% copper. The rest is nickel.
What percentage is nickel?

2 Mr Green decided that he should recycle his rubbish if possible.
In one week his rubbish weighed 25 kg. He was able to recycle 16 kg of it.

   a What fraction did he recycle?

   b What percentage is this?

3 Write these amounts as percentages.

   a 16 out of 50

   b 5 kg out of 200 kg

   c 3 cm out of 12 cm

   d 4 litres out of 25 litres

4 a Stella scores 48 marks out of a possible 80 in a French test. What is this as a percentage?

   b Simon scores 32 marks in the same test. What is his percentage?

5 12 out of 60 calculators have flat batteries within two years.
   What percentage do not need new batteries?

Building skills

Example outside the Maths classroom

Nutritional content

Toolbox

Here are two methods for calculating a percentage of a quantity. They are illustrated by an example:
Find 54% of 450.

> **To find 1%, divide by 100.**
> **To find 10%, divide by 10.**

The unitary method

In this method, it helps to have a mental picture of a percentage bar.

100% is 450

So 1% is $\dfrac{450}{100} = 4.5$

> Remember that "of" means × .

54% is $54 \times 4.5 = 243$

Multiplying by the percentage

In this method you make the percentage into a fraction or decimal.

54% of 450

> Remember that "of" means × .

$$= \frac{54}{100}_{10} \times \frac{450^{45}}{1}$$

> Make the calculation easier by cancelling first.

$$= \frac{54}{10_2} \times \frac{45^9}{1}$$

$$= \frac{54^{27}}{2_1} \times \frac{9}{1}$$

$$= 27 \times 9$$

$$= 243$$

Example – Calculating a percentage of a quantity

1 Calculate 40% of £60 million.

Solution

Either **the unitary method**

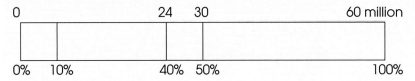

100% is 60 million

10% is 6 million

40% is 4 × 6 = 24 million, so £24 million

or **Multiplying by the percentage**

40% of £60 million

$\frac{40}{100}$ × 60 million

0.4 × 60 million

= 24 million

> Alternatively you could stay with fractions and do this as
> $\frac{40}{100} \times \frac{60}{1} = 24$

Remember:

✦ To find x% of y, calculate $\frac{x \times y}{100}$.

Skills practice A

1 Here are diagrams of some computer program download bars. For each one work out the total installation time.

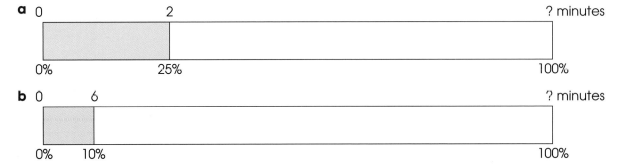

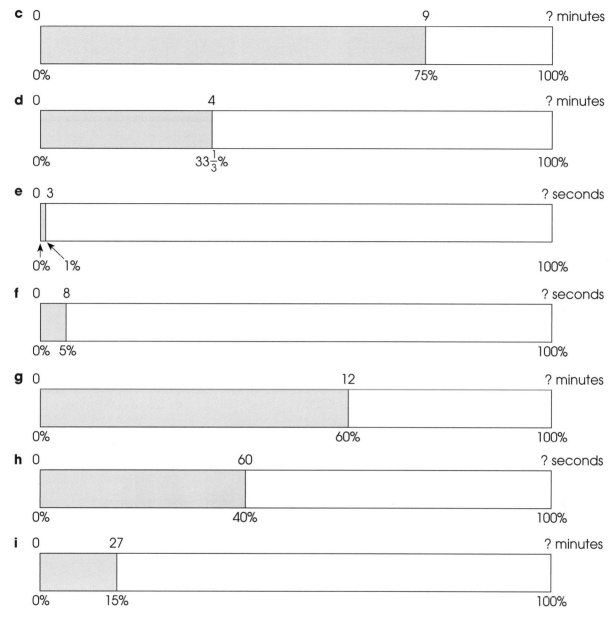

c 0   9   ? minutes

0%   75%   100%

d 0   4   ? minutes

0% $33\frac{1}{3}$%   100%

e 0 3   ? seconds

0%   1%   100%

f 0   8   ? seconds

0%   5%   100%

g 0   12   ? minutes

0%   60%   100%

h 0   60   ? seconds

0%   40%   100%

i 0   27   ? minutes

0%   15%   100%

2 For each diagram of a bottle, use your ruler to make suitable measurement. Then work out
  i   the percentage of the bottle that contains liquid
  ii   the amount of liquid in each bottle.

    a   200 ml bottle   **b**   150 ml bottle   **c**   200 ml bottle   **d**   250 ml bottle   **e**   100 ml
        bottle

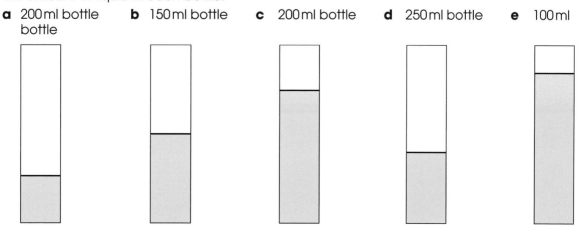

3 Match these red and blue cards in pairs.

a 50% of £10	b 1% of £7	c 10% of £1		£8.00	3p	20p
d 50% of £16	e 10% of £2	f 25% of £100		7p	25p	£3.00
g 100% of £15	h 100% of £6	i 10% of £4		£15.00	1p	£4.00
j 50% of £4	k 50% of £20	l 1% of £1		£5.00	£1.00	£10.00
m 10% of £6	n 25% of £1	o 100% of £4		40p	£25.00	50p
p 25% of £4	q 1% of £3	r 75% of £1		£6.00	10p	£2.00
s 75% of £4	t 25% of £2	u 75% of £2		£1.50	60p	75p

4 Calculate these amounts.

  a 10% of £400   **b** 15% of £1000   **c** 5% of 200 tonnes

5 A shop buys 500 batteries. 2% of them are faulty.
How many batteries are faulty?

6 A box contained 40 lettuces. 15% went bad and had to be thrown away.
How many lettuces remained?

7 Christine decides to save 20% of her pocket money. She receives £6. How much does she save?

8 Kim is buying a new house. The cost is £120 000. She has to pay a deposit of 15%.
How much is the deposit?

9 8% of a light margarine is fat. How many grams of fat are there in a 500 g tub?

10 32% of a tropical fruit drink is made from the juices of orange, lemon, pineapple and apricot.
How much of these juices is there in

  a a 1 litre bottle   **b** a 350 ml glass   **c** a 2.5 litre jug?

Skills practice B

1 There were 240 teenagers at a disco. 65% of them were girls. How many girls were at the disco?

2 Ryan set out on a 35 km hike but he only completed 60% of the course. How far did he walk?

3 A tub of 115 g of fruit fool contains 8% lemon.
How many grams of lemon are in the tub?

4 David buys a bike priced at £450.
He pays the shopkeeper a deposit of 35% of the price.
How much deposit does he pay?

5 There are 225 children at a primary school. 16% cannot swim. How many of the children can swim?

6 The contents of a jar of stuffed olives have a mass of 120 g. The label states that the amount of fat is 12.5 g per 100 g.
Write down
  a the percentage of fat in the stuffed olives
  b the amount of fat contained in the jar of stuffed olives.

7 In a dancing competition, 6 judges each give scores between 0 and 10.
  a Clare gets 43 points. What is this as a percentage?
  b John scores 80%. How many points out of 60 does he get?

8 Kate gets the bill for repairs to her car.

AL'S GARAGE
Parts £85.10
Labour £54

  a What is the total cost for parts and labour?
  b Value added tax (VAT) is charged at 20%.
     How much VAT does she have to pay?
  c Calculate the total cost of the parts, labour and VAT.

Reasoning

9 Use sensible guesswork to match these yellow and blue cards in pairs.
Then check your answers with a calculator.

a 64% of £320	b 72% of £250	£142.80	£80.34
c 94% of £165	d 68% of £210	£23.52	£99
e 47% of £245	f 11% of £900	£56	£38
g 103% of £78	h 70% of £80	£204.80	£115.15
i 19% of £200	j 56% of £42	£155.10	£180

10 A return flight from Malta to Athens costs £140.

   a The cost for a child is 60% of the full price. How much does a child's return flight cost?

   b A single flight for an adult costs £100. What percentage of the cost of a return flight is this?

Wider skills practice

1 Alvin buys a guitar. It costs £400.
He pays for it in instalments.

   a First he pays a deposit of 35%.
How much deposit does he pay?

   b Then he makes 12 monthly payments.
Each of these is 8% of the price.

      i What is each monthly payment?

      ii What is the total of all 12 monthly payments?

   c How much does he pay altogether?

   d How much more than £400 is this?

   e What percentage of £400 is this extra amount?

2 10% of the wood consumed each year is used as paper, 87.5% of which is used by rich countries.
What percentage of the wood is used by rich countries for paper?

3 a A salesperson receives commission at the rate of 10% of the value of everything he sells.

    i One week he sold £2240 worth of goods. How much commission did he receive?

    ii Another week he received £32 commission. What was the value of the goods he sold?

b Another salesperson receives commission at the rate of 15% of the value of the goods sold. One week she received £600 commission. What was the value of the goods she sold?

c A third salesperson made a sale worth £350. He received £42 commission. What rate of commission is being given?

4 Here is a diagram of a colony of bacteria.

At time 0, there are 200 000 of them.

At the end of every hour their number has increased by 10% of that at the start of the hour.

a Copy and complete this table.

Time (hrs)	Increase	Number of bacteria
0	–	200 000
1	20 000	220 000
2	22 000	
3		
4		
5		

Check that your last number in the table is 322 102.

b Use your calculator to work out $200\,000 \times 1.10^5$

Explain why this gives the same answer of 322 102.

Applying skills

1 Value added tax (VAT) is charged at 20%.

Find

    a the VAT to be added to each of these

    b the total bill

        i a restaurant bill of £50

        ii a garage bill of £70

        iii a telephone bill of £35

        iv a video recorder priced £450

        v a TV priced £250

New Bridge Restaurant

Meal for two	£44.00
plus VAT	
$\frac{17.5 \times 44}{100}$	£ 7.70
Total	£ 51.70

2 Fred is paid a salary each month of £1877, plus two allowances of £86.00 and £90.58. Before he receives his pay, money is deducted for various things. £123.21 is taken towards his pension, £338.34 is taken for income tax, £144.25 is taken for National Insurance.

    a What is his total monthly salary, before any deductions? Include the two allowances.

    b How much money Is he paid after deductions?

    c What percentage of his total salary goes towards his pension?

    d What percentage of his total salary is taken as income tax?

    e What percentage of his total salary does he pay for National Insurance?

Reasoning

Problem solving

Reviewing skills

1 Find

   a 20% of £300   b 3% of £5000   c 10% of 220 km   d 1% of 250 kg.

2 A school has 1200 students.

   55% of the students are girls. How many girls are there?

3 Sam buys a keyboard priced at £450. He pays the shopkeeper a deposit of 30% of the price of the keyboard.
How much deposit does he pay?

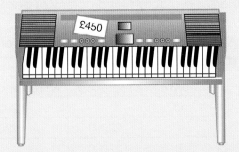

4 Helen buys a laptop priced at £180.

   a First she pays a deposit of 30%.
     How much deposit does she pay?

   b She then makes 12 monthly payments of £13 each.
     How much do these payments come to altogether?

   c What is the total of the deposit and the 12 monthly instalments?

   d How much extra does she pay for the laptop?

Example outside the Maths classroom

Building skills

Comparing discounts

 Toolbox

There are several methods for **converting fractions and decimals into percentages**.

They are based on finding an equivalent fraction with 100 on the bottom line.

The methods are shown here using the example of $\frac{1}{8}$.

Finding the equivalent fraction

$\times 50 \qquad \div 4$

$$\frac{1}{8} = \frac{50}{400} = \frac{12.5}{100} = 12.5\%$$

$\times 50 \qquad \div 4$

Using decimals

$$\frac{1}{8} = 0.125$$ $\longleftarrow$ **You need to divide 8 into 1.000**

$$0.125 \times \frac{100}{100} = \frac{12.5}{100}$$ $\longleftarrow$ **This is the equivalent fraction with 100 on the bottom line.**

$$= 12.5\%$$

Using a percentage bar

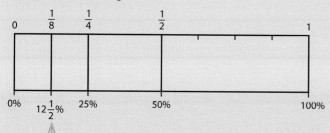

$\frac{1}{8}$ is the same as $12\frac{1}{2}\%$

To **convert a percentage into a fraction or decimal**, start by writing it as a fraction with 100 on the bottom line.

Converting to a fraction

$$12.5\% = \frac{12.5}{100}$$

$$= \frac{25}{200} \longleftarrow \boxed{\text{Multiply by 2 to remove the decimal.}}$$

$$= \frac{5}{40} \longleftarrow \boxed{\text{Simplify by dividing by 5.}}$$

$$= \frac{1}{8} \longleftarrow \boxed{\text{Simplify by dividing by 5.}}$$

Converting to a decimal

$$12.5\% = \frac{12.5}{100} = 0.125 \longleftarrow \boxed{\text{Using place value.}}$$

Example – Converting between fractions, decimals and percentages

a Write 42% and 28% as fractions, in their simplest form, and as decimals.

b Write $\frac{2}{5}$ and 0.37 as percentages.

Solution

a As a fraction: $42\% = \frac{42}{100} = \frac{21}{50}$

As a decimal: $42\% = \frac{42}{100} = 0.42$

Similarly, $28\% = \frac{28}{100} = \frac{7}{25} = 0.28$

b $\frac{2}{5} = \frac{20}{50} = \frac{40}{100} = 40\%$

$0.37 = 0.37 \times \frac{100}{100} = \frac{37}{100} = 37\%$

Remember:

+ Percentage means "out of 100", or "parts per 100".
+ To change a fraction or a decimal to a percentage, multiply by 100% (a whole).

Skills practice A

1 Convert these percentages to fractions.

   a 20%   **b** 30%   **c** 80%

2 Convert these percentages to decimals.

   a 10%   **b** 45%   **c** 17%

3 Convert these fractions to percentages.

   a $\dfrac{1}{2}$ **b** $\dfrac{7}{10}$ **c** $\dfrac{13}{20}$

4 Convert these decimals to percentages.

   a 0.4   **b** 0.15   **c** 0.05

5 Change these percentages to fractions.

   a 25%   **b** $33\dfrac{1}{3}$%   **c** $12\dfrac{1}{2}$%

6 Write these fractions as percentages.

   a $\dfrac{1}{8}$ **b** $\dfrac{3}{8}$ **c** $\dfrac{5}{8}$

7 Copy and complete this table.

Fraction	Decimal	Percentage
$\dfrac{4}{5}$		
		60%
	0.7	
$\dfrac{11}{20}$		
		44%
	0.32	
		35%
$\dfrac{9}{10}$		
	0.06	
$\dfrac{3}{5}$		
	0.85	
		16%
	0.13	
		65%

Skills practice B

1 Copy and shade the appropriate parts of these diagrams.

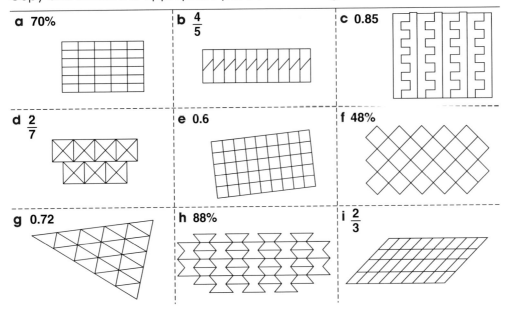

a 70%	**b** $\frac{4}{5}$	**c** 0.85
d $\frac{2}{7}$	**e** 0.6	**f** 48%
g 0.72	**h** 88%	**i** $\frac{2}{3}$

2 Write each of these lists in order, starting with the lowest.

  a $\frac{13}{20}$, 70%, 0.68, 60%   **b** 0.33, $\frac{1}{3}$, 30%, 0.34   **c** $2\frac{1}{4}$, 200%, 2.2, 22%   **d** 8.5, 8.6%, 0.08, 8

3 Write these fractions in order of size, lowest to highest.

  $\frac{9}{25}$ $\frac{19}{50}$ $\frac{1}{3}$ $\frac{3}{8}$ $\frac{2}{5}$ $\frac{7}{20}$

4 Copy and complete these. Write one of the symbols <, > or = between each pair.

  a $\frac{3}{5}$ ☐ 60%   **b** 25% ☐ $\frac{1}{5}$ **c** 35% ☐ $\frac{2}{5}$

  d $\frac{1}{7}$ ☐ $12\frac{1}{2}$%   **e** 200% ☐ 2.5   **f** 0.3 ☐ 3%

5 $\frac{9}{20}$ can be converted to a percentage as follows:

  $\frac{9}{20} \rightarrow \frac{45}{100} \rightarrow 45\%$

For each of the following fractions find
  • an equivalent fraction with 100 as the denominator
  • a percentage.

  a $\frac{19}{20}$ **b** $\frac{13}{20}$ **c** $\frac{3}{5}$

  d $\frac{18}{25}$ **e** $\frac{23}{25}$ **f** $\frac{36}{60}$

  g $\frac{69}{75}$ **h** $\frac{26}{40}$ **i** $\frac{102}{120}$

Reasoning

6 A number of four-year-old cars had their MOT test. Some failed.

At garage A, 150 cars were tested and 42 cars failed.

The percentage of cars that failed is

$$\frac{42}{150} = \frac{14}{50} = \frac{28}{100} = 28\%$$

This table shows the number of failures at each garage.

a Find the percentage of cars failing their MOT at each garage.

b Which garage would you go to? Give your reasons why.

Garage	Number tested	Number failed
A	150	42
B	320	128
C	180	54
D	480	84
E	72	27
F	256	64

7 A number of families in six towns were asked if they owned a video.

Find the percentage of families questioned who owned a video in each town.

Town	Number of families	Number owning a video
Gloucester	8 000	6 400
Harrogate	6 000	2 220
Jarrow	7 500	2 100
Keswick	15 000	2 550
Leicester	21 000	11 970
Margate	3 800	1 140

8 The tables show Nazma's marks for the autumn and summer terms.

a Convert the marks for the autumn term to percentages.

Use the two tables to answer these questions.

b In which term was Nazma's English mark better?

c What did you notice about her marks for technology?

d For which subject did she get a better mark in the autumn term than in the summer term?

e In which subjects did she improve her marks from the autumn term to the summer term?

f In which subject did she make the most improvement?

Autumn term

Subject	Mark
Physical Education	$\frac{19}{25}$
English	$\frac{34}{50}$
French	$\frac{14}{20}$
History	$\frac{17}{25}$
Geography	$\frac{15}{30}$
Mathematics	$\frac{41}{50}$
Science	$\frac{21}{30}$
Art	$\frac{28}{40}$
Music	$\frac{12}{24}$
Technology	$\frac{36}{40}$

Summer term

Subject	Mark
Physical Education	$\frac{17}{20}$
English	$\frac{32}{40}$
French	$\frac{21}{25}$
History	$\frac{8}{10}$
Geography	$\frac{13}{20}$
Mathematics	$\frac{35}{40}$
Science	$\frac{14}{20}$
Art	$\frac{17}{25}$
Music	$\frac{11}{20}$
Technology	$\frac{27}{30}$

Reasoning

Wider skills practice

1   Some fractions are awkward to express as decimals or percentages because they are recurring

decimals. We can write the fraction $\frac{1}{3}$ as a decimal or percentage in different ways:

• $\frac{1}{3}$ = 0.333 333 333...

• $\frac{1}{3}$ = 0.33 (2 d.p.)

• $\frac{1}{3}$ = 0.$\dot{3}$ ← **The " · " means "recurring".**

• $\frac{1}{3}$ = 33.333 333 33...% = 33.33% (2 d.p.)

• $\frac{1}{3}$ = $33\frac{1}{3}$ %

Write these fractions in the five ways shown above.

a $\frac{2}{3}$ **b** $\frac{1}{6}$ **c** $\frac{2}{9}$ **d** $\frac{5}{12}$ **e** $\frac{53}{99}$

Applying skills

1   In a raffle, tickets are sold for 50p each.
    The first prize is £100, the second prize is £50 and there are ten other prizes of £5 each.
    a How many tickets must be sold for the raffle to make a profit?
    b 452 tickets are sold. How much profit is made?
    c What is this profit as a percentage of the money collected from the ticket sales?
    d What is the profit as a percentage of the prize money?
    e The organisers hope to make a profit equal to 25% of the amount of money collected.
       How many tickets do they have to sell?

Problem solving

Reviewing skills

1   Copy and complete this table.

Fraction	Decimal	Percentage
$\frac{1}{2}$		
	0.15	
		75%
$\frac{1}{10}$		

2   Eva scores these marks in tests. Convert them to percentages and place them in order, smallest to largest.

French $\frac{15}{20}$ Maths $\frac{20}{25}$ RS $\frac{6}{10}$ Science $\frac{36}{40}$ IT $\frac{39}{50}$

3   Convert these percentages to fractions in their lowest terms.
    a   10% deposit required
    b   Music exam, distinction 80%
    c   Deposit of 30% required

4   Convert these decimals to fractions in their simplest terms.
    a   0.55   b   0.72   c   0.6   d   0.255
    e   0.07   f   0.7   g   7

Building skills

Example outside the Maths classroom

Sale prices

Toolbox

There are several ways to work out percentage increases and decreases.

These are shown here using, as an example, the question:

Find the amount when £120 is **a** increased by 15% **b** decreased by 15%

Finding the increase or decrease

100% is £120

1% is $\frac{1}{100} \times £120$

15% is $\frac{15}{100} \times £120 = £18$

a An increase of 15% gives

    £120 + £18 = £138

b A decrease of 15% gives

    £120 − £18 = £102

Using a ratio table

$$15\% = 10\% + 5\%$$

£120 − £18 = £102

%	100	10	5	15	115	85
Amount	120	12	6	18	138	102

b A decrease of 15% gives £102

£120 + £18 = £138

a An increase of 15% gives £138

This is the amount of the increase or decrease. In this case it is £18

Using a percentage bar chart

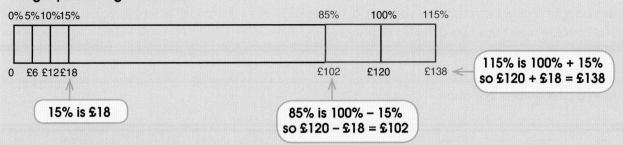

The chart shows that
a An increase of 15% gives an amount of £138
b A decrease of 15% gives an amount of £102

Using a multiplier

a The original amount is 100% so it is 100 + 15 = 115% when 15% is added.

So the new amount is 115% of £120 = $\frac{115}{100} \times$ £120 ← | You can also write this as 1.15 × £120 |

$= £138$

b In the same way, the amount is 100 − 15 = 85% when 15% is subtracted.

$$\frac{85}{100} \times £120 = 0.85 \times £120$$

$$= £102$$

Example – Percentage increase

Anneka earns £21 000 per year. She is given a 3% increase.
Calculate how much she now earns in a year. Use two different methods.

Solution

Using a ratio table

100%	1%	3%	103%
£21 000	£210	£630	£216 30

103% of £21 000 = £21 630

Finding the increase or decrease

100% is £21 000

1% is $\frac{1}{100} \times$ £21 000 = £210

3% is $\frac{3}{100} \times$ £21 000 = £630

An increase of 3% gives
£21 000 + £630 = £21 630

Example – Percentage decrease

William bought a new bicycle three years ago. It cost £300. Now it has lost 30% of its value. What is its value now? Use two different methods.

Solution

a   Using a percentage bar chart

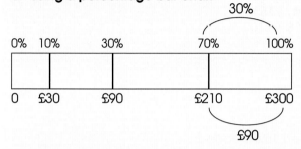

70% of £300 = £210

b   Using a multiplier

The new amount is 100% − 30% = 70%

This is $\frac{70}{100}$ × £300 = 0.7 × £300 = £210

Remember:

   ✦ Find the amount to increase or decrease the amount by first, then add it on.
   ✦ Alternatively, add or subtract the percentage from 100 and then find that percentage of the original amount.

Skills practice A

1   For each item below, work out the sale price. Use percentage bars like the one shown to help you.

   a   Normal price = £600. Reduced by 10% in the sale.

   b   Normal price = £590. Reduced by 10% in the sale.

   c   Normal price = £640. Reduced by 15% in the sale.

   d   Normal price = £560. Reduced by 5% in the sale.

   e   Normal price = £700. Reduced by 25% in the sale.

2 a Copy and complete this ratio table to find the amount when £ 250 is increased by 40%

100%	10%	40%	140%
£250	£25	£100	?

b What is the amount when £250 is reduced by 40%?

3 Use ratio tables to find
a £200 increased by 30%
b £5500 increased by 12%
c 720 metres decreased by 15%
d 80 kg decreased by 40%

4 In a sale the price of a pair of shoes is reduced by 20%. Before the sale the shoes cost £80.
a Calculate the reduction in price.
b What is the price in the sale?

5 The price of each of these items goes up by 20% What are the new prices?
a CD £15
b jeans £45
c video recorder £250
d football ticket £25

6 These items go down in value by the percentage shown. What is the new value of each item?
a bicycle £300, down 20%
b guitar £440, down 25%
c model car £30, down 50%

7 A shop is selling goods at 10% off. Find the sale price of each of these items.
a shoes £30
b jeans £55
c jumper £42

8 Find the sale price of each of these items.

SALE 10% off

A

€40

B

€65

C
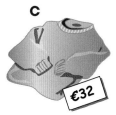
€32

9 Sarah gets a 4% pay rise. Her salary before the rise was £22 000.
a Calculate her increase in pay.
b Calculate her new salary.

10 When a piece of elastic is stretched, its length increases by 22%.
The elastic is 30 cm long before being stretched. What is its length when stretched?

Skills practice B

1 Match the boxes which have the same answer.

a 35 increased by 80%	90 reduced by $33\frac{1}{3}$%
b 70 decreased by 10%	15 raised by 40%
c 50 increased by 20%	80 decreased by 70%
d 18 increased by $33\frac{1}{3}$%	84 decreased by 75%

2 These people work for Avonford zoo. They are all given a 3% pay increase.
Work out their new salaries.

  a Abigail, a trainee, who earned £13 000

  b Alka, the big cats keeper, who earned £27 000

  c Alf, the maintenance man, who earned £22 000

3 A car goes down in value (depreciates) by 20% after one year.
Work out the values of these cars, which are all one year old.

  a Fiat Brava, new price was £8500

  b Peugeot 406, new price was £13 700

  c Peugeot 806, new price was £17 000

  d Vauxhall Astra Coupe, new price was £16 250

4 a The cost price of a guitar is £350. A music shop sells it at a profit of 11%.
   What is the selling price?

  b A book of popular music costs £9. More recent tunes have been written by the same
   composer, so the music shop sells the book at a loss of 23%.
   What is the selling price?

  c The cost of a tracksuit is £45. It is sold at a profit of 40%.
   What is the selling price?

  d The cost price of a pair of jeans is £30. They are sold at a profit of 60%.
   What is the selling price?

5 A shopkeeper bought a box of 200 chocolate bars for £50.

  a How much did she pay for each bar?

  b She made a profit of 20% on each bar. How much did she sell each bar for?

  c How much money did she receive from the sale of all the bars?

  d How much profit did she make from selling all the bars of chocolate?

  e The shopkeeper paid £50 for the bars of chocolate and made a profit of 20% on each bar.
   Find 20% of £50. What do you notice about your answer to part **d** and this value?

Reasoning

6 There were 15 000 women and 18 000 men living in the town of Allerton.

The population increased over the next few years.

The number of women increased by 10%.

The number of men increased by only 4%.

a How many men and how many women lived in Allerton after this increase?

b What was the total increase as a percentage of the original population?

7 A shopkeeper buys ringbinders at £2.20 each. He add 25% to this to get the selling price.

a Show that the selling price is £2.75 and that the profit is 55p.

b Calculate the shopkeeper's profit and the selling price for each of these items.

Item	Buying price	Percentage profit
i	80p	25%
ii	£1.70	10%
iii	£5.40	30%
iv	£5.00	15%
v	£9.70	20%

c In a sale, the selling prices of some articles were reduced.

Calculate the price reduction and the sale price of each of these items.

Item	Original price	Percentage reduction
i	70p	10%
ii	£18.00	25%
iii	£15.50	20%
iv	£8.70	$33\frac{1}{3}$ %
v	£4.40	15%

8 A shop has this offer on all its office chairs.

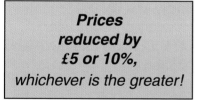

Prices reduced by £5 or 10%, whichever is the greater!

a What would be the cheapest sale price for a chair which normally cost

i £20   **ii** £35   **iii** £60   **iv** £74?

b Emily buys an office chair. The sale price is the same whichever way the discount is given.

i What is the normal price of the chair Emily buys?

ii What is the sale price?

iii Explain why it does not matter which way the discount is given.

Reasoning

9 A chemist buys hair gel at £2.40 per tube. She makes a 30% profit.

   a What is the selling price of the hair gel?

   b In a special offer, she sells three tubes for the price of two.
      Does she still make a profit? What is her percentage profit or loss?

Reasoning

10 A Youth club has some special offers as shown in the diagrams.
     If you wanted to spend exactly £10, how could you do it?

CINEMA usually £4.52 25% OFF!	*Salsa Dancing* *normally £4.50* *save 18%*	reduced from £5.07 by $33\frac{1}{3}$ % **TEN** **PIN** **BOWLING**
DIVING CLASSES 12% off £4.00 usual charge	*Standard price £3.80* *Get 15% off* *Clay pigeon shooting*	*Abseiling* *normal price* *£3.90* *now 10% off*

Wider skills practice

Reasoning

1 When water is frozen, its volume increases by 4%.

   a 5 litres of water is frozen. How many cm³ of ice will be made?   ⟵   **1 litre = 1000 cm³**

   b A machine makes identical ice cubes, each with a volume of 10 cm³.
      2.5 litres of water are used to make these ice cubes. How many ice cubes are made?

Reasoning

2 Ankur has been working in the same job for two years. His starting salary was £20 000.

   a After one year he received a 3% pay increase. What was Ankur's salary after one year?

   b The following year he received another 3% increase. What was Ankur's salary after two years?

   c How much more did he earn after two years than when he first started?

   d Find 6% of £20 000.

   e Is your answer to part **d** more or less than your answer to part **c**? Explain why this is.

Applying skills

1 These people all work at the same company. They are talking about their jobs.

I am the managing director of a small firm. I have six employees. I earn £60,000 a year.

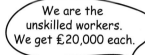

We are the unskilled workers. We get £20,000 each.

I am the foreman. I earn £40,000 a year.

We are the skilled workers and we each earn £30,000 a year.

At a union meeting, the workers decided to ask for higher wages.

I'm afraid there is only £21,000 to spare this year. We will have to share this between us.

The money should be shared out equally.

As foreman, I suggest that we all have a 10% increase in our salaries.

219

Problem solving

a Work out how much each person would get if their salaries were increased by 10%.

b Work out how much each person would get by sharing the £21 000 equally between them all.

c Which way would you vote if you were

  i the managing director

  ii a skilled worker? Why?

d Which method do you think most people voted for?

Reviewing skills

1 The government awards a 4% pay increase to all public sector workers.
   Work out the new salary for
   a Beatrice, who earned £15 000
   b Brett, who earned £24 000
   c Bert, who earned £17 000.

2 Cars depreciate in value as they get older.
   What is the value of each of these cars after one year's depreciation?
   a Peugeot 806 originally £17 500, depreciation 9%
   b Chrysler Neon originally £13 496, depreciation 25%
   c Vauxhall Astra originally £16 140, depreciation 15%

3 The value of these items has increased. Find their new values.
   a old postage stamp £5, increased by 20%
   b antique pottery £150, increased by 65%
   c diamond ring £1500, increased by 124%
   d vintage car £1800, increased by 26%

Building skills

 Example outside the Maths classroom

Inflation rates

 Toolbox

To calculate a percentage change, follow the method illustrated in this example.

The population of an island increases from 500 to 650 people. What is the percentage increase?

The increase is 650 − 500 = 150 people

As a fraction this is $\dfrac{150}{500}$ ⟵ **The increase.**

⟵ **The original population.**

Either

Find the equivalent fraction with 100 on the bottom line

$$\dfrac{150}{500} = \dfrac{30}{100} = 30\%$$

Or

Write the fraction as a decimal

$$\dfrac{150}{500} = 0.3$$

Then multiply by $\dfrac{100}{100}$ to make it a percentage

$$0.3 \times \dfrac{100}{100} = \dfrac{30}{100} = 30\%$$

You may find it helpful to use a percentage bar or a ratio table to illustrate this.

Example – Percentage increase

Maya deals in musical instruments. She buys a guitar for £75 and restores it. She sells it for £120. Find her percentage profit.

Solution

Profit = £120 − £75 ⟵ **Profit = sale price − cost price**

$\qquad$ = £45

As a fraction this is $\dfrac{45}{75}$ ⟵ **Remember to always put the original value on the bottom line.**

$$\dfrac{45}{75} = \dfrac{90}{150} = \dfrac{30}{50} = \dfrac{60}{100}$$

So Maya's profit is 60%

Example – Percentage decrease

Zorro was an overweight dog. He was 14.0 kg
His owner put him on a programme of long daily walks. After six months his weight is 9.8 kg.
What percentage weight has Zorro lost?

Solution

Weight lost = 14.0 – 9.8 = 4.2 kg

As a fraction $\frac{4.2}{14.0}$

Percentage decrease = $\frac{4.2}{14.0} \times \frac{100}{100}$ ← **Find an equivalent fraction with 100 on the bottom line.**

$$\frac{\cancel{420}}{\cancel{1400}} \quad \frac{\cancel{60}}{\cancel{200}} \quad \frac{30}{100} = \frac{420}{1400} = \frac{60}{200} = \frac{30}{100}$$ ← **This is the equivalent fraction.**

The fraction lost is $\frac{30}{100}$

So Zorro has lost 30% of his weight.

Remember:

✦ When you write the calculation as a fraction, it is always the original amount on the bottom line and never the new amount.

Skills practice A

1 The cost price of a personal stereo is £40. It is sold for £45.
What is the percentage profit?

2 The cost price of a mobile phone is £49. It is sold for £70.
What is the percentage profit?

3 The cost price of a poster is £4.50. It is sold for £3.60.
What is the percentage loss?

4 The cost price of a T-shirt is £15. It is sold for £12.
What is the percentage loss?

5 For each situation below, calculate
  a the profit made
  b the percentage profit.
  Give your percentage answers to the nearest whole number.
  i cost price £50, selling price £90
  ii cost price £30, selling price £40
  iii cost price £8, selling price £9.99
  iv cost price £15, selling price £24.50

6 For each situation below, calculate

    a the loss   **b** the percentage loss.

    Give your percentage answers to the nearest whole number.

        i   cost £20, selling price £15

        ii cost 90p, selling price 75p

        iii cost £500, selling price £410

7 For each situation, calculate the percentage profit.

    Give your answers to the nearest whole number.

    a cost price 20p, selling price 45p   **b** cost price 75p, selling price 85p

    c cost price £100, selling price £124.90   **d** cost price £1500, selling price £2300

8 For each situation below, calculate the percentage loss.

    Give your answers to the nearest whole number.

    a cost £45, selling price £30

    b cost 50p, selling price 18p

    c cost £1200, selling price £900

Skills practice B

1 **a** Sally has 60 books on her shelf. She buys 15 more. What is this as a percentage increase?

    b Sometime later Sally gives 15 of her books away. What is the percentage decrease in her number of books?

2 **a** A colony of bees is 400 strong in April. By the end of June the number has increased to 528. What is the percentage increase?

    b The colony is then struck by a disease and goes down to 132. What is the percentage decrease?

3 **a** A bottle of a brand of soft drink contains 30 grams of sugar. To make it more healthy the factory reduces the sugar to 18 grams. What percentage reduction is this?

    b Sales of the drink go down and the company increase the sugar content back to 30 grams. What percentage increase is this?

4 Jack has a long day driving.

He leaves home and goes first to A and then to B.

After B he could go straight home.

Instead he decides to go to C. What percentage does this add to his journey?

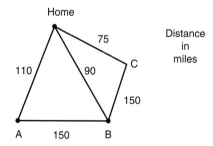

5 Find the percentage change that takes you from A to B in each case.

A	B
70	84
120	174
88	110
40	52

A	B
75	66
140	63
110	88
125	80

Look at your answers for going from 88 to 110 and from 110 to 88, what do you notice?
Would you expect them to be the same? Explain why they are not.

6 a Nigel's rent increased from £200 to £220 per week. Find the percentage increase in his rent.

b At the same time, Nigel's wages increased from £470 to £490 per week. Find the percentage increase in his wages.

c Comment on your answers.

7 The number of pupils in a school increased as given in the table.

Year	2009	2010	2011	2012
Number	581	620	641	672

In which year was the percentage increase in the number of pupils the greatest?

8 This table gives the prices of seven foods in six successive years.

Food	1972	1973	1974	1975	1976	1977
1 lb sausages	21p	24p	29p	32p	37p	44p
4 oz coffee	29p	30p	32p	40p	41p	72p
1 lb potatoes	2p	2p	2p	3p	7p	12p
12 eggs	20p	20p	47p	31p	39p	48p
2 lb sugar	10p	9p	10p	29p	23p	21p
1 pt milk	6p	6p	6p	5p	9p	10p
1 lb carrots	3p	4p	5p	7p	7p	14p

a The prices of sausages and sugar increased by different amounts but in each case the price roughly doubled between 1972 and 1977.
Copy and complete this table for the rest of the foods.

Food	1972 price	1977 price	Price increase	Price increase ÷ 1972 price	Percentage increase
1 lb sausages	21p	44p	23p	$\frac{23}{21}$ = 1.095	1.095 × 100% = 109.5%
4 oz coffee	29p	72p			
1 lb potatoes	2p	12p			
12 eggs	20p	48p			
2 lb sugar	10p	21p	11p	$\frac{11}{10}$ = 1.1	1.1 × 100% = 110%
1 pt milk	6p	10p			
1 lb carrots	3p	14p			

b Mrs Brown's shopping list is shown here.

What was the percentage increase in the cost of Mrs Brown's shopping?

1 lb sausages
8 oz coffee
5 lb potatoes
6 eggs
3 pts milk
1 lb carrots

Wider skills practice

1 Find the error and the percentage error in each of these measurements.

   a measurement = 4.6 cm, actual length = 4.5 cm

   b measurement = 4.5 cm actual length = 4.6 cm

   c measurement = 360 g, actual mass = 350 g

   d measurement = 290 g, actual mass = 280 g

   e measurement = 580 ml, actual volume = 640 ml

Applying skills

1 This information is taken from government statistics on transport and travel since 1961.

Transport and travel	1961	1971	1981	1991	2001	2011
Road vehicles (millions)						
Licensed road vehicles	9.0	14.0	19.3	24.5	28.9	34.5
Motor vehicles registered for the first time	1.3	1.7	2.0	1.9	2.9	2.4
Length of network (thousand km)						
All public roads	314.0	325.0	342.0	360.0	392.0	393.0
Motorways	0.2	1.3	2.6	3.1	3.5	3.6

Give your answers to the following questions to 1 decimal place.

   a How many more licensed vehicles were on the road in 2001 compared to 1961?

   b Calculate this increase as a percentage of the number of vehicles in 1961.

   c Which 10-year period had the greatest percentage increase in the number of road vehicles?

   d Calculate the percentage increase in the length of motorways over each 10-year period.

Reviewing skills

1 A shop bought DVD players at £88 each and sold them for £123.20.
   What was the percentage profit?

2 Tom buys a new car for £8270 and sells it three years later for £5789.
   What is his percentage loss?

3 **a** A house was bought for £160 000 and sold for £210 000. Calculate the percentage profit.

   b A flat was bought for £90 000 and sold for £83 000. Calculate the percentage loss.

Building skills

Example outside the Maths classroom

Reclaiming VAT

Toolbox

Sometimes you know the value of something and the percentage change but not the original value. Finding the original value involves reverse percentages, as in this example.

A coat costs £45 in a sale. It has been reduced by 10%. What was its original cost?

This percentage bar shows what you know and what you need to find out.

0		90%	100%
0		£45	?

0%	10%		90%	100%
0	£5		£45	£50

The original cost was £50.

Alternatively,

90% is £45

1% is $\frac{45}{90} = 0.5$

100% is 0.5×100
$= £50$

Example – When an amount is reduced

1 The sale price of a pair of designer sunglasses is £96.
  a The reduction in the sale is 20%. What percentage of the original price is the sale price?
  b Find the original price.

Solution

1 a The sale price is 80% of the original price.
  b 80% is £96

 100% − 20% = 80%

1% is $\frac{96}{80} = £1.20$

100% is 1.2×100
$= £120$

So the original price was £120.

Example – When an amount is increased

2 A shop sells boots for £56 a pair. The shop makes a profit of 40%.
What price did the shop pay for the boots?

Solution

2 Cost price = 100%; profit = 40% so the selling price = 140%.
140% is £56

1% is $\dfrac{56}{140}$ = £0.40

100% is 0.4 × 100

= £40

so the shop paid £40 for the boots.

Remember:

✦ The original amount is always taken to represent 100%.

Skills practice A

1 Sale prices in a department store are 80% of the original price.
Find 1% and then 100% (the original price) for each of these items in the sale.

  a towels £12   **b** table lamp £35   **c** table and chairs £90   **d** cutlery set £450

2 House prices in London have risen by 3% in the last month.

  a Taking last month's value as 100%, what percentage is the current value?

  b A house in London is sold for £785 000.
What percentage of the value of the house one month ago is this?

  c What is 1% of the value of the house one month ago?

  d What was the value of the house one month ago?
(Round your answers to the nearest pound.)

3 Sale prices in a shoe shop are 70% of the original price.
Find 1% and then 100% (the original price) for each of these items.

  a trainers £35   **b** boots £42   **c** shoes £45.50

4 These prices include VAT at 20%, so they are 120 % of the original prices.
For each item, find 1% and then 100% (the original price).

  a £72   **b** £240   **c** £2160   **d** £64.80

5 VAT (value added tax) is 20%. It is added to the original price (100%) of an item.
The prices of the items shown include VAT. For each of these items, find

   a 1%

   b 100% (the original price).

   c the amount of the VAT.

     i £300   **ii** £168   **iii** £204

  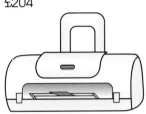

Skills practice B

1 A telephone bill is £180. This includes VAT at 20%. Find
the cost before VAT.

2 These items are reduced in a sale. Find their original prices.

   a a chess set selling at £19.80 after a 20% reduction in price

   b a quartz watch selling at £11.05 after a 15% reduction

   c a mobile phone selling at £52.50 after a 25% reduction

   d a CD selling at £11.90 after a 15% reduction

3 **a** Goalkeepers' gloves are sold at £34.50 per pair. The shop makes a profit of 15%.
What did the gloves cost the shop?

   b A silver ring is sold for £11.70. The retailer makes a loss of 35%. What was the cost price?

   c A guitar is sold for £325. The music shop makes a profit of 30%. Find the cost price.

   d A bicycle is sold for £728. The sports shop makes a profit of 25%. What was the cost price?

4 Ranulf pays tax at 23%. Find how much money he earns when the amount left after tax is

   a £18 480   **b** £64 80   **c** £84.

5 Juanita stays at three different hotels on Friday, Saturday and Sunday.
Her hotel bills are

   a Friday £79.20   **b** Saturday £64.80   **c** Sunday £84.

All the bills include VAT at 20%. Find the cost at each hotel before VAT is added.

6 House prices in the Midlands have risen by 22% in the last year.
A house in the Midlands is sold for £97 500. What was the house worth a year ago?

7 A shop sells trainers for £56 a pair and make a 40% profit. What was the cost price?

0 Peter bought a suit for £60 after a 20% reduction. What was the original price?

9 Geoff bought a video player for £180 including 20% VAT.
What was the cost before VAT was added?

10 These prices include VAT at 20%. Find the pre-VAT price. (Give your answer to the nearest penny.)

    a printer cartridge £22.50   **b** telephone bill £103.20

    c burger and chips £9.12   **d** polo-neck sweater £43.20

11 A market stallholder sells fruit and vegetables at a profit of 42%.

Find the price the stallholder paid for these items. (Round your answers to the nearest penny.)

    a cauliflowers sold for 45p each

    b apples sold for £1.20 per kg

    c new potatoes sold for £2.50 per bag

    d bananas sold for £1.60 per kg

    e mushrooms sold for £8 per kg

12 Carla opened a savings account.

One year later, with interest at 5%, she had £2100 in her account. How much did she invest initially?

Wider skills practice

1 In 2012 the population of a country is 36 million.

The population is decreasing at an annual rate of 2.5%.

Write your answer to these questions to the nearest thousand.

    a What was the population

        i in 2011

        ii in 2010?

    b What will the population be in 2015?

    c When will the population fall below 30 million?

2 The price of a CD player in November was £400. On 1 December the price was increased by 15%. In the January sales the price of the CD player was reduced by 15%. The sale price was not £400. Why not?

Applying skills

1 The VAT rate is 20%.

    a Find a rule for working out the VAT on a cost that includes VAT.

    b Check your ruling on an item costing £150 before VAT:

        i What is the VAT to be added?

        ii What is the cost including VAT?

        iii Now apply your rule from part **a**.

Reasoning

Reasoning

Problem solving

2 When a business or self-employed person earns more than a threshold amount (£77 000 per year in 2013), they have to register for VAT, which means:

i They have to charge VAT on their bills

ii They can claim back any VAT they pay when they buy anything for the business.

The second point is important, as it is money the business can get back from the taxman. They have to do the calculations first though and work out how much they can claim. Many invoices just give the total, you have to calculate backwards to the VAT (20%).

a Your friend Will is running his own business, but does not understand this very well. How would you explain to him how to calculate how much VAT he could claim back?

You might want to make use of the diagram below to help explain. Remember – you are the expert – make the explanation very clear **in writing** so Will has something he can refer to in the future.

For a bill of £24 that includes VAT:

Bill to company = 120%
Bill to company = £24

Cost of product = 100%   VAT = 20%
Cost of product = £20   VAT = £4

b Not so long ago, VAT was charged at 17.5%. How would Will have to calculate what to claim back if this happened again?

What about if VAT goes up to 22.5%?

c Sally has her own landscape gardening business. She is earning about £35000 each year and is wondering whether to register for VAT. She does not **have** to as she is earning way under the government threshold.

She asks you whether it would pay her to register anyway and claim back the VAT on the things she has to buy. If she registers though, she will have to charge her customers VAT. Would you advise her to register or not? What sort of information might you need to ask her to help make the decision?

Reviewing skills

1 These items are marked with the sale prices.

SALE 20% off

A

€40

B

€65

C

€32

a What percentage of the original prices are the sale prices?

b For each of the sale items find

i 1% of the original price

ii the original price.

2 Find the original price of these items.

a designer label jeans selling at £51.20 after a 20% reduction

b designer label shirt selling at £31.50 after a 30% reduction

3 The prices below include VAT at 20%.

Find the price of each of these items before VAT was added.

a video recorder £336   **b** DVD £19.20   **c** computer printer £132   **d** CD £13.92

Strand 6 • Ratio and proportion

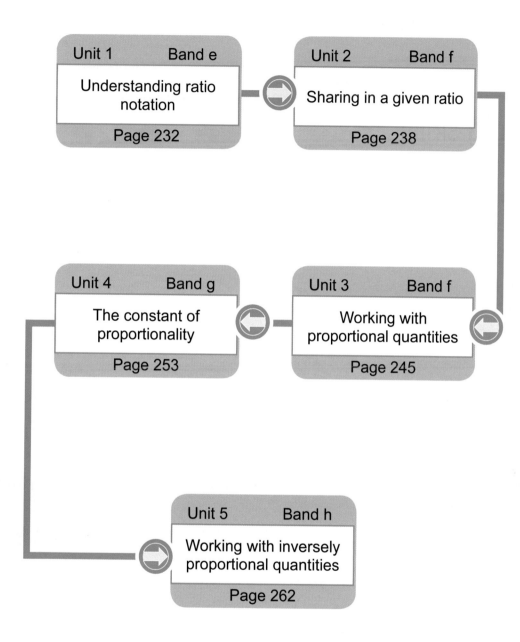

Unit 1	Band e
Understanding ratio notation	
Page 232	

Unit 2	Band f
Sharing in a given ratio	
Page 238	

Unit 4	Band g
The constant of proportionality	
Page 253	

Unit 3	Band f
Working with proportional quantities	
Page 245	

Unit 5	Band h
Working with inversely proportional quantities	
Page 262	

Building skills

Childcare ratios

Toolbox

There are various ways of writing ratios.

In the necklace you can see a repeating pattern.

black, red, brown, brown, brown / black, red, brown, brown, brown / ...

The ratio of black : red : brown is 1 : 1 : 3.

It is also possible to see a black : red : brown ratio of 2 : 2 : 6.

There are several other ways of seeing the ratio, such as 8 : 8 : 24.

The ratios   8 : 8 : 24

and   2 : 2 : 6

and   1 : 1 : 3

are all **equivalent ratios**.

1 : 1 : 3 is the **simplified ratio** of 8 : 8 : 24.

You may find it helpful to use a ratio table to solve problems.

Example – Working with ratios

In a class, there are 12 boys and 16 girls.

a What is the ratio of boys to girls in its simplest form?

b In another class, the ratio of boys to girls is the same. There are nine boys.
How many girls are there?

Solution

a

Number of boys	12	6	3
Number of girls	16	8	4

> You can divide both 12 and 16 by 2.
> You get 6 and 8.

> Then you can divide by 2 again to get 3 and 4.
> Nothing divides into both 3 and 4 so that is as far as you can go.

In its simplest form the ratio is 3 : 4.

b

Number of boys	3	9
Number of girls	4	12

> You are told there are 9 boys.
> You multiply 3 by 3 to get 9 so you multiply 4 by 3 to find the number of girls.

There are 12 girls.

Remember:

✦ Multiplying or dividing each part of a ratio by the same number does not change the ratio.
✦ Ratios are always given in terms of the smallest possible integers.

Skills practice A

1 Copy the three boxes below and write each of the ratios in one of the boxes.
All the ratios in each box must be equivalent.

1 : 2	2 : 1	1 : 3

2 : 4   5 : 15   8 : 4   6 : 12   8 : 16

18 : 9   4 : 12   10 : 5   2 : 6   9 : 27

2 Simplify these ratios.

a 8 : 2	**b** 5 : 10	**c** 10 : 5	**d** 12 : 20
e 35 : 25	**f** 16 : 24	**g** 50 : 45 : 30	**h** 24 : 16 : 32

3 a All the doors in a school are purple.
The purple paint is made by mixing red paint and blue paint in the ratio 1 : 2.
What does this ratio mean?

b Karl mixes 2 litres of red paint with 6 litres of blue paint.
Does he make the correct purple colour?
Explain your answer.

Reasoning

4 Pete and Jack are designing a new football shirt for their school.

The school colours are purple and yellow.

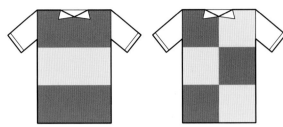

a Pete's design is one part yellow and two parts purple. Which design is Pete's?

b What is the ratio of colours for Jack's design?

Write the ratio in its simplest form.

c Look at these designs by other students.

Write down the ratios of yellow : purple.

Write each answer in the simplest form.

i 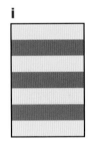 **ii**  **iii** 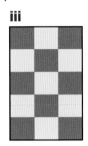 **iv**  **v** 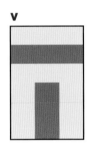 **vi**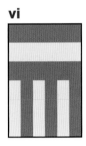

5 These shapes are in the ratio 1:3.

The copy is three times the size of the original.

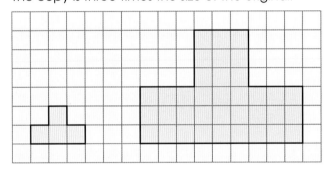

Write down the ratio of the lengths of each of these.

The original is on the left and the copy is on the right.

a 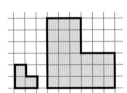 **b** **c**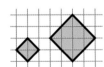

d 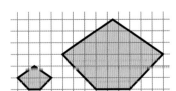 **e** 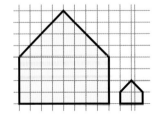 **f**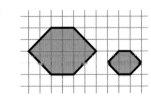

6 In a box there are 20 pink tissues and 30 white tissues.

    a Write down the ratio, pink tissues : white tissues.

    b Simplify the ratio.

7 Concrete is a mixture of cement, sand and gravel in the ratio 1 : 2 : 3.
How many bags of cement and gravel are needed when four bags of sand are used?

Skills practice B

1 Ben buys eight ice lollies for £3.20.

    a How much would four ice lollies cost?

    b How much would 12 ice lollies cost?

2 Sarah buys 12 USB drives for £9.60.

    a How much would three USB drives cost?

    b How much would 15 USB drives cost?

3 Sam buys 12 red roses for £6.00 and 12 tulips for £4.80.

    a How much do 18 red roses cost?

    b How much do 15 tulips cost?

    c How much do 9 red roses and 9 tulips cost together?

4 'Orange Fizz' is made by mixing orange juice and lemonade in the ratio 2 : 7.
Paul has 250 ml of orange juice.

    a How much lemonade does he need to use all the orange juice in making Orange Fizz?

    b How much Orange Fizz does he make?

5 'Berry Nice' is made by mixing cranberry juice and tonic water in the ratio 3 : 5.
Saskia uses 450 ml of tonic water.

    a How much cranberry juice does she need to use all the tonic water in making Berry Nice?

    b How much Berry Nice does Saskia make?

6 'Fruit Flip' is made by mixing fruit cordial, milk and yoghurt in the ratio 2 : 5 : 3.
Daniel uses 220 ml of fruit cordial.
How many millilitres of Fruit Flip does he make in total?

7 Sylvia has to travel 15 km to school.
She walks for 500 m then catches the bus for the rest of her journey.

    a Write down the ratio of the distance Sylvia walks to the distance she travels by bus.

    b Simplify your answer.

8 In 2000, Harry was ten and Leo, his brother, was six.

    a Find and simplify the ratio of their ages.

    b Find and simplify the ratio of their ages in 2010.

    c In what year will their ages be in the ratio 6 : 5?

    d Will their ages ever be in the ratio 1 : 1?
       Explain your answer.

Reasoning

Wider skills practice

1 Rewrite these ratios in correct ratio form (without units). Give then in their simplest form.
You will need to write them in the same units first.

    a £1 : 50p
    b 10 km : 600 m
    c 8 hours : 1 day

    d 2 cm : 5 mm
    e 3 minutes : 80 seconds
    f 500 ml : 1 litre

    g 2 days : 4 hours
    h one week : 4 hours
    i 400 kg : 1 tonne

    j 2 hours : 15 minutes
    k 18 mm : 2.4 cm : 0.12 m
    l 35 seconds : 2 minutes : 20 seconds

2 Write each ot these ratios in its simplest form.

    a $\dfrac{3}{4}$: 90%
    b $\dfrac{1}{2}$: $\dfrac{2}{3}$
    c $\dfrac{11}{20}$: 0.8
    d $\dfrac{3}{10}$: $\dfrac{1}{3}$

Reasoning

3 Ninety girls are asked what their favourite sport is.
The answers are shown in the pie chart.

    a Write down the ratio of the angles, hockey : tennis : netball.

    b Simplify this ratio.

    c How many girls like each sport best?

    d Check that your answer to part c makes a total of 90.

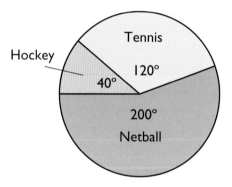

Applying skills

1 On a map the scale is 1 : 200 000.

    a What distance is shown by 1 cm on the map?
       Give your answer in metres.

    b The distance from Avonford to Bridleton is 4.5 cm on the map.
       How far is this in real life?

Problem solving

2 **a** It takes 1 hour to tumble dry a pair of socks.

       Two students are discussing how long it would take to tumble
       dry three pairs of socks.

       Joel says it would take 3 hours.

       Kamran says it's a trick and it would take 1 hour.

       Who is right?

    b Can you think of some other situations that are similar to this?

Reviewing skills

1 A shop sells boxes of plain and milk chocolates.
   One box contains three plain chocolates and nine milk chocolates.
   a Write down the ratio, plain chocolates : milk chocolates.
   b Simplify your answer.
   All the other boxes have the same ratio of plain chocolates : milk chocolates.
   c A box contains 27 milk chocolates.
      How many plain chocolates does it have?
   d Another box contains 12 plain chocolates.
      How many milk chocolates does it have?

2 In each part, one ratio is different from the other two.
   Find the odd one out.
   a 2:4   4:6   5:10
   b 1:2   7:14   5:12
   c 1:3   3:9   2:4
   d 1:7   2:12   3:18

3 Write each of these ratios in its simplest terms.
   a 6:9:15:12
   b 5 days : 5 weeks
   c 1000:200

Building skills

Example outside the Maths classroom

Mixing concrete

Toolbox

In sharing problems, start by finding the total number of "parts". Then decide how the parts are allocated.

You can use a rectangular bar as in this example.

Kate and Pam share the cost of their £8.40 pizza in the ratio 3:4. How much does each pay?

The ratio is 3:4

3 + 4 = 7 so there are 7 parts.

Draw a bar with 7 equal parts.

K	K	K	P	P	P	P
£1.20	£1.20	£1.20	£1.20	£1.20	£1.20	£1.20

Kate has 3 shares and Pam has 4.

Divide £8.40 into 7 shares £8.40 ÷ 7 = £1.20

So Kate's share is 3 × £1.20 = £3.60

Pam's share is 4 × £1.20 = £4.80

Alternatively, you can use proportions.

These fractions are called proportional

Kate pays $\frac{3}{7}$ of £8.40 = £3.60

Pam pays $\frac{4}{7}$ of £8.40 = £4.80

$\frac{1}{7}$ of £8.40 is £1.20

Example – Sharing in a given ratio

Nigel and Robert go to a car boot sale.

They have a lucky find and buy a box of old Star Wars figures for £10.

Nigel pays £4 and Robert pays £6.

There are 40 figures in the box.

a Do you agree with Robert? Why?

b The ratio of their money is 2 : 3.

They share the figures in this ratio.

Find how many each of them gets

Using **i** proportions **ii** a rectangular bar.

Nigel

That's 20 each.

No, that's not fair.

Robert

Solution

a Yes. Robert paid more than Nigel so it seems right that Robert should get more of the figures than Nigel.

b The ratio is 2:3

$2 + 3 = 5$ so there are 5 parts

i Nigel gets $\frac{2}{5}$ of 40 = 16 figures

Robert gets $\frac{3}{5}$ of 40 = 24 figures

$\frac{1}{5}$ of £40 is £8

N	N	R	R	R	
2	2	2	2	2	10
8	8	8	8	8	40

Nigel:
$8 + 8 = 16$

Robert:
$8 + 8 + 8 = 8 \times 3 = 24$

There are two parts for Nigel and three parts for Robert so there are five parts altogether.

This row shows how the £10 they paid in total was shared between them.
Nigel paid £4 and Robert paid £6.

There are 40 figures to share.
$10 \times 4 = 40$ so multiply each number of in the row above by 4.

Nigel gets 16 figures.
Robert gets 24 figures.

 Remember:

✦ The order of the numbers in the ratio is important.

Skills practice A

1 In a football season Avonford Town take 48 penalties.
The ratio of penalties saved to penalties scored is 1:5.

  a Fill in the numbers in a copy of this rectangular bar.

Saved	Scored	Scored	Scored	Scored	Scored

  b How many penalties are saved?

  c How many are scored?

2 A fancy dress costume has a mouse's head.
The length from the chin to the tip of the ears is 28 cm.
The ratio of the length of the ears to the length of the face is 1:3.

  a Copy and fill in the numbers in this rectangular bar.

Ears	Face	Face	Face

  b What is the length of the ears?

  c What is the length of the face?

3 A different fancy dress costume has a mask for a mouse's head which is 24 cm wide.
The ratio of the width of one ear to the width of the face to the width of the other ear is 1:2:1.

  a Copy and fill in the numbers in this rectangular bar.

Ear	Face	Face	Ear

  b How wide is each ear?

  c How wide is the face?

4 In a netball match the ratio of goals scored to goals missed is 3:1.
60 shots are attempted altogether.

  a Draw a bar to represent the ratio.

  b How many goals are scored?

5 Share these in the ratio 1:2.

  a 15   **b** 9   **c** 24

6 Share these in the ratio 3:1.

  a 12   **b** 40   **c** 28

7 Share 30 in the ratio

  a 1:2   **b** 1:4

  c 2:1   **d** 2:3

8 **a** Divide 26 in the ratio 4:9.

  b Divide 72 in the ratio 1:2:3.

Skills practice B

Reasoning

1 Humza and Lucy buy a chocolate bar between them.

I will split it in half.

That's not fair! I paid 45p and you only paid 15p.

Humza   Lucy

a Why doesn't Lucy think this is fair?

b They decide to split the chocolate in the ratio 1 : 3.
 Why do they decide on the ratio 1 : 3?

c There are 12 pieces of chocolate.
 How many do each of them get?

Reasoning

2 In shortbread biscuits the ratio of butter to sugar to flour is 2 : 1 : 4.
 The total mass of the ingredients is 350 g.

a How much of each ingredient is used?

b Ellie accidentally writes down the ratio as 1 : 2 : 4.
 What will her biscuits taste like?

3

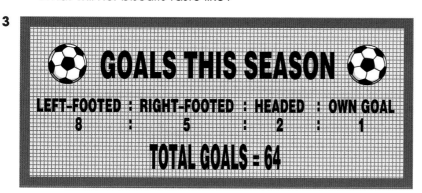

GOALS THIS SEASON

LEFT-FOOTED	:	RIGHT-FOOTED	:	HEADED	:	OWN GOAL
8	:	5	:	2	:	1

TOTAL GOALS = 64

How many of each type of goal were scored?

4 Mr Kelly invests £200 000 in a business.
 Mrs Lightwood invests £150 000 in the same business.
 In the first year they make £70 000 profit.
 How much of the profit should each of them get?

5 The total mass of a cake is 1050 g.
 It uses flour, rice flour, fat, sugar, currants and candied peel in the ratio 12 : 4 : 6 : 8 : 4 : 1.
 How much of each ingredient was used?

Problem solving

6 Martin says he could share this bar of chocolate in the ratio 1:3.

Sam says he could share it in the ratio 5:7.
How many different ratios could the bar be shared into?

7 The table below refers to goals scored in a local football league.
It shows the total number of goals scored by each team and the ratio of how the goals were scored.
Work out how many of each type were scored by each team.

	Left-footed		Right-footed		Headed		Total
Shellbury	4	:	7	:	4	:	45
Plystar	3	:	5	:	1	:	36
Swynton	2	:	6	:	1	:	27
Avonford	4	:	6	:	1	:	55

Reasoning

8 How many *different* ratios can the value 24 be shared in?

Reasoning

9 Cameron says that sharing in a ratio of 1:3 is like sharing into one-third and two-thirds.
Dale disagrees and says that it's like sharing into one-quarter and three-quarters.
Who is right?
How do you know?

Wider skills practice

1 In the diagram, the ratio of $a:b:c$ is 2:3:4.
Work out the size of each angle.

2 The sides of a pentagon are in the ratio 1:2:3:4:5.
The perimeter of the pentagon is 60 cm.
Work out the length of each side.

3 The angles of a quadrilateral in clockwise order are in the ratio 4:5:4:5.
a Work out the sizes of the angles.
The corresponding lengths of the sides of this quadrilateral are in the ratio 2:3:2:3.
b Make a possible sketch of the quadrilateral and state what type of quadrilateral it is.

Applying skills

1 Sally is six and Jane is eight.

For Christmas their dad, Richard, gives them £56 on the condition that they divide it between them in the ratio of their ages.

a How much does Jane receive?

Richard promises to give them £56 every time that the money will work out as a whole number of pounds each when they share it in the ratio of their ages.

b He tells them that he did this when Sally was one and Jane was three.

Check that this gave a whole number of pounds each.

c Richard says he has already done this at one other Christmas and that he expects to be able to do it twice more in the future.

Find out the ages of Sally and Jane at these three times.

2 Josef sets up a small business selling cupcakes.

Sheila and Matt are his business partners. They have decided it is fair that any profit they make should always be divided in the same ratio as the money they each invested in the business.

Josef invests £600 of his own money to buy equipment and ingredients.

Sheila invests £250 and Matt invests £150.

a In what ratio is the profit divided?

b In the first month, the business makes a profit of £500.

How much will each partner receive as their share?

c They all decide to leave their original investment in the business to keep it growing and also to put back £50 each of their profit from the first month into the business.

How much does each partner have invested in the business now?

d They make £500 profit in the second month.

How much profit will each partner get in the second month?

e i What percentage of the profit did Matt receive in the first month?

ii What about in the second month?

f What do you think of Matt's strategy of ploughing the same amount of profit back into the business as the others?

g Businesses have to decide all the time how much money to hand out to their shareholders and how much to invest in the business.

What might any business have to think about when it decides what to invest and what to spend?

Reviewing skills

1 Divide 100 in the ratio 2 : 3 : 5

2 Two neighbours club together to buy some lottery tickets.
Mrs Patel puts in £6 and Mrs Jones puts in £4.
One of their tickets wins £50 000.

   a In what ratio should they share the money?

   b How much do they each win?

3 7.2 kg of fertiliser is spread evenly over three small lawns.
The areas of the lawns are 7 m², 8 m² and 9 m².
How much fertiliser is used on each lawn?

Building skills

Example outside the Maths classroom

Supermarket prices

Toolbox

It is important to choose the most suitable method to solve a problem involving ratio and proportion.

- A ratio table can be very helpful for understanding a situation.
- The unitary method is good when the numbers are not quite straightforward and can be helpful for comparing quantities using unit costs.

Example – Comparing unit costs

Orange juice can be bought in different-sized cartons.

Holly needs 6 litres of orange juice for a party.

Which size cartons should Holly buy?

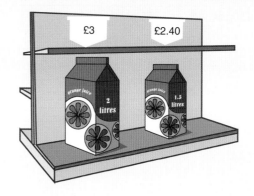

£3   £2.40

Solution

Smaller carton

1.5 litres cost £2.40

1 litre costs $\frac{1}{1.5} \times$ £2.40 = £1.60

Unit cost = £1.60

Larger carton

2 litres cost £3.00

1 litre costs $\frac{1}{2} \times$ £3.00 = £1.50

Unit cost = £1.50

The larger carton has a lower unit cost.

Holly should buy the larger carton.

Example – Using the unitary method

These ingredients for apple crumble make enough to serve two people.

> **Apple Crumble** (serves 2)
> 1 large cooking apple
> 25 g white sugar
> $\frac{1}{4}$ teaspoon cinnamon
> 90 g wholemeal flour
> 40 g butter
> 75 g brown sugar

Inga needs to make an apple crumble for five people.
How much of each ingredient should she use?

> In the unitary method you find for 1.

> Then you scale up by multiplying.

Solution

Ingredients	For 2	For 1 (÷2)	For 5 (×5)
Cooking apple	1	$\frac{1}{2}$	$2\frac{1}{2}$
White sugar	25 g	12.5 g	62.5 g
Cinnamon	$\frac{1}{4}$ tsp	$\frac{1}{8}$ tsp	$\frac{5}{8}$ tsp
Wholemeal flour	90 g	45 g	225 g
Butter	40 g	20 g	100 g
Brown sugar	75 g	37.5 g	187.5 g

> This column gives all the answers.

Example – Solving problems with a ratio table

40 blank CDs cost £20.

a Find the cost of 50 blank CDs.

b Find the cost of 24 blank CDs.

Solution

a

Number of CDs	40	20	10	50
Cost (£)	20	10	5	25

> 10 + 40 = 50

> 20 + 5 = 25

50 CDs cost £25.

b

Number of CDs	40	20	4	24
Cost (£)	20	10	2	12

> 20 + 4 = 24

> 10 + 2 = 12

24 CDs cost £12.

Remember:

✦ Ratio tables are a helpful way of organising your working.
✦ The unitary method helps you to work with more complicated numbers.

Skills practice A

1 A pack of three DVDs costs £9.00.
   a How much does one DVD cost?
   b How much do nine DVDs cost?

2 Six bottles of flavoured water cost £4.50.
   a How much does one bottle cost?
   b How much do ten bottles cost?

3 A car travels 60 km on 12 litres of petrol.
   a How far does it travel on 1 litre of petrol?
   b How far does it travel on 7 litres of petrol?

4 Karen uses a recipe for cream of mushroom soup which serves four people.
   Copy and complete the table to help Karen work out how much of each ingredient she will need for six people.

Ingredients	Quantity for 4 people	Quantity for 1 person	Quantity for 6 people
Mushrooms	240 g		
Stock	300 ml		
Small onions	1		
Plain flour	30 g		
Milk	400 ml		
Egg yolks	2		

5 Andy has a recipe for Bolognese sauce which serves eight people.
   Copy and complete this table to help him find the quantities needed for six people.

Ingredients	Quantity for 8 people	Quantity for 1 person	Quantity for 6 people
Shallots	12		
Margarine	40 g		
Minced beef	240 g		
Chopped tomatoes	480 g		
Tomato puree	32 ml		
Garlic cloves	4		

6 Dan is cooking Tuna and Cheddar Stuffed Peppers.

His recipe serves four people.

a For one person the quantity of breadcrumbs is 25 g.

What are the quantities of the other ingredients for one person?

b One day, Dan makes the meal for five people.

How much of each ingredient does he use?

c By accident, he uses 30 ml of pickled chillies in the recipe for five people.

Will the meal taste more or less spicy than usual?

4 red peppers
100 g bread crumbs
4 tomatoes
30 ml pickled chillies
50 g mild cheddar cheese
400 g tinned tuna

7 Louis is allowed to claim for use of his car for work.

One month he claims £68 for driving 170 miles for work.

a What is the charge per mile?

b Louis's boss wants his claim to be not more than £50 per month.

How many miles can Louis drive for work per month?

Skills practice B

1 Four nectarines cost £1.20.

Use **a** a ratio table

     b the unitary method to find the cost of **i** seven nectarines **ii** nine nectarines.

2 Three pens cost £1.20.

Use **a** a ratio table

     b the unitary method to find the cost of **i** two pens **ii** eleven pens.

3 Red roses are priced at £9.60 for 12.

Use **a** a ratio table

     b the unitary method to find the cost of **i** 3 roses **ii** 16 roses.

4 Three ice-lollies cost £2.40.

How much do 7 ice-lollies cost?

5 Five Mp3 downloads cost £25.50.

How much do 3 cost?

6 One day, Jacqueline gets paid £60 for doing five hours' work.

  a How much does she get paid per hour?

She always gets paid at the same rate.

Here is her time sheet for a week.

  b Work out how much she gets paid each day.

Day	Hours worked
Monday	6
Tuesday	8
Wednesday	0
Thursday	8
Friday	10

7 Jo is making a chocolate cake.

She wants to make it for 12 people.

Work out how much of each ingredient she needs using the information on the right.

1 egg for every three people.

100 g of flour for every egg.

Half as much sugar as flour.

10 g of butter for every person.

Half as much chocolate as butter.

Reasoning

8 Jam is sold in two sizes of jar.
Which size jar gives the better value for money?

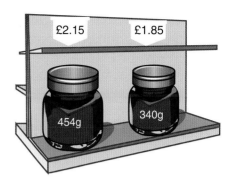

9 a What is the cost of 100 grams for each box of cornflakes?
b Which box is the better buy?

10 Jack is making ham sandwiches for a party.

 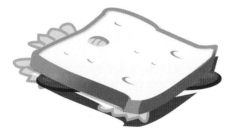

He butters a piece of bread and puts on one slice of ham and three slices of tomato.
He puts another piece of buttered bread on top.
Then he cuts it into four sandwiches.

Jack uses 12 slices of ham altogether.

a How many slices of bread does he use?
b How many slices of tomato does he use?
c How many ham sandwiches does he make?

Wider skills practice

1 Marc sees a flash of lightning and starts counting.
He counts 8 seconds before hearing the thunder.
The speed of sound is 1190 kilometres per second.
How far away was the lightning?

Reasoning

2 A standard size of photograph is 4 inches high and 6 inches wide.

Larger prints can be ordered but the ratio of the height to the width must remain the same otherwise the picture will look stretched.

Write down eight sizes of photo that would be appropriate.

Applying skills

1 When you go shopping, do you or your parents ever compare the price of different items?

Sometimes a special offer might not be so special!

Comparing packages of different shapes and sizes is very hard, but not if you can work out the price for the same amount of each.

a Which of these packets of chocolates offers the best value for money?

Work out the price for one chocolate for each of the packets.

| 89p | £1.99 | £2.45 |

Most items in supermarkets, for example cheese, are sold in packs with the weight or volume given.

It's not always easy to see if a deal, for example buy one get one half-price, really is worth having, but checking out the price for a gram (or a millilitre) of each (like with the chocolates) is the best way.

Many supermarkets put the price per gram or millilitre on the shelf edge to help you.

b Which is better value in each case?

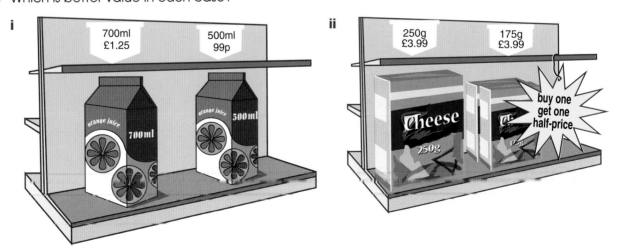

c Why might you decide to buy the more expensive option?

d What techniques do you think retailers use to make you spend more than you need to?

2 Jasmina has just got her first job after university.

She studied civil engineering and her new company has projects designing and building new roads all around the world.

She is keen to travel and see new places, but she has heard that some countries have very high income tax rates and she is worried that she might have to pay a lot of her money in tax.

She does some searching on the internet and finds out some information.

From: HR Department
To: Jasmina Pula

Dear Jasmina,
We are delighted to offer you the job of Graduate Engineer with us. We confirm that your starting salary will be £21 000 per year paid in the country where you are working. If you are posted overseas, please let us know your local bank details as soon as possible so we can organise to pay your salary into it.

In Australia, no tax is paid for earnings under A$18 000 per year.

For every Australian dollar you earn over A$18 000 you pay roughly 20 cents in tax.

You can earn 200 000 Indian rupees (INR) without paying any tax.

After that you have to pay 20% of any extra money you earn.

UK government website says no tax is paid for earnings under the UK Personal Allowance, but for every pound you earn above that you pay tax at 20%.

1.00 AUD	=	0.609 581 GBP
Australian dollar	↔	British pound
1.00 INR	=	0.011 144 7 GBP
Indian rupee	↔	British pound

U.K. allowance	2013 to 2014 tax year
Born after 5 April 1948 – Personal Allowance	£9440

a What advice would you give Jasmina about where she will pay least tax?

b What else might influence Jasmina's choice of where she would like to work?

Reviewing skills

1   Karen uses a recipe for Cream of
    Mushroom soup which serves four people.

    Copy and complete the table to help Karen
    work out how much of each ingredient she
    will need for six people.

Ingredients	For 4	For 1	For 6
Mushrooms	240 g		
Stock	300 ml		
Small onions	1		
Plain flour	30 g		
Milk	400 ml		
Egg yolks	2		

2   Jars of pickled gherkins are available in two sizes.

    A 420 g jar costs 85p.

    A 700 g jar costs £1.10.

    Which size jar is the better buy?

Building skills

Example outside the Maths classroom

Converting money

Toolbox

A **conversion graph** is a way of showing how one value is related to another.
It allows you to convert between two units easily.

Direct proportion means there is a connection between two **variables**: as one variable increases, the other increases at the same rate.

For example, if one variable is trebled, the other will also be trebled.

The sign $\propto$ means 'is proportional to' and can be used to help create a formula.

If $a \propto b$ then $a = kb$ where k is called the **constant of proportionality** so $k = a \div b$.

Example – Creating a formula

In physics, the current (I) in an electric circuit is directly proportional to the voltage (V) when the resistance (R) is constant.

In one circuit, when $I = 0.2$, $V = 10$.

a Write a formula connecting I and V.

b Find I when $V = 100$.

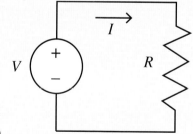

Solution

a $I \propto V$ so

$I = kV$ ⟵ **k is the constant of proportionality.**

When $I = 0.2$, $V = 10$

$0.2 = k \times 10$

$k = 0.2 \div 10$

$k = 0.02$

So the formula is

$I = 0.02V$

b When $V = 100$,

$I = 0.02V$

$I = 0.02 \times 100$

$I = 2$

Example – Drawing a conversion graph

One day, £6 is worth the same as €9.

a Draw a conversion graph between
pounds (£) and euros (€).

b An ice-cream costs £1.40.
How much is this in euros?

Solution

a You need two points to plot the graph. However it is good practice to use at
least one more point as a check.

Make a table.

£	6	0	3
£	9	0	4.5

This is the check point.

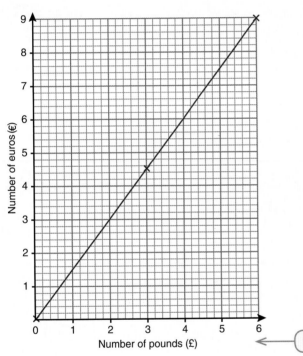

Number of euros (€)

Number of pounds (£)

Label the axes.

b Reading from the graph, £1.40 = €2.10.

Remember:

✦ A conversion graph will always go through (0, 0).

✦ You need two points to plot a conversion graph, but should use at least one more as a check.

✦ The sign ∝ means 'is proportional to'.

✦ Two variables a and b in direct proportion are connected by the formula $a = kb$ where k is the constant of proportionality.

Skills practice A

1 This conversion graph converts euros (€) to Japanese yen.

   a Convert these amounts to Japanese yen.

     i €1   **ii** €15

     iii €19

   b Convert these amounts to euros.

     i 300 yen   **ii** 150 yen

     iii 950 yen

   c Convert €30 to Japanese yen.

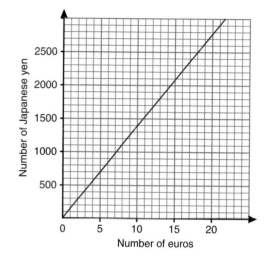

2 Jo is on holiday in France.

She takes this graph with her to help convert between British pounds (£) and euros (€).

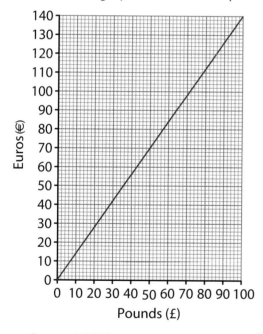

   a Convert £65 into euros.

   b Convert €105 into pounds.

   c Copy and complete this conversion table.

Number of pounds (£)	25	50	70			
Number of euros (€)				21	77	126

   d Explain how you can use the graph to convert £250 into euros.

3 A quantity p is directly proportional to another quantity q. When q is 7, p is 21.

   a Find the value of p when q is 42.

   b find the value of p when q is 10.

   c Write an equation connecting p and q.

4 Two quantities x and y are connected by the equation $y = kx$.

   When $x = 5$, $y = 10$

   a Find the value of k.

   b Find the value of x when $y = 8$.

   c Draw a graph of y against x.

5

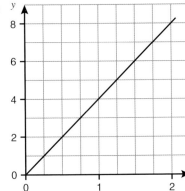

This graph shows the relationship between x and y.

   a Complete this statement: y is directly ….. to x.

   b Find the constant of proportionality.

   c What is the value of y when $x = 1.5$?

6 David does an experiment to see how electrical resistance varies with the length of wire used.

   Here are his results.

Length of wire (cm)	10	20	30	40	50
Resistance (ohms)	2	4	6	8	10

   a Draw a pair of axes.

      Use values from 0 to 50 centimetres on the horizontal axis and from 0 to 10 ohms on the vertical axis.

      Plot the points and join them with a straight line.

   b The resistance is 7.4 ohms.

      What is the length of the wire?

   c David says, 'If you double the length of the wire, it doubles the resistance.' Is he right?

7 r is proportional to s.

   a Write this in symbols.

   b When $s = 5$, $r = 40$.

      Find the constant of proportionality.

   c Write down a formula connecting r and s.

   d **i** Find r when $s = 10$.

      ii Find s when $r = 7$.

Problem solving

8 You are told that $a \propto b$ and also that $b \propto c$.

  a When $c = 8$, $b = 5$

    When $b = 10$, $a = 0.2$

    What are the constants of proportionality for a to b and for b to c?

  b Show that a is proportional to c.

    How is the constant of proportionality for a to c related to values you found in part **a**?

9 The table shows some values for two variables d and e.

  Is d directly proportional to e?

d	$\frac{1}{2}$	$\frac{1}{5}$	$\frac{1}{10}$
e	$\frac{5}{16}$	$\frac{1}{8}$	$\frac{5}{80}$

Reasoning

10 You are told that $a \propto b$ with a constant of proportionality k.

  Is $b \propto a$ and, if so, what is the constant of proportionality?

  Hint: You could use some of the examples from previous questions and see if they work the other way round.

Skills practice B

Reasoning

1 You are going on holiday to Mars.

  Dave the spaceman and his dog are going as well.

  The gravitational pull on Mars is weaker than on Earth.

  This means that things weigh less on Mars.

  Dave weighs 1000 N on Earth.

  He only weighs 400 N on Mars.

  a Use this information to draw a conversion graph between weight on Earth and weight on Mars.

  b Dave's dog Pluto weighs 250 N on Earth.

    Use your graph to find how much Pluto weighs on Mars.

  c Pzork the Martian weighs 360 N on Mars.

    Use your graph to find how much Pzork weighs on Earth.

  d A Mars buggy weighs about 6000 N on Mars.

    Explain how to work out how much it weighs on Earth.

2 When reading from a graph, it can be difficult to be accurate.

  a Jordan reads from a graph that 30 minutes of tennis burns 240 calories.

    Calculate how many calories Jordan would burn doing 1 hour of tennis every day for a week.

  b Andrew thinks that Jordan has read the graph incorrectly and that 30 minutes of tennis burns 220 calories.

    Using Andrew's reading, how many calories would Jordan burn doing 1 hour of tennis every day for a week?

  c What is the difference in the results based on the two different readings of the graph?

3 Tom sells packs of playing cards on the internet.

For each pack of cards he sells, he makes 80p profit.

a Write a formula connecting the profit he makes (P) and the number of packs of cards he sells (d).

b One month, Tom sells 13 packs of cards.

How much profit does he make?

c Tom wants to buy a magic trick that costs £30.

How many packs of cards does he need to sell to have enough to buy the trick?

4 On a particular day £1 will buy

Canadian $2.09

2.3 Swiss francs

€1.6

US$1.37

a Find the cost in pounds (£) of

i a bicycle costing €150

ii a pair of jeans costing US$28

iii an ice cream costing 2 Swiss francs

iv a cable car ride costing Canadian $29.

b Jake has £190.

Approximately how many euros can he buy?

5 A recycling company knows that the mass of newspaper can be estimated when it is stacked up.

A 30 cm stack of newspaper weighs approximately 15 kg.

Melody says that you can estimate the mass of newspaper in kilograms by finding half of the height of the stack of newspaper in centimetres.

a Copy and complete this word formula.

Mass in kilograms = ... × ....

b Write a formula connecting the mass, M, and the height, H, of stacks of newspapers.

c Use your formula to estimate the mass of a stack of newspapers 70 cm high.

6 When newspaper is compacted using a machine, the mass in kilograms can be estimated based on the volume in cubic metres (m^3).

5 m^3 of compacted paper weighs 2400 kg.

a Calculate the mass of 1 m^3 of compacted paper.

b Write a formula connecting the mass, M, and the volume, V.

c A recycling bank can hold 6.5 m^3 of compacted paper.

How much will this paper weigh?

7 A pedometer is an instrument that counts how many steps you take.

Sometimes, pedometers are not very accurate, especially if you are doing exercises.

This chart shows the equivalent number of steps you would make when taking part in three activities.

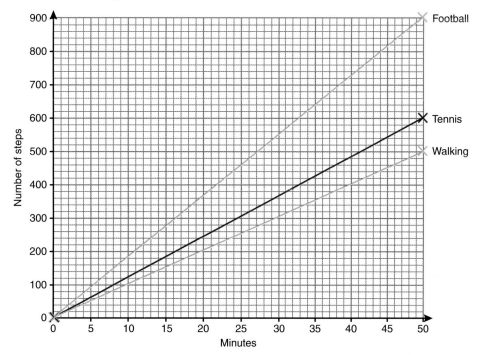

a Oliver takes part in a tennis match which lasts 40 minutes.
How many steps is that equivalent to?

b Naomi does 30 minutes each of walking, tennis and football.
How many steps is that equivalent to in total?

c Priya needs an extra 1500 steps to achieve her weekly target.
How many minutes of football should she play?

Wider skills practice

1 The circumference of a circle is directly proportional to the diameter of the circle.
What is the constant of proportionality?

2 A ship travels s kilometres in t hours. s is directly proportional to t with equation $s = kt$
When $t = 5, s = 120$.

a Find the value of s when
   i $t = 10$ **ii** $t = 1$

b Find the constant of proportionality, k.

c What does the constant of proportionality tell you?

Applying skills

1 Clear plastic bottles can be recycled.

The value of the bottles is in direct proportion to the mass of bottles.

1 tonne of clear plastic has a value of £260.

A 1-litre clear plastic bottle has a mass of 40 g.

How many of these bottles do I need to have a value of £500?

2 Abigail is at a garden centre and sees this giant spade.

She thinks it belongs to a giant and wonders how tall the giant would be.

Estimate the height of the giant that would use this spade.

3 A water tank is in the shape of a cuboid with a base measuring 50 cm by 40 cm.

The depth of water in the tank is in direct proportion to the volume of the water.

a The depth of water in the tank is 3 cm.

What is the volume?

b Write a formula connecting the volume (V) to the depth of the water (d).

c Charlotte doesn't know exactly how tall the tank is, but it is shorter than she is.

She wants to know if it is likely to hold the 400 litres of water she needs to water her garden fully.

Is the tank likely to be able to hold 400 litres of water?

Hint: 1 litre = 1000 cm³

Reviewing skills

1 The exchange rate from US dollars to Indian rupees is $1 = 62.5 rupees.

a Write a formula connecting the number of dollars (D) and the number of rupees (R).

b Find the cost in $ of a taxi ride costing 600 rupees.

2 The table gives corresponding values for the variables g and h.

g	5	7	9	13
h	70	98	126	182

It is thought that g and h are directly proportional.

Do the values in the table support this?

3 The area of wall to be painted and the number of litres of paint needed are directly proportional.

   a 6 litres of paint will cover an area of $30\,m^2$.

     Write a formula connecting the area of wall (A) and the number of litres of paint needed (L).

   b Michaela wants to paint walls with a total area of $80\,m^2$.

     How many litres of paint will she need?

Building skills

Example outside the Maths classroom

Road works

Toolbox

Inverse proportion means there is a connection between two **variables**: as one variable **increases**, the other **decreases** by the same proportion.

For example, if one variable is doubled, the other will be halved.

The sign $\propto$ means 'is proportional to'. Inverse proportion is represented using the reciprocal. Where a and b are inversely proportional, then ab is a constant.

$a \propto \dfrac{1}{b}$ means a is inversely proportional to b.

So $ab = k$ where k is a constant.

Example – Solving problems involving inverse proportion

A company is testing four electric cars on a journey from Edinburgh to London.
All the cars travel the same route.

a One car travels for 6 hours at an average speed of 60 miles per hour.
How long is the route from Edinburgh to London?

b The second car travels at an average speed of 30 miles per hour.
How long does the journey take this car?

A formula connecting the speed (s) and the time (t) taken for this journey is

$$st = 360$$

c The third car took 9 hours to complete the journey.
Use the formula to find its average speed.

d The fourth car had an average speed of 50 miles per hour.
Use the formula to find the time taken.

Solution

a In 1 hour the car travels 60 miles so, in 6 hours the car travels 60 × 6 = 360 miles.
The route from Edinburgh to London is 360 miles.

b At 30 mph the journey takes 360 ÷ 30 = 12 hours.
Notice that this is a case of inverse proportion.
Travelling at half the speed takes twice as long. ⟵ $\boxed{\textbf{2 × 6 hours = 12 hours}}$

c $st = 360$
$s \times 9 = 360$ ⟵ $\boxed{\textbf{The car takes 9 hours.}}$

$s = 360 \div 9$ ⟵ $\boxed{\textbf{Dividing both sides by 9.}}$
$s = 40$

The third car travelled at an average speed of 40 miles per hour.

d $st = 360$
$50 \times t = 360$ ⟵ $\boxed{\textbf{Average speed was 50 mph.}}$

$t = 360 \div 50$ ⟵ $\boxed{\textbf{Dividing both sides by 50.}}$
$t = 7.2$

0.2 hours = 0.2 × 60 = 12 minutes
The fourth car takes 7 hours 12 minutes to complete the journey.

Example – Looking for inversely proportional relationships

The table shows values for two variables, c and d.

c	8	12	24
d	30	20	10

Martin thinks that $c \propto \dfrac{1}{d}$.

Is Martin correct?
Explain how you know.

Solution

If c and d are inversely proportional, then $cd = k$. ⟵ $\boxed{\textbf{This is the same as } c = k \times \dfrac{1}{d} \textbf{ or } d = k \times \dfrac{1}{c}}$
 8 × 30 = 240   12 × 20 = 240   24 × 10 = 240

In each case the answer is the same, 240, so c and d are indeed inversely proportional.

Remember:

✦ If two variables are inversely proportional, it means that as one variable is increased, the other is decreased at the same rate.

✦ When two variables, x and y are inversely proportional, $xy = k$ where k is a constant.

Skills practice A

Reasoning

1 Sarah and Claire are planning a party but they are not sure how many people will turn up.

They make 60 cupcakes.

   a There are 20 people altogether at the party.

     How many cupcakes do they get each?

   b Claire thinks that if there had been *more* people, they would have had *more* cakes each.

     Give an example to show that Claire is wrong.

   c How many people could be at the party so that the cakes could be shared equally without having to cut the cakes?

     List all the possible answers.

2 Five of Sam's colleagues buy him a leaving gift that will cost them £6 each.

In the end, only four of his colleagues contribute towards the gift.

   a What is the value of the leaving gift?

   b How much do the four colleagues each need to pay?

3 Here is a table showing values for two variables, a and b.
Show that a and b are inversely proportional.

a	100	200	70
b	14	7	20

4 $c \propto \dfrac{1}{d}$. Copy and complete this table of values.

c	16	8		32
d	2		8	

Reasoning

5 j Is Inversely proportional to k.

Which of these could be correct formulae connecting j and k?

$$jk = 500 \qquad j = \frac{500}{k} \qquad j = 500k \qquad \frac{j}{k} = 500$$

6 Copy and complete this table of values for the variables m and k, given that m is inversely proportional to k.

m		3	22	
k	11		6	66

7 s and b are inversely proportional.
Copy and complete the table.

s	0.6	0.3		24
b	8		12	

Skills practice B

1 A bridge needs to be painted. It would take eight painters 15 days.

   a If six painters are employed instead of eight, how long will it take them?

   b How long will it take if 12 painters are employed?

   c How long would it take one painter working alone?

   d How many painters would be needed to complete the work in just one day?

Reasoning

2 When a gas camping stove is used for 2 hours a day, the gas in the cylinder lasts for 70 days.

   a How many hours does the gas last in total?

   b How many days will the gas in the cylinder last if the stove is used for 3 hours a day?

   c The gas needs to last for at least two weeks.

     What is the maximum number of hours per day the stove can be used for?

3 Eight men can plaster a block of flats in six days.

   a How many men are needed to plaster the flats in four days?

   b How many days would it take one man to plaster the block of flats on his own?

Reasoning

4 A farmer has enough feed to keep 80 cows for five days.

   a How long would the same amount of feed last if the farmer had

     i 40 cows   **ii** 100 cows   **iii** 50 cows?

   b The farmer decides to retire from farming.

     He keeps one cow as a pet.

     He has enough feed left over to keep 60 cows for six days.

     How long will the feed last for his one pet cow?

   c Why might your answer to part **b** not be quite right?

5 A campsite has enough food to feed 120 scouts for 35 days.

   a How long will the food last if there are 15 fewer scouts?

   b How long will the food last if there are 20 extra scouts?

Reasoning

6 The frequency of a vibrating guitar string is inversely proportional to its length.

   a A guitar string 0.7 metres long vibrates at a frequency of 6 times each second.

     What frequency would a string 0.3 metres long vibrate at?

   b What length of string vibrates 7 times every two seconds?

7 In a factory, six pipes are used to fill a large tank with water.

The six pipes take 12 hours to fill the tank from when it is empty.

   a How long will the tank take to fill if only four pipes are used?

   b The factory's owner is considering buying two extra pipes.

     How much time would having two extra pipes save?

   c Write a formula connecting the time taken, t hours, and the number of pipes, n.

Wider skills practice

Problem solving

1 Investigate this claim.

The exterior angle of a regular polygon is inversely proportional to the number of sides.

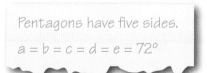

Pentagons have five sides.

$a = b = c = d = e = 72°$

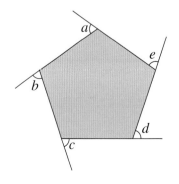

2 Investigate the shape of a graph where y is inversely proportional to x.

a Complete this table of values.

x	12	6	4			
y	1	2				

b Draw the graph using equal scales for both x and y.

c What are the values of y when

  i $x = 0.5$ **ii** $x = 0.1$?

d Describe the shape of the graph.

e Do all inverse proportion graphs look like this?

3 In the table, the variables d and e are inversely proportional.
Some values for d and e are given using algebraic expressions.

d	$2a$	$2a^2$	$6am$	
e	$6a$			$3a^3$

a What is $d \times e$?

b Copy and complete the table.

Applying skills

1 A farmer needs to build a rectangular fence around part of his field.
The length is l and the width is w metres.
The fenced-off section needs to have an area of 100 square metres.

a Make a table of some possible values for l and w.

b Add another row to your table, giving the length of fencing the farmer needs.

c What is the minimum length of fencing needed?

2 A pump can empty a swimming pool in six hours.
How long would it take to empty the pool using

a two pumps

b three pumps

c 12 pumps?

Reviewing skills

1 Use the values in the table to find out whether w and y are inversely proportional or not.
Explain how you know.

w	52.5	35	21	14
y	4	6	10	15

2 In an electrical circuit, for a fixed voltage, the current (I) is inversely proportional to the resistance (R).
When the current is 40 amps, the resistance is 280 ohms.

a Write a formula connecting I and R.

b Use your formula to calculate the resistance when the current is 60 amps.

3 It will take four workers five hours to repair a road.
The boss wants it finished in two hours or less.
How many workers are needed?

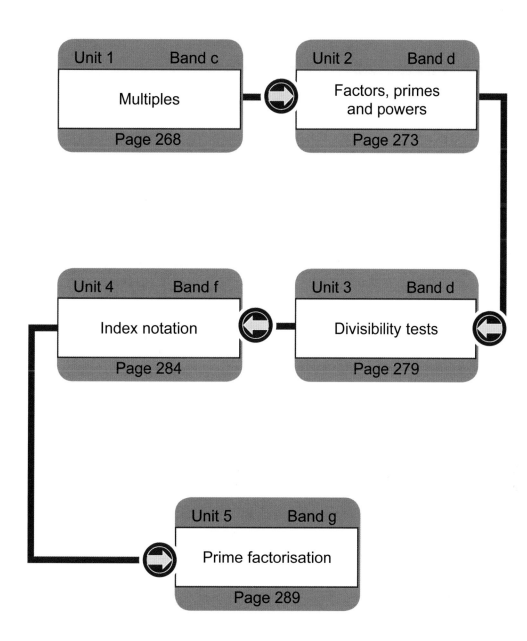

Unit 1   Band c

Multiples

Page 268

Unit 2   Band d

Factors, primes and powers

Page 273

Unit 4   Band f

Index notation

Page 284

Unit 3   Band d

Divisibility tests

Page 279

Unit 5   Band g

Prime factorisation

Page 289

Building skills

Example outside the Maths classroom

Selling eggs

Toolbox

To find the multiples of 5, start at 5 and count up in 5s, 5, 10, 15, 20 and so on.

To find the multiples of 8, start at 8 and count up in 8s, 8, 16, 24, 32 ....

So the multiples are the numbers you find in a times table.

Large numbers have multiples and not just those you know the tables for.

For example, the multiples of 53 are

$1 \times 53 = 53$

$2 \times 53 = 106$

$3 \times 53 = 159$

$4 \times 53 = 212$ and so on.

Multiples of 2 are called 'even' numbers.

Whole numbers that are not even are called 'odd'.

Example – Finding multiples of larger numbers

What is the sixth multiple of 23?

Solution

$6 \times 23 = 138$

So the sixth multiple of 23 is 138.

Remember:

✦ Multiples of a number are never smaller than the number.

✦ A times table square is helpful for finding multiples.

Skills practice A

1 a List the first ten multiples of 6.
 b List the first five multiples of 12.
 c What is the relationship between the lists in part **a** and part **c**?

2 Here are some multiples of a number:

   8   32   64

 What numbers could these all be multiples of?

3 What is
 a the fifth multiple of 3
 b the eighth multiple of 16
 c the third multiple of 72?

4 Write down
 a all the multiples of 8 between 11 and 30
 b all the multiples of 12 between 100 and 200
 c all the multiples of 7 between 15 and 50.

5 Copy and complete this multiplication grid.

×				
	15			
		2	11	
		20		40
	30		66	

6 Find the answers to the following sums.
 a The third multiple of 3 plus the second multiple of 20.
 b The seventh multiple of 2 multiplied by the second multiple of 7.
 c The fourth multiple of 4 minus the third multiple of 3.
 d The tenth multiple of 7 divided by the seventh multiple of 5.

7 a i List all the even numbers up to 20.
   ii List the first ten multiples of 2.
   iii What do you notice about parts **i** and **ii**?
 b i List all the odd numbers up to 20.
   ii List all the multiples of 3 up to 30.
   iii What do you notice about parts **i** and **ii**?

Skills practice B

1 Steve thinks of a number. It is in the 5 times table and the 9 times table.
Steve's number is less then 200.
What could Steve's number be? How many possible answers are there?

2 Copy all the numbers from the box below. Draw a circle around each multiple of 3. Draw a square around each multiple of 4. Draw a triangle around each multiple of 5. Some numbers will need two shapes.

6	18	45	4	9	27
20	15	35	8	24	10
12	28	25	21	16	

3 Jack makes buns. He sells them in packs of four.

a Copy and complete the table.

Number of packs	1	2	3	4	5	10
Number of buns	4					

b Describe any patterns that you can see in the numbers of buns.

c Shade in your answers on a copy of this grid.

1	2	3	4	5	6	7	8	9	10
11	12	13	14	15	16	17	18	19	20
21	22	23	24	25	26	27	28	29	30
31	32	33	34	35	36	37	38	39	40
41	42	43	44	45	46	47	48	49	50
51	52	53	54	55	56	57	58	59	60
61	62	63	64	65	66	67	68	69	70
71	72	73	74	75	76	77	78	79	80
81	82	83	84	85	86	87	88	89	90
91	92	93	94	95	96	97	98	99	100

d Shade in the numbers of buns for 6,7,8 and 9 packs onwards. What patterns are there?

4 Christina makes triangle shapes with matchsticks.

a Draw the next two diagrams.

b Copy and complete this table.

Height of Δ-shape	2	3	4	5	6
Number of matchsticks					

c Copy and complete this sentence.
These numbers are ____ of 3.

d The number of matchsticks increase by 3 each time. Why is this?

e Christina makes a Δ-shape of height 10. How many matchsticks does she use?

f Christina has 100 matchsticks. She makes the biggest Δ-shape possible.
What is the height of the Δ-shape?

Reasoning

5 John, Megan, Humza and Lucy have to get through the multiples maze.
They can only move up, down, left or right.

		John			Exit A			
	9	97	18	26	31	84	91	13
	17	29	27	33	9	77	47	59
Lucy	7	14	63	49	21	70	5	85	**Exit D**
	2	42	56	1	3	50	32	40	**Exit B**
Megan	4	36	23	19	15	55	20	71
	43	44	8	48	60	16	28	67
Exit C	6	24	12	30	35	25	45	10	**Humza**

- John follows multiples of 3.
- Megan follows multiples of 4.
- Humza follows multiples of 5.
- Lucy follows multiples of 7.

a Write down the numbers in the route each person follows.
   Where does each person come out?

b Which number do John, Megan and Humza all use?

c You can change this number to stop them getting through the maze.
   Give one of the numbers you can change it to.

6 A class is playing a game called 'Fizz Buzz'.
The children say the numbers in turn but, if their number is a multiple of 3 they say 'fizz' or if it's a multiple of 5 they say 'buzz'. If the number is a multiple of 3 and of 5 they say 'fizz buzz'.
The first part of the game goes like this:

'one'   'two'   'fizz'   'four'   'buzz'   'fizz'   'seven'   'eight'

The children reach 100 and stop.

a How many times did someone say 'fizz'?

b How many times did someone say 'buzz'?

c How many times did someone say 'fizz buzz'?

7 The children now play a game called 'Fizz Buzz Bang'.
The rules are the same as for 'Fizz Buzz' but now, if the number is a multiple of 7, they say 'bang'.
What's the first number that is reached where the child playing will say

a 'fizz bang'?

b 'buzz bang'?

c 'fizz buzz bang'?

Wider skills practice

1 Say whether each of these statements is true or false.

a All multiples of 2 are even numbers.

b All multiples of 3 are odd numbers.

c Apart from 1 and 12, the number 12 is a multiple of three other numbers

d Apart from 1 and 17, the number 17 is not a multiple of any number.

e If you add two odd numbers, your answer is a multiple of 2.

Applying skills

1 a Shade in the multiples of 4 on a copy of the 'spiral' grid below. What patterns do you notice?

73	74	75	76	77	78	79	80	81	82
72	43	44	45	46	47	48	49	50	83
71	42	21	22	23	24	25	26	51	84
70	41	20	7	8	9	10	27	52	85
69	40	19	6	1	2	11	28	53	86
68	39	18	5	4	3	12	29	54	87
67	38	17	16	15	14	13	30	55	88
66	37	36	35	34	33	32	31	56	89
65	64	63	62	61	60	59	58	57	90
100	99	98	97	96	95	94	93	92	91

b Try shading multiples of a different number. Use another copy of the grid.

2 Here is a list of the first six multiples of a number.
Each of the digits has been replaced by a coloured circle.
What digit does each colour represent?
Explain how you know,

Problem solving

Reviewing skills

1 a Write down all the multiples of 5 between 34 and 61.

   b Write down all the multiples of 4 between 27 and 45.

   c Write down all the multiples of 9 between 35 and 82.

2 Christina makes cross shapes with matchsticks.

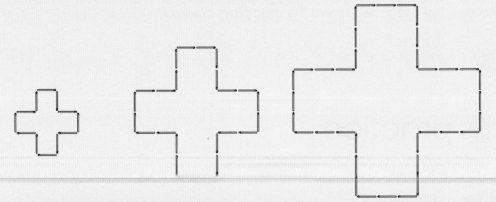

   a Copy these diagrams and draw the next two.

   b Write the number of matchsticks underneath each diagram.

   c What do you notice?

Building skills

Example outside the Maths classroom

Maths problems

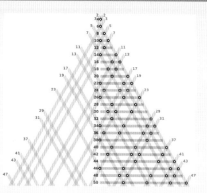

Toolbox

A factor of a number divides into it exactly.

A factor is also called a divisor of the number.

The factors of a number come in pairs that multiply together to make the given number.
Think of the number as a set of dots.

If the dots are arranged to make a rectangle, then you have found factors.

For example, 2 and 3 are factors of 6 because $2 \times 3 = 6$.

1 and 6 are also factors of 6 because $1 \times 6 = 6$.

Every number has at least one pair of factors. Every number of dots can be made into a rectangle that is one dot high and has all of the dots in a row. The only way that five dots can be made into a rectangle is

This means that the only factors of 5 are 1 and 5. Such numbers, with only two factors, are called **prime numbers**.

The prime numbers up to 50 are

  2, 3, 5, 7, 11, 13, 17, 19, 23, 29, 31, 37, 41, 43 and 47

1 is not a prime number because 1 has only one factor.

For some numbers, 4 for example, the dots can be arranged into a square.

These numbers are called **square numbers**. $2 \times 2 = 4$, which is written $2^2 = 4$.
2 squared is 4.

The square numbers up to 100 are

  1, 4, 9, 16, 25, 36, 49, 64, 81 and 100

$2^3 = 2 \times 2 \times 2 = 8$, 8 is called a cube number.

The **cube numbers** up to 100 are 1, 8, 27 and 64.

Example – Finding all the factors

Find all the factors of 30.

Solution

Starting at 1	$1 \times 30 = 30$
Try 2	$2 \times 15 = 30$
Try 3	$3 \times 10 = 30$
Try 4	Not a factor
Try 5	$5 \times 6 = 30$
Try 6	We already have 6 as a factor
	This means we have them all.
	The factors of 30 are 1, 2, 3, 5, 6, 10, 15, 30

Remember:

✦ Factors (or divisors) are numbers that divide into a given number exactly.
✦ Factors come in pairs.
✦ Prime numbers have exactly two factors.
✦ 1 is not a prime number.
✦ Factors are lower in value than the number itself.

Skills practice A

1 a Copy and complete these number sentences.

    i $1 \times \boxed{} = 24$

    ii $2 \times \boxed{} = 24$

    iii $3 \times \boxed{} = 24$

    iv $4 \times \boxed{} = 24$

  b List the factors of 24.

  c Explain why 24 is not a prime number.

2 List all the prime numbers from 1 to 20.

3 There are two prime numbers between 20 and 30. What are they?

4 Which factor pair is missing for the number 40?

    1×40 2×20 4×10

5 Which factor pair is wrong for the number 56?

    1×56 2×28 4×14 6×9 7×8

6 **a** Find all the factors of 35

   b Find all the factors of 36

   c Find all the factors of 37

   d **i** Which of the numbers 35, 36 and 37 is a prime number?

   ii How can you tell from its factors?

   e **i** Which of the numbers 35, 36 and 37 is a square number?

   ii How can you tell from its factors?

7 **a** Copy and complete this calculation in as many ways as you can.

   $\square \times \square = 50$

   b Is 50 a prime number?

8 Which of these numbers are prime?

   5   19   27   37   39   46

9 **a** Which of these numbers are square numbers?

   6   9   22   25   45   64   100

   b Which of these numbers is also a cube number? How do you know?

10 Copy and complete these.

   a $9 = \square^2$ **b** $25 = \square^2$ **c** $100 = \square^2$

11 Copy and complete this table.

Number	1	2	3	4	5	6	7	8	9	10
Number of factors	1	2	2							

   a List the numbers which have only two factors.

   b What type of numbers are these?

   c List the numbers with an odd number of factors.

   d What type of numbers are these?

Skills practice B

1 You know that 4 × 4 = 16 and so $4^2 = 16$.

   Another way to write this is $4 = \sqrt{16}$.

   Find

   a $\sqrt{81}$ **b** $\sqrt{64}$ **c** $\sqrt{1}$ **d** $\sqrt{400}$

2 You know that 3 × 3 × 3 = 27 and so $3^3 = 27$.

   So the cube root of 27 is 3.

   Find the cube roots of

   a 64   **b** 1000   **c** 1   **d** 125.

3 Find all the cube numbers between 1 and 300.

For questions 4–7, you will need some copies of this multiplication grid.

	1	2	3	4	5	6	7	8	9	10	11	12
1	1	2	3	4	5	6	7	8	9	10	11	12
2	2	4	6	8	10	12	14	16	18	20	22	24
3	3	6	9	12	15	18	21	24	27	30	33	36
4	4	8	12	16	20	24	28	32	36	40	44	48
5	5	10	15	20	25	30	35	40	45	50	55	60
6	6	12	18	24	30	36	42	48	54	60	66	72
7	7	14	21	28	35	42	49	56	63	70	77	84
8	8	16	24	32	40	48	56	64	72	80	88	96
9	9	18	27	36	45	54	63	72	81	90	99	108
10	10	20	30	40	50	60	70	80	90	100	110	120
11	11	22	33	44	55	66	77	88	99	110	121	132
12	12	24	36	48	60	72	84	96	108	120	132	144

4 a 48 appears in the grid four times.

    i On a multiplication grid, colour each 48 red.

    ii Use the grid to find the pairs of factors that give the red numbers. For example, 4 × 12 = 48.

    iii Find the other factors of 48 that are not shown on the grid.

    iv Find some other numbers which appear several times. Use different colours to shade them. Write the multiplication facts.

b Which numbers appear an odd number of times in the grid?

    i Shade each one a different colour on another multiplication grid.

    ii What is special about these numbers?

5 a Use the grid to find some of the factors of 36.

b What are the other factors of 36?

6 a Use the grid to find some of the factors of 105.

b What are the other factors of 105?

7 a The number 7 appears just 2 times.
    What type of number is 7?

b The number 108 also appears just twice.
    Is this the same type of number?
    Explain your answer.

8 a List the factors of 96.

b Identify the factors of 96 that are

    i odd numbers

    ii prime numbers

    iii multiples of 4

    iv cube numbers

    v the product of two of the other factors.

Reasoning

Reasoning

Wider skills practice

1 Pip is a gardener. She has 100 flowers to plant in a bed.
There are 48 red flowers, 32 yellow flowers, 12 blue flowers and 8 white flowers.

The garden designer has said that each colour of flower should be planted to make a rectangle and that all four rectangles should be arranged to make a square. Pip has to use all of the flowers.

a How many flowers will be along each side of the square?

b What size will each of the four rectangles need to be in order to make the square?

2 The grid on page 276 is symmetrical.

a Draw the line of symmetry on a copy of the grid.

b Explain why the multiplication grid is symmetrical.

c The line of symmetry goes through some numbers.
What is special about these numbers?

d How do you find the square root of a number on the line of symmetry?

Applying skills

1 Find

a a three-digit number that doesn't have 2 as a factor.

b a three-digit number that doesn't have 2 or 3 as a factor.

c a three-digit number that doesn't have 2, 3 or 5 as a factor.

d a four-digit number that doesn't have 2, 3, 5, 7 or 11 as a factor.

e a four-digit number with exactly three factors.

2 Find

a two square numbers that add to give another square number

b three square numbers that add to give another square number

c two prime numbers that add to give another prime number

d three prime numbers that add to give another prime number

e two prime numbers that add to give a square number

f two square numbers that add to give a prime number.

Reviewing skills

1 Copy this diagram.

a For each number along the bottom, shade or colour the boxes to show the factors.
The first three numbers have been done for you.

b What patterns do you notice?

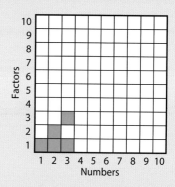

2 **a** List the factors of 16.

   b Which of these factors are

     i square numbers

     ii prime numbers

     iii cube numbers?

3 Find all the square numbers between 27 and 56.

4 Find

   a $\sqrt{81}$ **b** $\sqrt{144}$ **c** the cube root of 8.

Building skills

Example outside the Maths classroom

Maths puzzles

Toolbox

A **factor** or **divisor**, divides into a number exactly.
The given number is **divisible** by its factors.
Here are some common tests for divisibility.

Divisor	Test	Example	Explanation
2	Is the number even?	$6814 = 2 \times 3407$	The last digit, 4, is even
3	Add the digits together. Is the total a multiple of 3?	$786 = 3 \times 262$	$7 + 8 + 6 = 21$ $21 = 3 \times 7$
4	Are the last two digits a multiple of 4?	$61724 = 4 \times 15431$	$24 = 4 \times 6$
5	Is the last digit either 5 or 0?	$51325 = 5 \times 10265$	The last digit is 5
6	Is the number divisible by both 2 and 3?	$576 = 6 \times 96$	It is even; the last digit is 6 $5 + 7 + 6 = 21 = 3 \times 7$
8	Are the last three digits a multiple of 8?	$13288 = 8 \times 1661$	$288 = 8 \times 36$
9	Add the digits together. Is the total a multiple of 9?	$1584 = 9 \times 176$	$1 + 5 + 8 + 4 = 18$ $18 = 9 \times 2$
10	Is the last digit 0?	$62590 = 10 \times 6259$	The last digit is 0

Example – Using divisibility tests to solve puzzles

5 A B is a three-digit number.

This number is a multiple of 9 and a multiple of 4.

What digits could the letters A and B represent?

Solution

The number is a multiple of 9, so the digit-sum must be a multiple of 9.

Options are 504, 513, 522, 531, 540, 594, 585, 576, 567, 558, 549

The number is a multiple of 4, so the last two digits must be a multiple of 4.

504, 540, 576 are the only ones that are multiples of 4.

The possibilities are

A = 0 and B = 4

A = 4 and B = 0

A = 7 and B = 6

Remember:

✦ Divisibility tests won't give you an answer to a division calculation but they will tell you if the answer is going to be a whole number.

✦ The key divisibility tests are for 2, 3, 4, 5, 9 and 10.

Skills practice A

1 Which of these numbers are divisible by 2?

42   103   3078   96   2114   500 796

2 Which of these numbers can be divided by 10?

40   650   1090   65   702   20 070

3 Which of these numbers can be divided by 5?

203   735   920   661   805   40 300

4 Which of these numbers are divisible by 3?

83   257   4 196   102   1137   200 736

5 Which of these numbers are divisible by 9?

108   7135   103 284   243   8226

6 Which of these numbers are multiples of 4?

124   4082   11 335   421   4096

7 If a number can be divided exactly by 2 and by 3, then it can be divided exactly by 6.
This is because 6 = 2 × 3.

Which of these numbers are multiples of 6?

105   1734   7814   306   2871

8 Which of these numbers are multiples of 8?

4084   11 335   4096   11 336

Skills practice B

1 Copy this number grid.

0	1	2	3	4	5	6	7	8	9
10	11	12	13	14	15	16	17	18	19
20	21	22	23	24	25	26	27	28	29
30	31	32	33	34	35	36	37	38	39
40	41	42	43	44	45	46	47	48	49
50	51	52	53	54	55	56	57	58	59
60	61	62	63	64	65	66	67	68	69
70	71	72	73	74	75	76	77	78	79
80	81	82	83	84	85	86	87	88	89
90	91	92	93	94	95	96	97	98	99

a Find the digit total of the numbers in a yellow square.

b Find the other numbers with the same digit total. Colour those squares yellow.

c Now do the same for the green and blue squares.

d Colour the squares with digit totals of 12, 15 and 18.

e What number divides into all the coloured numbers?

2

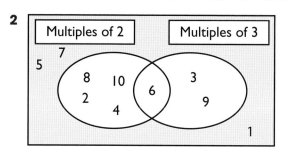

a Copy the diagram and add all the numbers from 11 to 50 to it.

b List all the numbers in the intersection.

c What can you say about the numbers in the intersection?

3 Work out the missing digits in these numbers.

a 307☐ is a multiple of 5 and 2.

b 1☐5☐ is a multiple of 9, 5 and 2.

c 7☐☐2 is a multiple of 3 and 4.

4 The lock on Christina's bike has a three-digit code.
Each digit is either 5, 6, 7, 8 or 9.

    a The whole number is divisible by 5. Write the last digit in a copy of the lock.

    b The second digit is odd. What digits can it be?

    c The number made by the last two digits is divisible by 3. What are the last two digits?
Fill in the middle digit in your copy of the lock.

    d The first digit is even. What digits can it be?

    e The whole number is divisible by 3. Fill in the first digit in your copy of the lock.

5 The lock on Andy's mountain bike also has a three-digit code.
Each digit is either 1, 2, 3, 4 or 5.

    a The code is even. What digits can the last digit be?

    b The number made by the last two digits is divisible by 3.
Write down the possible pairs for the last two digits.

    c The whole number is divisible by 3. Write down the possible code numbers.

    d The whole number is *not* divisible by 4. What is the code number?

Wider skills practice

1 Use all or some of the digits 8, 7, 6, 0, 0 and 3 to make

    a a six-digit multiple of 8

    b a six-digit multiple of 10

    c a four-digit multiple of 9.

2 A message is to be encoded like this
    • Replace A with 01
      Replace B with 02 ...
      ... Z with 26
    • Add a check digit at the end to make each encoded word a multiple of 9.
      So FUN would be 0621144.
    a Decode the message
       07150914072   20151   130118193
    b Replace the final word in part **a** by a place of your choice.

Applying skills

1 Here are some three-digit numbers that are divisible by 11
       165, 396, 935
    a Write down some more three-digit numbers that are divisible by 11.
    b Use your numbers to find a divisibility rule for 11 for three-digit numbers.
    c Extend your rule to for four-digit numbers that are divisible by 11.
    d What happens with numbers that have five digits or more?

Reasoning

Problem solving

Problem solving

2 Find a three-digit number that is
- divisible by 4
- less than 300
- a multiple of 3
- a multiple of a square number between 50 and 100

What is the number?

Reviewing skills

1 Copy this diagram.

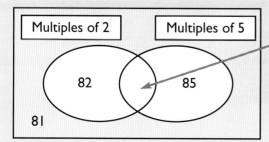

Multiples of 2   Multiples of 5

82   85

81

The overlap is called the intersection.

a Sort all the numbers from 50 to 100.

b What can you say about the numbers in the intersection?

2 Copy this table.

Multiples of 2	Multiples of 3	Multiples of 4	Multiples of 6	Multiples of 8	Multiples of 9

Put these numbers in the correct columns.

606, 350, 225, 3000, 3678, 5376, 2480, 360, 131, 4096

Building skills

Example outside the Maths classroom

Growth patterns

Toolbox

Repeated multiplications can be written using index notation like this:
- $5 \times 5 \times 5 = 5^3 = 125$.
- $3 \times 3 \times 3 \times 3 \times 3 = 3^5 = 243$.

Numbers written using index notation can be multiplied and divided easily.

To **multiply numbers** written using index notation,

$$3^5 \times 3^4$$
$$= (3 \times 3 \times 3 \times 3 \times 3) \times (3 \times 3 \times 3 \times 3)$$
$$= 3^9$$

The powers have been added 5 + 4 = 9

To **divide numbers** written using index notation,

$$3^5 \div 3^4$$
$$(3 \times 3 \times 3 \times 3 \times 3) \div (3 \times 3 \times 3 \times 3) = \frac{3 \times \cancel{3} \times \cancel{3} \times \cancel{3} \times \cancel{3}}{\cancel{3} \times \cancel{3} \times \cancel{3} \times \cancel{3}}$$

$$= 3^1$$

The powers have been subtracted 5 – 4 = 1

$$= 3$$

Notice that $3^1 = 3$

Using brackets with index notation means that the powers are multiplied.

$$(3^5)^4 = 3^5 \times 3^5 \times 3^5 \times 3^5$$
$$= (3 \times 3 \times 3 \times 3 \times 3) \times (3 \times 3 \times 3 \times 3 \times 3) \times (3 \times 3 \times 3 \times 3 \times 3) \times (3 \times 3 \times 3 \times 3 \times 3)$$
$$= 3^{20}$$

4 lots of 5 is 20

Example – Equivalent amounts

Match these cards into pairs of the same value.

4×4^3	$4^9 \div 4^2$
$4^9 \div 4^3$	$4^5 \times 4^2$
$(4^3)^3$	$(4^2)^2$

Solution

Simplify each amount

$4 \times 4^3 = 4 \times 4 \times 4 \times 4$

$\qquad = 4^4$

$4^9 \div 4^3 = \dfrac{\cancel{4} \times \cancel{4} \times \cancel{4} \times 4 \times 4 \times 4 \times 4 \times 4 \times 4}{\cancel{4} \times \cancel{4} \times \cancel{4}}$

$\qquad = 4^6$

$(4^2)^3 = (4 \times 4) \times (4 \times 4) \times (4 \times 4)$

$\qquad = 4^6$

$4^9 \div 4^2 = \dfrac{\cancel{4} \times \cancel{4} \times 4 \times 4 \times 4 \times 4 \times 4 \times 4 \times 4}{\cancel{4} \times \cancel{4}}$

$\qquad = 4^7$

$4^5 \times 4^2 = (4 \times 4 \times 4 \times 4 \times 4) \times (4 \times 4)$

$\qquad = 4^7$

$(4^2)^2 = (4 \times 4) \times (4 \times 4)$

$\qquad = 4^4$

So $4 \times 4^3 = (4^2)^2$

$\quad 4^9 \div 4^3 = (4^2)^3$

$\quad 4^9 \div 4^2 = 4^5 \times 4^2$

Remember:

✦ Index notation shows how many numbers are to be multiplied.

Skills practice A

1 Write each expression as a power of 2.

  a $2 \times 2 \times 2 \times 2$

  b $2 \times 2 \times 2 \times 2 \times 2 \times 2 \times 2$

  c $2 \times 2 \times 2 \times 2 \times 2 \times 2 \times 2 \times 2 \times 2 \times 2 \times 2 \times 2$

2 Copy and complete these.

   a $4^2 = \square$ **b** $\square^3 = 125$ **c** $2^\square = 32$

3 Copy and complete this cross-number puzzle.

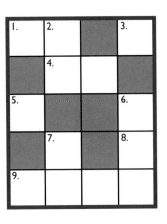

Across
1 2^4
4 7^2
5 The square root of 25
8 The cube root of 8
9 11^3

Down
2 4^3
3 3^1
6 11^2
7 The square root of 169

4 Write 64 as a power of

   a 2   **b** 4   **c** 8   **d** 64

5 Work out the missing digits in these. There may be more than one answer.

   a $\square^2 = 25$

   b $\square\square^2 = \square\square 5$

   c $\square^3 = \square\square 6$

   d $\square^6 = \square^2$

6 Calculate the difference between 3^2 and 2^3.

7 Find $3^3 + 4^2 + 2^4$

8 5^4 can be written in several ways.
Here are some.
    $5 \times 5 \times 5 \times 5$
    $5^2 \times 5^2$
    $5^3 \times 5^1$
Write 4^5 in as many different ways as you can.

Skills practice B

1 Write each expression as a single power of 2.

   a $2^5 \times 2^2$ **b** $2^8 \div 2^3$ **c** $(2^3)^2$

   d $2^4 \div 2^4$ **e** $2^4 \div 2^6$ **f** $\dfrac{2^3 \times 2^5}{2^2}$

2 Write each expression as a single power of 3 or 5.

   a $3^4 \times 3^2$ **b** $3^5 \div 3^2$ **c** $(3^2)^4$

   d $5^2 \div 5^2$ **e** $5^2 \div 5^4$ **f** $5^2 \div 5^3$

Reasoning

Reasoning

3 Find the missing digits.

    a $7^{\square} = 7^5 \div 7^2$ **b** $7^3 = 7^3 \times 7^{\square}$

    c $(7^{\square})^4 = 7^8$ **d** $7^6 \div 7^2 = 7^{\square} \times 7^3$

4 The expressions on these 12 cards can be matched into six pairs. All the missing numbers are the same.

    a Match the cards into pairs.

    b What is the missing number?

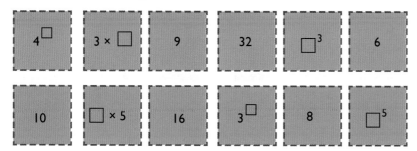

| $4^{\square}$ | $3 \times \square$ | 9 | 32 | $\square^3$ | 6 |
| 10 | $\square \times 5$ | 16 | $3^{\square}$ | 8 | $\square^5$ |

5 Which is the larger number of each of these pairs, or are they the same?

    a 2^5 and 6^2 **b** 5^3 and 2^7 **c** 4^3 and 3^4

    d 2^9 and 8^3 **e** 10^3 and 2^{10}

Wider skills practice

1 **a** Write down the value of $49 \div 49$.

    b Write 49 as a power of 7.

    c Write $7^2 \div 7^2$

        i as a power of 7   **ii** as a number.

    d what is the value of 7^0?

    e What are the values of

        i 2^0 **ii** 3^0 **iii** 17^0?

    f State a general value for the power zero.

2 Find the smallest number (other than 1) which can be written as A^2 and as B^5, where A and B are whole numbers.

Reasoning

Applying skills

1 This game is called 'The tower of Hanoi'.

a Cut out two strips of paper of different lengths.
Put the strips on tower 1.

Move one strip at a time from tower to tower until it looks like this.

The rule is that you can only put a smaller strip on top of a bigger strip.

b Play the game with three strips. Start like this:

c Try it with four strips.
d What is the smallest number of moves for one strip? for two strips? for three strips? for four strips?
e What do the smallest numbers of moves have to do with the powers of 2?

Reviewing skills

1 Write each of these calculations as a single power.
   a $4^5 \times 4^9$ **b** $7^9 \div 7^2$ **c** $(13^7)^8$

2 Find the values of these.
   a $(2^2)^3$ **b** $2^2 \times 2^3$ **c** $2^2 + 2^3$ **d** $2^3 \times 2^3$

   e $2^3 \times 2^3$ **f** $32 \div 2^3$ **g** $2^{99} \div 2^{96}$ **h** $\dfrac{2^5}{(2 \times 2 \times 2 \times 2 \times 2)}$

3 Which of these is the odd one out?
   a **i** $7^9 \times 7^2$ **b** **i** $(5^2)^3$
   ii $7^5 \times 7^6$ **ii** $5^2 \times 5^3$
   iii $7^2 \times 7^9$ **iii** $5^2 + 5^3$
   iv $7^{11} \div 4^9$ **iv** $5^3 \times 5^3$
   v $\dfrac{7^{11}}{7}$ **v** $5^3 + 5^3$
   vi $5^5 \div 5^0$
   vii $5^6 \div 5^1$

Building skills

Internet security

 Toolbox

The factors of a number divide into it exactly.

The factors of 12 are 1, 2, 3, 4, 6 and 12

Prime factors are the factors of a number that are also prime numbers.
The prime factors of 12 are 2 and 3.

Every number can be written in terms of its prime factors.

> Remember 1 is not a prime number.

$$12 = 2 \times 2 \times 3 = 2^2 \times 3$$

A factor tree is often used to write a number as a **product of its prime factors**.

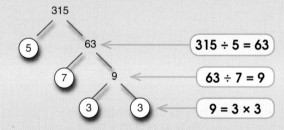

$$315 \div 5 = 63$$

$$63 \div 7 = 9$$

$$9 = 3 \times 3$$

From this diagram, you can see that $315 = 5 \times 7 \times 3 \times 3 = 3^2 \times 5 \times 7$.

Any number's set of prime factors is unique. A different set of prime factors will give a different number.

The **highest common factor (HCF)** of two numbers is the largest factor that they share.

You can find the HCF of two numbers by listing their factors, as in this example for 20 and 30.

Factors of 20	1	2	4	5	⑩	20		
Factors of 30	1	2	3	5	6	⑩	15	30

The highest number in both lists is 10 and this is the HCF. ← The HCF is often quite a small number.

The **lowest common multiple (LCM)** of two numbers is the lowest multiple that they share.

You can find the LCM of two numbers by listing their multiples, as in this example, again using 20 and 30.

Multiples of 20   20   40   ⑥⓪   80   100

Multiples of 30   30   ⑥⓪   90   120   150

The lowest number in both lists is 60 and this is the LCM. ◄─── **The LCM is often quite a large number.**

Another way of finding the HCF and LCM of two numbers is to place their prime factors in a Venn diagram. In the following example this is done for 315 and 270.

315 = 3 × 3 × 5 × 7   270 = 2 × 3 × 3 × 3 × 5

Placing these factors in a Venn diagram gives

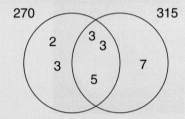

270   315

The HCF is found by multiplying the numbers in the intersection:

   3 × 3 × 5 = 45

The LCM is found by multiplying all of the numbers in the diagram:

   2 × 3 × 3 × 3 × 5 × 7 = 1890

Example – Finding prime factors using a factor tree

Write 1540 as a product of its prime factors.

Solution

Using a factor tree:

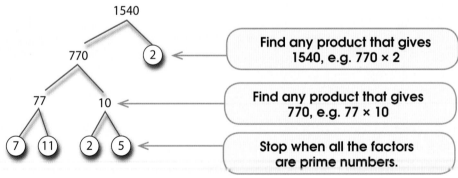

1540

770   2   ◄─── **Find any product that gives 1540, e.g. 770 × 2**

77   10   ◄─── **Find any product that gives 770, e.g. 77 × 10**

7 11   2 5   ◄─── **Stop when all the factors are prime numbers.**

So 1540 = 7 × 11 × 2 × 5 × 2

   = $2^2 × 5 × 7 × 11$

Example – Prime factors

Find the HCF and LCM of 24 and 90 by

a using a Venn diagram

b listing factors and multiples

Solution

a The prime factors of 24 are $2 \times 2 \times 2 \times 3 = 2^3 \times 3$

The prime factors of 90 are $2 \times 3 \times 3 \times 5 = 2 \times 3^2 \times 5$

On a Venn diagram these are placed like this

24   90

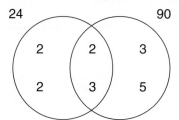

$HCF = 2 \times 3 = 6$ ← ❴ **The numbers in the intersection give the HCF.** ❵

$LCM = 2 \times 2 \times 2 \times 3 \times 3 \times 5 = 360$ ← ❴ **All the numbers are needed for the LCM.** ❵

b
Factors of 24	1	2	3	4	⑥	8	12	24			
Factors of 90	1	2	3	5	⑥	9	10	15	18	30	45	90

The HCF is 6. ← ❴ **The highest number which is in both lists is 6.** ❵

Multiples of 24	24	48	72	96	120	144	168	192	216	240	264	288
	312	334	③⑥⓪	384								
Multiples of 90	90	180	270	③⑥⓪	450 ...							

The LCM is 360. ← ❴ **360 is the first number which is in both lists.** ❵

Remember:

✦ Writing a number as a product of its prime factors means writing all of the prime factors as a multiplication.

✦ Use index notation to write a product of prime factors neatly.

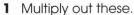
Skills practice A

1 Multiply out these.

   a $2^2 \times 3^2$ **b** 3×5^2 **c** 2^3

   d 2×7^2 **e** $2^3 \times 3^3$

2 Multiply out these.

   a $2^2 \times 3$ **b** 2^4 **c** $2 \times 3 \times 5$

   d $3^2 \times 5$ **e** $3 \times 5 \times 7$ **f** $3 \times 7 \times 11$

   g $2 \times 3 \times 11$ **h** $2^2 \times 5^2$

3 **a** Complete this list of the factors of 60.

      1, 2, 3, ..., 60

   b Write a list of the prime factors of 60.

   c Write 60 as a product of prime factors.

4 **a** Copy and complete this diagram to find the prime factors of 18.

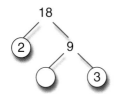

   b Write 18 as the product of prime factors.

5 Draw factor trees to find the products of the prime factors of these numbers.

   a 12   **b** 84   **c** 420

6 Write each of these numbers as a product of its prime factors.

   a 8   **b** 15   **c** 20

   d 50   **e** 70   **f** 240

7 Write each of these as a product of its prime factors.

   a 21   **b** 35   **c** 24

   d 25   **e** 48   **f** 120

   g 144   **h** 39   **i** 65

   j 1000

8 **a** What are the first ten multiples of 5?

   b What are the first ten multiples of 6?

   c What is the Lowest Common Multiple (LCM) of 5 and 6?

9 **a** List the first eight multiples of 30.

   b List the first eight multiples of 24.

   c What is the LCM of 30 and 24?

10 Find the LCM of each pair of numbers.

   a 3 and 5   **b** 4 and 6   **c** 9 and 12

11 Find the LCM of each of these pairs of numbers.

    a 10 and 15   **b** 20 and 30   **c** 4 and 12

    d 15 and 20   **e** 12 and 18   **f** 7 and 8

    g 9 and 11   **h** 11 and 15

12 a What are the factors of 12?

    b What are the factors of 16?

    c What is the Highest Common Factor (HCF) of 12 and 16?

13 Find the HCF of each pair of numbers.

    a 15 and 20   **b** 18 and 24

14 Find the HCF of each of these pairs of numbers.

    a 6 and 8   **b** 6 and 9   **c** 12 and 16

    d 36 and 42   **e** 42 and 70   **f** 66 and 121

    g 72 and 36   **h** 45 and 90

Skills practice B

1 Find the LCM of these sets of numbers by first finding their prime factors.

    a 64 and 72   **b** 20 and 35   **c** 16 and 28

    d 32 and 25   **e** 90, 80 and 75   **f** 2430 and 32

2 Find the HCF of these sets of numbers by first finding their prime factors.

    a 8 and 14   **b** 24 and 9   **c** 6 and 15

    d 4 and 20   **e** 7 and 8   **f** 35 and 30

    g 15 and 28   **h** 10 and 100   **i** 42 and 49

    j 4, 10 and 12   **k** 15, 25 and 30

3 a Write the numbers 90 and 56 as the product of their prime factors.

    b Place these prime factors in a Venn diagram.

    c Find the HCF and LCM of 90 and 56.

4 a Find the HCF of 90 and 360.

    b Find the LCM of 90 and 360.

    c What do you notice about your answers to parts **a** and **b**?
       Find another pair of numbers with this pattern.

5 a Find a number with prime factors of only 13, 17 and 19.

    b Find a number between 100 and 200 with prime factors that are all even.

    c Find a pair of numbers that have prime factors of only 2, 3, and 5.
       One of your pair should be a two-digit number and one should be a three-digit number.

6 You can write 24 as a product of its prime factors like this. $24 = 2^3 \times 3$

    a Write 60 as a product of its prime factors.

    The HCF of 24 and 60 is 12.

    b Write 12 as a product of its prime factors.

    c How can you use the products of primes of 24 and 60 to find their HCF?

Reasoning

Reasoning

7 A gear wheel with 30 teeth drives another wheel with 55 teeth.

At the start a certain pair of teeth are touching.

How many turns must each wheel make before the same pair of teeth are touching again?

8 A toy train track is made up of identical interlocking straight pieces.

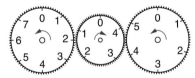

The toy designer needs to be able to make straight sections of track exactly 75 cm, 120 cm and 150 cm long.

75 cm

120 cm

150 cm

How long does each interlocking piece of track need to be?

9 Mrs Darker has three jars of sweets to give to three classes of five-year-olds at the end of term.

Each jar contains the same number of sweets.

There are 20 children in class A, 24 in class B and 25 in class C.

Each of the three classes is given one jar of sweets to share equally among the children in that class.

a In which class do the children receive the most sweets?

In class A, when the sweets are shared out, and each child gets the same number, there is exactly one sweet left over for the class teacher.

Mrs Darker was surprised to discover that there was also just one sweet left over for the class B teacher and one left over for the class C teacher.

b What is the minimum number of sweets in each jar for this to happen?

10 These dials are set at 0:

After the left dial has been turned through one complete turn they look like this:

a Draw a diagram to show what they will look like after two complete turns of the left dial.

b How many complete turns of the left dial are needed before the first two dials are both set to 0?

c How many complete turns of the left dial are needed before all three dials are again set to 0?

11 Pete makes rosewood jewellery.

Pieces of wood are joined together to make bracelets, necklaces and anklets.

All the pieces of wood are the same length.

Look at the poster on the right.

 a Write down the common factors of 18, 48, 54 and 24.

 b What are possible lengths for the pieces of wood?

 c What length do you think is best?

Pete's jewellery	
Bracelets	18 cm
Short Necklaces	48 cm
Long Necklaces	54 cm
Anklets	24 cm

GUARANTEED TO BRING YOU LUCK

12

BUSES AVAILABLE FROM THIS STOP

	1b	3a	4
Departing every	5 mins	8 mins	10 mins
First departure	9.00 am	9.00 am	9.00 am

All three buses leave together at 9.00 a.m. When is the next time that all three buses leave together?

Wider skills practice

1 The prime factors of a square number can be written in pairs like this:
 - 36 = (2 × 2) × (3 × 3) is the square of 2 × 3.
 - 16 = (2 × 2) × (2 × 2) is the square of 2 × 2.

 a Explain why $3^2 \times 5^2$ is a square number.

 b What is its square root?

 c 24 = 2 × 2 × 2 × 3. Write down the square of 24.

 d Find the square root of $2^2 \times 3^2 \times 7^2$.

2 The prime factors of a cube number can be grouped in threes like this:
 - 216 = (2 × 2 × 2) × (3 × 3 × 3) is the cube of 2 × 3.

 a 15 = 3 × 5. Write down the cube of 15.

 b What is the cube root of $3^3 \times 7^3$?

3 64 = 2 × 2 × 2 × 2 × 2 × 2 = 2^6 is a square number and a cube number.

 a Show that its factors can be grouped in pairs and in threes.

 b Find two more numbers that are both square numbers and cube numbers.

4 Nomsa thinks she has found a counter-example to the rule that any number has only one set of prime factors. She says "My number is 24871. I can factorise it in two ways. It can be 209 × 119 or it can be 187 × 133. I have found an exception to the rule!" Is Nomsa correct?

5 a Write 20 as a product of its prime factors.

b Write 24 as a product of its prime factors.

c Write 120 as a product of its prime factors.

d 120 is the LCM of 20 and 24. Look at your answers to parts **a**, **b** and **c**.

    i What do you multiply 20 by to get 120?

    ii What do you multiply 24 by to get 120?

Applying skills

1 Linda has her car serviced every 6000 km.

Here are some of the checks they carry out.

Check	Required every
Brake fluid	6000 km
Change oil filter	12 000 km
Tyres	6000 km
Wiper blades	18 000 km
Change timing belt	24 000 km

Service	6000	12 000	18 000	24 000
Check	Brake fluid Tyres	Brake fluid Tyres Oil filter		

a Copy and continue the table to show all the services up to the 48 000 km service.

b How many kilometres does the car travel before it has a service that includes all five checks?

2 In a motor race, the faster car completes the circuit in 5 minutes and the slower car takes 7 minutes.

a How long is it before the faster car overtakes the slower car at the same time as they pass through the starting position?

b How many laps has each car completed?

c Does the faster car overtake the slower car anywhere else on the circuit?

d If so, where does this happen and after how long?

Problem solving

Problem solving

Problem solving

3 The map shows the route of a charity walk.

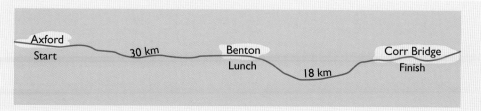

Marshals stand at equally spaced intervals along the route including at the lunch stop, the start and the finish.

a Find the HCF of 18 and 30.

b What distance is there between each marshal? There are several possible answers. Give two of them.

c What is the smallest possible number of marshals?

Reviewing skills

1 Multiply out these.

  a 2×3^2 **b** $3^3 \times 5^2$ **c** 3×13 **d** 3×7^2

2 Write each of these numbers as a product of its prime factors using index notation.

  a 8   **b** 15   **c** 20

  d 50   **e** 70   **f** 240

  g 312   **h** 729   **i** 52

  j 224   **k** 11 240

3 Find the LCM and HCF of each of these sets of numbers.

  a 6 and 10   **b** 42 and 70   **c** 72, 36 and 18

  d 12 and 64